BEHIND BARS

Sunetra Choudhury started her career at the *Indian Express* newspaper where she headed the city team. Three years later she moved to TV news and joined NDTV. After covering the 2009 election campaign travelling across the country on a bus for two months, she wrote *Braking News*. In 2016, she received the Red Ink award and is the 2018 Jefferson Fellow. Most recently she is the recipient of Mary Morgan Hewett Award that recognizes the achievements of women journalists. Choudhury is currently the political editor at *Hindustan Times*. Her most recent book, *Black Warrant: Confessions of a Tihar Jailer* is co-authored with Sunil Gupta.

'Based on extensive secondary research and detailed interviews with people who have spent time in jail as well as those who have worked in or on jails, Choudhury presents a series of stories which are nothing short of eye-opening – dare I say, even eye-popping – in their revelations.'
The Wire

'Choudhury has a fluid writing style and makes her book a compelling read. However, you may not want to breeze through it and instead take your time in savouring these 13 stories.'
Khaleej Times

'The author compels us to confront the agonies of people who are hauled up on charges of terrorism. But there are others too, who have been released and may be broken in body but not in spirit after several years inside. They come to life in these pages as evidence of injustice and failure of the system.'
Business Standard

'…*Behind Bars* is a fascinating effort, especially since the book is dripped in palpable anger against the many privileges of the elite, even inside jails. In that, it is a first draft of a sociological mapping of contemporary India, its many immoral famous ones, its heart-wrenching cruelties, the many individual sacrifices and the hidden secrets of its wealthy and powerful.'
The Hindu

'With unbelievable details of the life inside prison and the sorry state of hundreds of undertrials languishing in jails, this book questions the primary purpose of imprisonment – is it actually reform, punishment or just misusing the system we are a part of?'
Literary Yard

'These are heartbreaking stories – as is much of the book. Prison is heartbreaking. There is no soft landing in Tihar, no matter who you are. No matter how rich and famous you may be, jail is a terrible experience.'
Biblio

'This isn't a book for the faint-hearted with its stomach-churning descriptions of filth and violence but it casts a strong light on an area of darkness. It will prick your conscience and invite you to reflect on the conspiracy of silence that accompanies the gross human rights abuse in judicial custody.'
The Open Magazine

'With extraordinary details of the life inside prison and the sorry state of hundreds of undertrails languishing in jails, the book questions the primary purpose of imprisonment – is it actually reform, punishment or just misusing the system we are a part of.'
The Sunday Guardian

'In clean and engaging language, rich with detail and well-chosen adjectives, the book presents interesting facts about jail food, extraordinarily sincere jail employees as well as corrupt and perverted ones, rituals such as *mulakat* – and more.'
Hindustan Times

'Through Choudhury's smooth-flowing narrative, the book makes for an easy read. Her commendable access and references to chargesheets, court orders, research studies reassure the reader of her credibility, and builds faith in her content.'
Deccan Chronicle

BEHIND BARS

PRISON TALES OF INDIA'S MOST FAMOUS

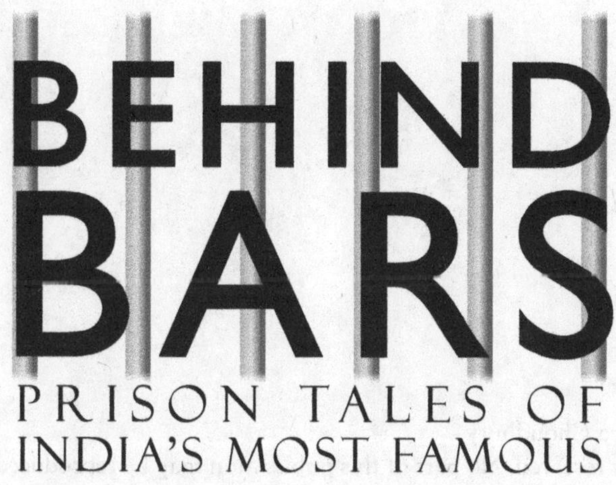

SUNETRA CHOUDHURY

ROLI

for
Neel & Sudeep

First published in April 2017
Third impression, 2021

Roli Books Pvt. Ltd
M-75, Greater Kailash II Market, New Delhi 110 048
Phone: +91 (011) 40682000
E-mail: info@rolibooks.com
Website: www.rolibooks.com

Also at Chennai & Mumbai

Cover: Sonali Zohra
Author photo (on the back cover): Hridayesh Joshi

ISBN: 9789351941316

Typeset in Sabon LT Std by Roli Books Pvt Ltd.

CONTENTS

INTRODUCTION

It was sometime in early 2016 that I got a call from an undisclosed number. The woman on the other end of the line had a foreign accent and when she told me her name was Anca, it took me only a couple of seconds to figure out who she was. I was a little confused because the last I heard about Anca Neascu Verma was that she was in jail for various CBI cases along with her husband, Abhishek Verma. 'Oh, you are now...,' I asked. 'Yes, I am now outside,' she finished what I was trying to say, and I could sense her smiling. This sense of humour warmed me a bit, though I was intrigued because while I had reported on CBI and a few of cases that involved her and her husband, I had not shown any particular interest in cases which were more obsessively followed by defence beat reporters. I had never spoken to either of them but I was in touch with their lawyers for legal developments. So when she suggested we meet at Hyatt one afternoon, I thought it was perhaps some lead to a story, so I agreed. I wasn't really sure what I was going to gain from it but the fact that she sought me out soon after coming out of prison, had me curious.

'I'm feeling so good because I just went to the spa after so long,' she declared when she saw me. She looked almost six feet tall and was striking with her blonde hair and a fitted designer dress. 'I tell people that I was away to the ashram. That's what I call my four years in jail – ashram.' I was fascinated to say the least. I guessed she had called me to make a case for her husband who was still in jail at the time. I knew she wanted me to perhaps do stories on what had happened to CBI's investigation after so many years, but what we ended up talking about was her time in jail. I have done stories on jail experiences throughout my career, but never before had I got this kind of insight into prison life.

Anca was rich, beautiful, a Romanian married to an influential Indian businessman who was forever being chased by law authorities, and she was now sitting outside jail, literally cooling her pedicured heels and willing to dish the dirt on what goes on inside. Until now we only had an inkling of what may be happening inside through sporadic news headlines – Mohammad Shahabuddin being caught taking selfies with his phone inside prison, the Punjab jailbreaks revealing that they had been updating their Facebook status from inside the jail till the time they ran away, the Nirbhaya rapist committing suicide in jail. Each of these news breaks would quickly be hushed away by a spokesperson, like statement ordering an inquiry, and then everything would get brushed under the carpet again. For the first time, I was meeting a woman who had been in the slammer and was willing to talk about how she figured out the system to her advantage.

So I fixed a TV interview with Anca where she shocked audiences by revealing that well-off women inside jail, like her, hired servants for a fee. The servants, also inmates, would do all their menial tasks for meagre amounts of money, which meant that you could spend your jail term at least not worrying about cleaning the toilet and doing any other task assigned to you.

It would have ended with that – a good interview and a good TV show – but when she sent me a picture of herself wearing Louis Vuitton inside jail, it was beyond my imagination. She said that it wasn't for publication but there were a whole series of pictures taken like that which I couldn't get off my mind. Anca may be a CBI accused, but she told me something which I found very honest: 'If you steal 1,000 rupees, the hawaldar will beat the shit out of you and lock you up in a dungeon with no bulb or ventilation. If you steal 55,000 crore then you get to stay in a 40-foot cell which has four split units, internet, fax, mobile phones and a staff of ten to clean your shoes and cook your food (in case it is not being delivered from Hyatt that particular day) – Incredible India!'

None of these things she could say on camera but she was willing to give me all the information. How she managed to live with an LCD TV and Star World Premiere, not missing a single episode of 'Orange is the new Black' inside jail. That's when the idea of a book occurred to me and I decided to look for others like Anca, who are basically so influential that they didn't mind telling us what really happens in our jails. If they hid their own comforts of how rules were bent for them, they didn't hesitate to talk about others and, in return, the others filled in on their jail antics.

Initially, getting people to talk was tough. For instance, in Dasna Jail, Rajesh and Nupur Talwar had clearly figured out a survival system. One of the first things that struck me during our meeting at the superintendent's room of the jail was how nicely ironed their kurtas were. They were both stunned with the prospect of spending their lives incarcerated for their teenage daughter Aarushi's murder, but they didn't have to worry about laundry, apparently. Neither of them had also lost any weight even though at that time, they had already spent more than a year at Dasna. This had always intrigued me. How could most affluent people manage to not look any different despite being in jail? Indrani Mukerjea was an exception in being the rich TV executive whose blow dried long bob soon became all-roots exposed grey mass, but people like A. Raja, Sanjay Dutt and others came out betraying no sign of change. The reason, in Talwar's case at least, was evident. They were doctors and the jail officials were delighted to have their services in house. So they had traded in their skill in servicing the jail staff and their families in return for a relatively comfortable life inside. But the problem was talking to me about it would only jeopardise their interests.

Then there was the case of Saharasri Subrata Roy. The Supreme Court may have sent him to prison in 2014 for not paying back his depositors ₹20,000 crore, but they had also given him benefits which had never been seen by anybody in prison before. Subrata Roy is the first person in the history of Tihar Jail to have comforts of air-conditioning. Whether you are A. Raja, Pappu Yadav, Manu Sharma or Sanjeev Nanda, the best you could have in luxury was a cooler, tiled floors and a cell to yourself which you could furnish with a bed. But because the court allowed Roy to use the video conference facilities, he was moved from Ward 9 of Jail Number 1 to the old court complex of Tihar Jail. It had meeting and conference rooms and because it was meant to be like an office, it had air-conditioning too. 'Even Indira Gandhi didn't have this comfort when she came to stay here.'

When I went to meet Roy, he was staying in the presidential suite of the Maurya Sheraton in Delhi. He had agreed to see me after I harangued his secretary about my book. I was warned though that Saharasri already had a three-book deal with another publisher and so he couldn't really be a part of my book. But I thought I could perhaps convince him otherwise.

After walking through a long corridor inside the Chandragupta suite that had been used by heads of state (Clinton had used the Grand Presidential Suite), and after passing by a room that only had his shoes, I was ushered into a sitting room with Roy. He was very polite and spoke to me in Bangla, appreciating my work as I'm sure his secretary may have briefed him. Someone brought in some *mishti doi* and *sandesh*. As soon as I took out my notebook he said, 'Listen, don't include me in this book of yours. I'm not a criminal.' I told him that not everyone featured in my book would be a criminal. Many would be those wrongly accused of crimes which led them to unfairly spend long years in custody. 'But I am different. There isn't even an FIR against me,' he clarified.

That was it. I was disappointed because every time you think of the rich and famous in jail in India, you immediately think of Subrata Roy. However, I wasn't too heartbroken because I knew that in his own writings published so far he wasn't really giving away any scandalous details. If anything, many inmates resented him for the facilities he got in Tihar, even though he paid ₹1.23 crore for them as directed by the court. During my interviews with jail officials, one handed me a document which didn't just confirm the gossip that surrounded Roy but showed actual evidence of a transgression.

A police communication from IPS officer Anisa Husain, commandant, Tamil Nadu Special Police (TSP) VIII battalion, dated 3 September 2015, addressed to the Director General (DG) of Prisons, said this:

Subject: Inmate Manu Sharma of Semi Open Jail met with inmate Subradha Rai (sic) along with jail official

It is submitted that on 15.08.2015 at 14.30 hours Assistant Superintendent Sh SGK Murthi came into Special Jail along with the inmate of semi open jail Manu Sharma and met inmate Subradha Rai and went out at 17.50 hours, and again 16.08.2015 DJ warder 1244 Mukesh Mor came into Special Jail along with semi open jail inmate Manu Sharma at 1750 hours and went out 1822 hours.

This is for favour of kind information and appropriate action may please be taken in this regard at an early date.

Yours faithfully,

Complainant (signed)
TSP VIII Bn, New Delhi

This perhaps is the only violation that has some documentary evidence against Subrata Roy. It is unthinkable for an inmate to leave his own jail, forget about going to another area and hanging out with another inmate in their cushy air-conditioned environment. The only reason why it was reported was that the TSP's lady constable lived up to their reputation of being very meticulous about reporting any violation. However, despite this complaint, neither faced any action. Roy got bail for his mother's cremation in May 2016 and never went back to jail till the time of this writing. Manu Sharma was getting the benefit of being an exemplary convict, which meant being out on parole for good behaviour.

Senior jail officials told me how they were instructed to go all out to make Roy comfortable, allowing food from outside, allowing him to not have his room locked and to receive all kinds of visitors. One official I spoke to said that he couldn't accept the kind of violations that were taking place under his nose. So he decided to go see Chief Minister Arvind Kejriwal. The chief minister heard him out but said that he couldn't really do much since Roy's case was directly under Supreme Court's supervision. The officer came back dejected but was stunned to learn that Subrata Roy already knew that he had complained about him. 'If you had any complaint against me, you could have just told me,' Roy allegedly said to him. The officer, intimidated, told me that he vehemently denied the complaint. However, since then he was bypassed for all of Roy's files.

Special treatment in jail is, of course, not a new phenomenon. One of the first beneficiaries of this was the infamous Charles Sobhraj who went by the moniker 'Bikini killer' because most of the people he allegedly seduced and killed were female tourists. Sunil Gupta, who retired in July 2016 after four decades of service at Tihar Central Jail, says that the day he joined work as a young officer in 1981, he saw Sobhraj was like the king of the jail, roaming around freely in the administrative areas. 'I was surprised. How could a criminal be sitting with officers, I thought.' Gupta didn't have to wonder for very long because soon Sobhraj offered his services to him, too.

'He said to me, "Mr Gupta, can I help you with office work?" I asked him how and he said, "I can type for you and help with your briefs."' Gupta got the go ahead from his bosses and soon Sobhraj's work was shining through. 'It was a pleasant surprise. Whenever we would get any notice from the court, he would quickly draft a reply with citations. His communication skills were exemplary, and soon people started noticing the work. I ended up getting all the kudos for *his* good work.'

Of course, the pay-off was that Sobhraj did whatever he pleased, including using the room next to the jail superintendent's office. Gupta was told that Sobhraj had some recording of the superintendent which was so explosive that he even allowed Sobhraj to have private, intimate meetings with women in that office. 'Whenever some woman was expected in Tihar, he would dress up smartly.' And apparently, the dress up would usually work. 'I have walked in on him sitting objectionably with a woman journalist at one time,' said Gupta.

So it wasn't an utter shock when one day in 1986, Doordarshan started carrying news that Sobhraj had escaped jail. 'I rushed to my office and saw horrific scenes there. The jail gates were all open, the guards were in semi-sleepy state; they all looked like they had been drugged.' Gupta recalled how even after he'd made the 14-kilometre trek from his home to Tihar they were yet to get started on shutting the jail gates down, but they couldn't do anything immediately about Sobhraj and twelve others who had run away. A probe later found that Sobhraj had thrown himself a birthday party by ordering sweets and giving a crisp 50-rupee note to each guard along with a drug-laced *barfi*. Money power had made him get away with prison break in the 1980s, and it would help other VIPs make their own rules even three decades later when I was writing this book. Incidentally, a decade later, after Sobhraj had been rearrested, Sushil Sharma tells the story of how Sobhraj was again fatally drugging another inmate because he didn't want to share his cell space!

But this is not all that is unfathomable about jail life. How is it that the number of deaths in Tihar Jail went from 35 in 2014 to 43 in 2015 and then 40 in 2016, without anyone asking questions? It seems that because jails are supposed to house the unsavoury characters of our society, no one really cares what happens to them. Whether they are tortured or they enjoy extravagant lifestyles, we only sit up and take notice when it is a familiar face that's gone behind bars.

For instance, take a look at the 2014 Comptroller and Auditor General (CAG) report on prison conditions that was submitted to the Delhi Government for action. According to the report, 14,209 prisoners have been squeezed into a jail which has space for only 6,250. The report also states that between 2009 and 2014, there were 146 deaths due to illnesses, suicides, accidents or attacks by fellow inmates and that 'the prison authorities were not able to ensure safe custody and detention of inmates in jail.' This comes alive brilliantly in the experiences of Kobad Ghandy, the Doon School alumnus who is jailed under suspicion of being a Maoist. He describes living under the threat of the 'bladebaaz' – the slashers who roam around jails waiting to brand anyone for a small fee. Imagine having to be wary of that when you are 70 years old.

While senior citizens like Kobad were denied even a special diet which their medical condition required, the CAG report shows that others were getting away with keeping mobile phones, pistols, cash, and ropes – all contraband items that were found with prisoners. One senior police officer told me that if I wanted I could even get an iPhone7 in jail, but it would cost be a bit more than it would in open market.

You could get the latest phone but you couldn't get an ultrasound done in jail. As the CAG report pointed out the jail didn't have a lab, endoscopy facility or even proper staff for medical care. This has to be by design because it allows the influential to leave jail on the pretext of treatment. So the two young convicted murderers Vikas and Vishal Yadav, who killed Nitish Katara, were hauled up by the Supreme Court for making 87 visits to All India Institute of Medical Sciences (AIIMS) for no apparent ailment which couldn't be tackled at the medical centre in the jail premises. Nilam Katara, the mother fighting for punishment of her son's killers, told me that she got a call from an AIIMS doctor who wanted to tip her off about the parties that the convicts were enjoying in their hostel where they were allegedly being 'treated'. AIIMS refused to entertain her Right to Information (RTI) application and so she had to sit and sift through the logbooks of the prison to figure out how many times the Yadav cousins were being taken in and out of jail for medical treatments. On many occasions, this would coincide with New Year's Eve or other festivals. Nilam Katara and Gupta also confirmed that Manu Sharma's father had specially opened a hotel in Janakpuri, next to Tihar, called Piccadily which caters to jail staff. They are guaranteed a good time in the hotel in return for a favourable treatment for the boy who murdered Jessica Lal.

So, what was initially meant to be a how-to-survive-in-jail guide of the unlikely, influential and wealthy prisoners like Anca Verma, A. Raja, Pappu Yadav, Peter Mukerjea, Amar Singh and Somnath Bharti, also took on the need to find out about the other jailed inmates. How could I write a book on prison life and not write about those who are powerless and without a voice or are wrongly incarcerated? And that's how I met Wahid. His was a high-profile case. He was a man in the news and yet his story had got lost in the sameness of a brutal judicial system which puts the burden of proof on the innocent.

Even after two decades of reporting, his account gave me sleepless nights. I realized how in daily journalism we err in relying too much on what authorities say, in not questioning the prosecution agency. Wahid stands acquitted today after a decade in jail and yet there is no compensation for the time he has lost, for the wounds that he bore from prison. Wahid has given real names of his tormentors, not just to me, but to courts and judges. All of them are decorated police officers – A.N. Roy, K.P. Raghuvanshi, Vijay Salaskar. You cannot dismiss his words because he and the others who have been convicted can show you a Mumbai High Court judgement which upholds how they were beaten in jail, their rights violated and then denied medical treatment. I called the former top cop A.N. Roy about the horrendous details that Wahid and the others have accused him and his team of. They point out that they have a conviction in the 7/11 case in their favour and that the judge has already dealt with accusations of torture. I asked him how he could explain the specific allegations, the time, the dates, the names of officers they have provided. 'They are advised by their lawyers to do this so that they can buy some time. They know that they can't deny the terror evidence but they can get away with human rights violation charges.'

I asked him the question Wahid kept asking me – why would a terrorist keep appearing for questioning every day after a blast? To that Roy didn't give a very convincing answer. He said only some of them were questioned daily before being arrested, others were caught after an exhaustive investigation. Did he use any third degree, I asked him, to which he responded: 'We have not used any third degree method, but we have used psychological means. We would not let them sleep, our team would sit with them. I can assure you beatings did not happen, but other kinds of pressures did happen.' I don't know why that would give Wahid a permanent slow gait and a slight limp, but I asked him how Wahid was now going blind, a direct fallout of his eyes being tied up. He replied, 'I don't know this. What happened to him 10 years ago, can the impact be visible now?'

I didn't have the answers either. As a journalist, we're only told to go by facts and make no assumptions. And so I can't take a judgement call about any of the subjects in my book. Some of them have been proved innocent, while others are in jail waiting for the judicial system to run its course. By writing about them, I am empathizing with their situation. After all, they have entrusted their faith in me to tell their stories to the best of my ability. Some like JP are hoping that by sharing their experiences others don't have to endure the same hell as they did. Some stories, like that of the teenager who ended up going to a juvenile home or baby jail are an eye-opener to what adolescent delinquency looks like in urban India. The headlines from one part of the country talk about Khap panchayats passing fatwas against jeans, and here seduction, rape allegations are all happening on Instagram and being dealt by Jat police personnel who are also now using social media to gather evidence as part of the Indian Penal Code.

I'll always regret not having three stories as part of this book. One is of Kanimozhi, the Dravida Munnetra Kazhagam (DMK) leader who was sent to jail because she was part of the party's mouthpiece Kalaignar TV, which allegedly received kickbacks in the 2G scam. She had done a sit-down interview with me a day before she went to prison but never spoke of her prison experiences afterwards, adopting a stoic silence about it all. When I met her for the book, she told me, 'I don't want cheap sympathy.' She was also very bitter even years later because she, and many others, believed that she was made a political scapegoat while her step-mother Dayalu Ammal, who was the actual director of the company, was let off. Kani wanted to talk but like other public figures was too wary of how it would play out. Her personality is also much more reserved, making her a tough subject for an interviewer.

The other two people I couldn't crack were R.K. Sharma, the Indian Police Service (IPS) officer and Director General of Prisons who went to jail in connection with the murder of journalist Shivani Bhatnagar; and Monica Bedi, the starlet who was arrested along with her boyfriend, underworld don

Abu Salem. Both Bedi and Sharma discussed the book with me in great detail but decided they would wait to tell the world their own stories through their own books. That's the thing about prisons – they make for one hell of a story.

THE FOUR DAYS THAT CHANGED AMAR SINGH

In the same season of discontent that saw A. Raja and the 2G gang go to Tihar, there was another entrant to the 'West Delhi jail of fame', although only for four days. The small-framed, once portly, now shrunk, Amar Singh was arrested in September 2011, exactly three years after he played a starring role in the Indo-US nuclear deal. By then, Dr Manmohan Singh had not just won the vote of confidence in Parliament, he had also won a second round as prime minister and so all such roles were forgotten as history. Those four days that Amar Singh spent in Tihar Jail don't even pop up in political profiles and journalistic copies anymore since the courts erased all allegations of bribery against him. But Amar Singh has neither forgotten nor forgiven, and when I meet him in Parliament as he had made a comeback to the Samajwadi Party (SP) as Rajya Sabha MP in July 2016, he is a changed man.

There are some members of Parliament who are reporter favourites and Amar Singh definitely used to be one of them. If you had a story that was a dull political copy and you needed something to just give it a zing, you could always rely on him for a great quote. Television reporters loved him because he never said no to anybody for a soundbite and he'd never hesitate making the most incredible claims on camera. Political correctness wasn't his forte and he was willing to bitch other netas out too. So, when I approached him to talk about the book, I was taken aback by his silence. I wrote emails, called his secretary numerous times, but there was no response at all. And this was the same Amar Singh who would often regale reporters with his version of inside stories of netas and their parties at his home. His office just told me that the MP hadn't had time to consider my request. And that's when I cornered him in Parliament House.

'I won't lie to you, I've seen your mails.' I waited for some one-liner or joke that was his usual trademark but they weren't coming. 'Those days were very painful and I don't want to talk about them.' I may have looked a little crestfallen at his response for he added to explain: 'You see, I'm not the man I used to be.'

If I hadn't been researching and working on this book, I might have dismissed this statement from him as a flippant remark. But by now I'd met so many people who said the same thing to me. A French national whose years in an Indian jail had left her so paranoid, she didn't want to leave the house while she was on bail; a former prison administrator who ironically also lands up in prison himself – they were just some of the characters I met who felt paranoid about sharing their stories. They felt as if talking about their jail days, even after being acquitted, might somehow bring them back or tempt their fate. As if talking about it in the past tense might invite hubris and might make those days of incarceration real again. And when Amar Singh said no to me that day, I noticed that he was no longer emerging from Parliament hall to surround himself with a gaggle of reporters. 'I am now careful of what I say.'

I respected his feelings and gave up the chase. A couple of months later, I again bumped into him in Parliament. 'Sir, by any chance, have you reconsidered your decision?' He smiled and said, 'Call my office, I'll give you time.'

THE 123 AGREEMENT THAT LED TO 120 IPC

Before the fear and loathing of jails, if there was one thing that the once Congressman-turned-SP general secretary was known for, it was networking. They say that's how he became close to Mulayam Singh Yadav – met him on a flight in 1995 and took his party out of Uttar Pradesh and gave it some sex appeal, introduced him to filmstars like Amitabh Bachchan and industrialists like Anil Ambani. It's the same kind of appeal that the United Progressive Alliance (UPA) approached him with in the summer of 2008 when they were seeking support for the Indo-US nuclear deal. It was not easy for the UPA because the Left was pulling out its support screaming against American Imperialism. So, in the kind of intrigue we've only seen in TV shows like West Wing and House of Cards, the Congress party was looking for miracle friends to survive a confidence vote and they hoped Amar Singh would oblige. That was tricky because, as he aptly describes it, the Left and the SP had a natural affinity, which the Congress and SP didn't: 'The relationship between SP–Congress was blow hot–blow cold. And the relationship between the SP and the Left was cordial and cozy to the extent that each time there was a discussion about the nuclear deal between Comrade [Prakash] Karat and UPA, he would come to my residence and brief us about the details of the discussion.'

If that's the kind of trust that Mulayam Singh and Amar Singh shared with not just Politburo chief Prakash Karat but Left's other senior leaders like Harkishan Singh Surjeet and Sitaram Yechury, their status with the Congress was 'it's complicated'. When the UPA was first formed in 2004, Sonia Gandhi wouldn't even let Amar Singh beyond her outhouse and he felt all slighted and angry after going uninvited to her dinner party. Then, they kept dangling a CBI case against Mulayam Singh, manipulating them for support whenever it was convenient. In 2008, however, the Congress tried to erase all that as the SP became indispensable with their 39 MPs. If the communists left with their 59 MPs over signing of the Indo-US nuclear deal, the band of Samajwadis would provide a great buffer. But could they turn their back on their old comrades?

Amar Singh claims that it was a secret meeting between him and the prime minister's top aide that got him involved in this entire deal. 'The twist came when the National Security Advisor M.K. Narayanan met me.' He doesn't elaborate on what actually transpired at that meeting, that is still classified. 'That is not to be discussed. I wouldn't have said even this much but Dr Manmohan Singh has revealed this after Dr Kalam's death.'

Indeed, Dr Manmohan Singh did confirm, in a 2015 interview to Karan Thapar, Amar Singh's crucial role in helping his government survive. In the interview he had said: 'I was discussing these matters with Amar Singhji and also with Mulayam Singhji and with great difficulty we managed to convince them to re-look at their objections. I remembered the regard Mulayam Singhji had and they went to meet Dr Kalam.'

This was some quick thinking by the good doctor. Because what many wouldn't recall was that Dr Kalam and Mulayam Singh shared a special bond. Way back in the 1990s when Mulayam Singh was the defence minister in the United Front government, he worked with Dr Kalam who was the top government scientist. And it was Mulayam Singh who apparently threw his name in the game when National Democratic Alliance (NDA) was looking for a new president in 2002. 'Why not have a Muslim president? It will send a strong message after Godhra,' he's reported to have suggested to L.K. Advani, Atal Bihari Vajpayee and Pramod Mahajan referring to the Gujarat riots where 3,000 people were killed. In one shot he had killed the other minority contender P.C. Alexander's chances. Mulayam Singh asked if they knew of a 'nationalist' Muslim and no one could dispute the credentials of the missile man, Dr APJ Abdul Kalam.

So when Dr Singh suggested that they speak to former president Dr Kalam about the benefits of the deal, the two thought it was a great idea. 'He was non-biased and not supported by the Congress. We realized his opinion would be beyond politics as he was a specialist in this field.'

They went to meet him and the quintessential teacher that Dr Kalam was, he gave them a bit of a crash course on nuclear energy and India's needs. The 123 Agreement or the Indo-US Civil Cooperation Nuclear Agreement was a greatly technical deal which most people didn't understand and so the two men asked him some basic questions – Is this deal good for India? If so, why and how? Are there any alternatives?

'Dr Kalam said it was a good deal because if India didn't become a member of the Nuclear Suppliers Group, then getting Uranium would become difficult and our atomic programme would suffer. We asked him, wasn't coal enough, and he laughed and said, "No, it was not and you'll see." He said that Hiroshima and Nagasaki could happen anywhere, and that Chernobyl-like nuclear catastrophes could happen anywhere. But nuclear power was the cheapest, and the most conducive power. We also went to the extent of asking if there were any alternative to Uranium for India. Dr Kalam said

Thorium but Thorium-based technology was not available in India and would take a lot of time.'

Mulayam Singh was satisfied, but then came the tricky politics of making the turnaround look right. He may have ditched Sonia Gandhi in 1999 by first pledging support and then going back on his word, but if he was to turn his back on the Left by bailing out the same Congress party now, he had to apparently make it look convincing. So, they struck an agreement and announced their stand in Dr Kalam's house – from being anti-nuke deal to calling it a great deal for the country.

'We said to him, Sir, we would like to announce this in your presence as we had already taken a political decision of supporting the Left. If we make a departure all of a sudden, then we will look like fools.' As smooth, dramatic political moves go, it was right up there as a classic, and for a while Amar Singh was the man about town. 'Throughout, Pranab Mukherjee, the minister of external affairs at the time was briefing me personally and saying I was crucial to the deal. I was also invited when Condoleeza Rice, the US Secretary of State came for an official visit [in 2008]. It was a small group meeting during her state visit and I was part of that.'

While it lasted, it was wonderful; right down to International Atomic Energy Agency (IAEA) head El Baradei giving Amar Singh credit for driving the deal home. Unfortunately for him, these fine diplomatic moments were all forgotten because what was actually seen on 22 July 2008 – the sight of MPs showing one crore rupees in Parliament – overwrote everything else. Amar Singh and Dr Manmohan Singh could claim their cause was nationalist, but the public could only see the dirty cash that had allegedly been paid to buy MPs. It was as if A.B. Bardhan, senior leader of the CPI knew exactly what was happening when he said a week before to the media: 'No one has principles anymore. It is not a question of few crores but ₹25 crore for horse-trading. I have never seen ₹25 crore in my lifetime. I am sure that none of you have seen it either.'

The TV-watching public didn't witness 25 crore rupees, but they did see one crore in cash and that too on the sacred floor of Parliament. And that's where it all slowly started to go very wrong for Amar Singh. From being privy to the most crucial strategy meetings, he was suddenly a bit of a pariah because CNN-IBN, a private news channel had done a sting operation along with the BJP, who claimed Congressmen and Samajwadis namely Amar Singh were the ones trying to buy MPs.

At that time, however, no one could imagine that Amar Singh or the BJP MPs would ever go to jail for this. It all happened very slowly and took its time. In fact, even CNN-IBN didn't air the footage until a month later. They said they were verifying the tapes but the speculation was that the government put too much pressure on them to not air it after they had won the trust vote. It would undermine the win that they were so clearly relishing. But the Opposition, the BJP and the Left, wasn't going to give up so easy. The three BJP MPs Ashok Argal, Faggan Singh Kulaste and Mahabir Singh Bhagora declared themselves whistle-blowers and finally, by the end of the month, a parliamentary probe panel was set up under Congress' K.C. Deo.

The day the panel asked CNN-IBN to depose and they submitted their tapes for the inquiry, they aired the footage. It showed another Samajwadi MP Rewati Raman Singh in a room with the BJP MPs and suggesting they meet 'Saheb' and work out an understanding. The BJP MPs are captured on camera constantly referring to Amar Singh as the person who is doing the deal and offering money for abstaining from the vote. The next day the tapes captured a car purportedly carrying a couple of those MPs (you can't see them because the windows are tinted) to Amar Singh's house. The next thing on the tape shows the MPs in a room and another man Sanjeev Saxena (said to be an aide of Amar Singh) laying out bundles of cash. He gets someone on the line, who the MPs speak and refer to as 'Amar Singh ji'. That's the substance of what's captured on tape.

'There was no evidence against me, no voice, or face of mine. So when the parliamentary committee freed all of us and the Speaker ratified it, the matter should have ended there. Because whatever you say or do within Parliament, is a matter granted immunity.'

And that's almost what happened. The committee looking into the charges against him and the other leaders gave everyone a clean chit by the end of the year. After all, this was the same reason in 1993 that the Jharkhand Mukti Morcha MPs, accused of manipulating the trust vote against Prime Minister P.V. Narasimha Rao, got a reprieve from court because you can't prosecute MPs for what happens inside Parliament.

'Never in Parliament's history has any crime inside been referred to the police. Maybe, because Mr Chidambaram was in immense love with me and had great affection for me, I saved the government of which he was home minister, but he referred my role to be investigated by the Delhi Police.'

Amar Singh's anger against the then Home Minister P. Chidambaram is understandable. He felt vulnerable because by 2011, he didn't have his MP status and neither was he in the SP. He had been sacked for anti-party activities as differences with other members like Azam Khan and Akhilesh Yadav had already cropped up. One of the accused MPs Ashok Argal wasn't even charge sheeted because the Prevention of Corruption Act requires sanction to prosecute a public person. But the saviour of the nuclear deal had no such shield three years down the line.

And in his mind, he couldn't come to terms with the fact that his colleague Rewati Raman Singh who is actually in the sting video, wasn't prosecuted. Others might argue that Amar Singh was far more high profile and the one the BJP was calling the mastermind of cash-for-vote, but Amar Singh doesn't see it quite like that.

'The person who was in the video wasn't touched and the argument given was "sound is blurred, images are hazy". That was true of him but what about me who was not seen in any video? The only evidence was that the co-accused, Sanjeev Saxena, I had helped his son get admission into Dyal Singh College. As an MP, I keep writing letters, but that was used as evidence.' The police was able to convince the judge that the letter of recommendation proved that Saxena was indeed a close associate of Amar Singh and so when he's seen on tape giving the money to the MPs for their vote, he was acting on his directions, especially because the MPs are seen referring to 'Amar Singh' on phone. His contention was, however, that by itself that letter doesn't count for anything because MPs give out recommendations to all.

'In the original case diary, Arun Jaitley and L.K. Advani were all players in the case, but nothing happened to them. V.K. Malhotra of the BJP was in the probe panel, and he said we don't want this probe to go on. My good friend Ram Gopal Yadav, who was our party representative on the panel, said the same thing. Everyone agreed that this should end because Congress had won the vote of confidence and survived, the chapter was closed.'

However, it didn't because at some point, it became much larger than all these politicians. A group called India Rejuvenation Initiative led by former Chief Election

Commissioner J.M. Lyngdoh filed a petition in the Supreme Court for a special probe into the matter. The Delhi Police, which had been sleeping on the case for the last few years, was prodded into action.

'It was a plea of judicial activism and since Lyngdoh was a high-profile person and Anna Hazare and Prashant Bhushan were active, Supreme Court ordered a probe. The person seen in the video talking to MPs was Rewati Raman Singh – he was not touched, and allowed to go scot free. Chidambaram thought I was a vulnerable lamb, a big name who does not have any strings attached with him now, a very nice slaughterable material. And I was slaughtered.'

On 6 September 2011 Amar Singh went to Tihar Jail along with the three BJP MPs, and also senior leader of the BJP, Sudheendra Kulkarni. Police felt that Kulkarni was behind the sting operation as he introduced CNN-IBN to the three MPs and facilitated the offer of cash-for-vote.

IN JAIL WITH MEMORIES OF SHAHRUKH KHAN

You would think that politicians find a way to spin their arrest, a way to take advantage of it all. Amar Singh was a consummate politician, but he wasn't an electoral politician, a man of the masses who would use the experience to meet a different set of people, or really use it to gain sympathy from his voters. He was a typical Rajya Sabha man who was known more for Page 3 parties, and wasn't afraid to flaunt his flamboyant lifestyle. Of course, life had altered in this sphere too, since 2008, as he wasn't being able to take that colourful lifestyle any longer and he had also lost many of his influential friends. A year later, in 2009, Amar Singh was away for months in Singapore getting treatment for his renal condition and then finally getting a kidney transplant. His transplant status was his biggest plea in the case.

'I argued in the Rajan Pillai biscuit baron case, it was established that the infirm and sick shall not be kept in jail. I am a kidney transplant patient who continues to be vulnerable. Sangita Dhingra, who was the Queen of Justice, didn't pay any attention to my plea.'

Rajan Pillai had died in custody in Tihar in 1995 because of lack of medical attention. It was the best instance to invoke. Amar Singh also hired Ram Jethmalani whose daughter Rani Jethmalani suffered from the same condition and had also had a kidney transplant. She eventually died of her condition in 2010, but in Amar Singh's bail hearing, her father gave her example explaining why Tihar could be dangerous for someone with this condition. A senior lawyer like him would never usually appear in the desolate Tis Hazari courts, but for Amar Singh, he made that exception too. But all of this amounted to nothing.

'The judge asked how come I didn't get myself treated in India, why did I go to Singapore? I told her that I am an influential person and I should have been arrested before so that I don't influence the investigation. Now that I have been charge sheeted, what is the point of arresting me? The trial should happen and afterwards I can be sent to jail.' Judge Dhingra, however, wasn't in the mood to listen and packed off the 55-year-old to judicial custody. Amar Singh immediately discovered the price of fame.

'I was told in Tis Hazari to give my chain, my watch and everything on my body. I handed over everything. I was made to sit in a black van. There was quite a media glare and I felt the ruthlessness, their hunger for headlines. I went to jail, and all the sentries started saluting me not realizing that I was a prisoner.'

The man who would actively seek out the media was now resenting its scrutiny, while his glamorous and influential friends were trying their best and going to great lengths to avoid him. For instance, even the Tihar boss, IPS officer Neeraj Kumar went on a long leave to avoid meeting him, or to expect him to do him any favours. In fact, so that he wouldn't even call him, he went to Singapore. Amar Singh dismisses the thought that it could have been just a coincidence.

Luxuries and indulgences are all relative. To the 14,000 odd inmates, the area where the 2G accused were imprisoned was super fancy because they had Western toilets, was clean and also had some open space. Amar Singh was lodged there along with them, but all he could see was the stripped-down version of living.

'I was given a small *chatai* [mat] with no pillow. I was given a bucket of water with a mug. So if I had to drink water, I had to drink from that and if I had to shit, I would have to wash myself using that mug. My friend Kiran Bedi had converted Tihar Jail into a classless jail. If you are of some status or if you are a rapist, you should be treated the same. That idea was in full implementation at that time.'

Part of the anxiety and bitterness was due to the setback to his status, what he saw as an affront to his position. The rest of it was vulnerability of his health. 'My creatinine level was becoming very high because a kidney transplant patient is a repaired commodity and not a rectified one. A borrowed kidney has to be maintained. Any nephrologist will tell you how transplant patients have to live in a clean atmosphere and eat hygienic food. Using the same mug for your arse and for your mouth, sleeping on a *chatai* and hospital where few are likely to be treated, you are sure to get an infection. It is certainly not conducive for any patient taking immune-suppressive drug. What is that drug? It is given to kidney patients to kill their immunity to help the organ survive. So, Amar Singh without immunity system, Amar Singh known for his kidney disease, Amar Singh who was charge sheeted, none of this was considered by Judge Sangita Dhingra, the right honourable judge! I thank her for her justice!' He doesn't mention because he perhaps doesn't know that Sangita Dhingra got a lot of media attention for being the brave and upright judge who sent this VIP to jail. There were profiles done in newspapers about her, and of course, the anti-corruption brigade outside, Anna Hazare and Arvind Kejriwal were calling all politicians thieves and asking them all to be locked up.

The atmosphere of those days is quite aptly captured in a story that Amar Singh loves to tell. 'There was once a giant who came to a village and started picking up people randomly to eat. One day, he picked on a couple, and took away the man, leaving the wife widowed. The head of the village went to meet the giant and said, you want flesh, we will provide you the flesh. We'll give you those who are old, who've already lived their lives. Let us give you the flesh. Just like that, the system is providing the people the victims of their choosing. For example, in Commonwealth Games Scam, Sheila Dikshit was the main person, Suresh Kalmadi was only a part, but he was sent to jail. Kanimozhi is also a part that's been given. The moral of the story is, the giant of the judiciary had suddenly risen. In CWG, instead of Sheila, Kalmadi was given. In cash-for-votes, they had given me. I was a big name and yet, my arrest wouldn't affect the government. Suresh Kalmadi's arrest wouldn't affect the government. The principle of democracy is collective responsibility. I am not defending Raja, but as a political science student, the prime minister is first among equals.'

For those four days that these selected, powerful few spent together in jail, new relationships were formed and some old baggage dumped. When Amar Singh saw Karim Morani in Tihar, initially it was a bit awkward. Karim Morani after all was best friends with Singh's frenemy Shah Rukh Khan and the last time that they met in 2004, they almost came to blows.

Apparently, it was a Zee TV show organized by Shah Rukh and the Moranis. Despite his terribly busy schedule, Amar Singh had cajoled his friend Amitabh Bachchan to make an appearance at the event. However, when Big B arrived with Amar Singh at the venue, they were given seats in the tenth row and obviously, they were not amused.

'We were leaving in a huff when Shah Rukh and Morani came and offered to shift us in the front row. We said if Amitabh Bachchan and Amar Singh need to request someone to get a front row, it was a very silly situation. We were not their sponsored or paid artistes, we were invited as guests. And since we felt we were not given our due dignity, we left and they didn't have a right to stop us. There was a scuffle between us.'

Obviously that scuffle was no small thing because just a couple of years down the line, and owing to Shah Rukh's challenge to Amitabh Bachchan's position in the film industry, Amar Singh and Shah Rukh kept fighting over silly things. Shah Rukh made fun of him at a film awards event, after which Amar Singh got a whole bunch of his protestors to demonstrate outside Shah Rukh's house which made his daughter cry. The two also fought when Amar Singh said snarky things about Shah Rukh's detention in the US and the star hit back with another snide remark about Amar Singh's health and wellness. These fights continued but when Amar Singh saw Karim Morani as his cellmate in Tihar, he knew jail trumps everything. 'Destiny made us land as strange bedfellows in Tihar. We had no option. Like if there is a flood, a snake and a human being both take shelter on the tree and they are both worried about their life. They forget the trait of fighting with each other as they are worried about their own lives. We were in gloom, we were in distress and we were thrown together in the same cell.'

Amar Singh had made all kinds of enemies because he was thick with the Bachchan family. The story goes that it was Amar Singh who turned things around financially when Bachchan's company ABCL was going bust. That long association, however, took a hit in jail. He can't forgive Bachchans for not coming to see him in jail.

'When I got bail, Mr Bachchan came to see me, but I was not impressed. I must mention, my very old friends Shyam and Hari Bhartia (of the Hindustan Times group) came to see me before I got bail. They were very normal. Bachchan only came after I was granted bail and was in hospital. I was very cold and formal with him because he waited. He is a politically correct, suave person. Subrata Roy was also the same. I went to see him in Tihar twice. I said that I must do to people what they did to me. He took far too long to come.'

Nothing tests a relationship like standing in the dock. Amar Singh may have resented others in the Bachchan family long before Tihar. For instance, he never forgot that once when he was going to Subrata Roy's party, his ride, a helicopter, was halted because it had to go back to pick up Aishwarya Rai. He also always nursed grudges against Jaya Bachchan for saying less than complimentary things about him in their SP circles. But Amitabh Bachchan had been a constant and even hung out with him in Singapore while he was recuperating from his kidney ailment. They may have been together in sickness and in health, but they couldn't do the same when in jail: 'When he came to meet me I didn't feel like talking to him because the feelings I had for him, the friendship had gone. They had got filtered from my mind and the realization had dawned that mostly people are weathercocks.'

As Amar Singh puts it, the Ambanis, the Bachchans, the 'it crowd', all 'vaporized'. And the deepest cut of all, his VIP doctor, Padma Shri winning nephrologist Dr Ramesh Kumar also deserted him. When Amar Singh's wife called the doctor and asked him to come visit him, he told them, 'No, no, I want to stay away from you, because you are a criminal.' The same doctor, who's also former PM A.B. Vajpayee's doctor, would before this incident call him all the time for 'small, petty favours'. Amar Singh said this betrayal really shocked his wife, more than anything else. At that time, his twin girls were just seven years old. Amar Singh is worth thousands of crores, but even he talks about the expense of hiring big lawyers for hefty fees and then the case being adjourned for 'some silly excuse like they are having some headache, there is a wedding or a funeral in the family.' Lakhs of rupees being spent and you have no choice because it's either that or endless stay in jail. 'My wife who is completely unaware of these worldly pursuits knew just Salman Khurshid, a friend who was also the law minister. However, he too refused to see her.' Amar Singh says she is yet to recover from the shock. His four days in jail have left her insecure and scared. 'She doesn't want to trust anybody, wants to remain closeted. She has almost become mental, she has not come out of that shock.'

It's all these betrayals, he says, that has made his bond stronger with actress-turned-politician Jaya Prada. He was the one who introduced her to politics and launched her as an SP MP from Rampur. In 2006, taped conversations between the two leaked where he's commending her for being a good 'follower'. He's also heard appreciating the way she 'waxes' her legs because he likes them that way. 'Jaya Prada was the only person who came out openly in my support. People keep talking shit about our relationship but nobody sees the pure dedication and commitment. When everybody from Bachchans to Ambanis to Saharas were not in sight, she was the only known face who came forward and because of her MP status, she got some privileges and ensured my wife could come and meet me. Otherwise my wife would not have been able to meet me. How can I forget Jaya Prada? People and their fertile imagination, but I will not forget her and Dr Ramesh Kumar, the two extremes.'

Amar Singh also left a deep impression on other inmates. In one of his letters, inmate Kobad Ghandy mentions meeting them together in Tihar:

The other day I bumped into Amar Singh and Jaya Prada when I went to meet the superintendent. Amar Singh was ever so warm saying he knew all about me and was himself a college (or school) student in Calcutta during the years of turmoil in the early 1970s. And they were on about a Bengali film they had recently made on the Naxalite movement, where Jaya Prada plays the main role as a Naxalite leader and Amar Singh a politician sympathetic to the Naxals. Interesting! They said the picture was doing well at the box office. The same night he was shifted to All India Institute of Medical Sciences (AIIMS). Teams of doctors were swarming the place at that time. (September 2011)

Sushil Sharma remembered a chance meeting with him in Tihar. 'I just appreciated what a fiery leader he used to be in Kolkata. He had tears in his eyes because he realized I remembered him from the good days.'

Amar Singh spent just four days in jail, then was moved to AIIMS where he stayed for months till he got bail. The Tihar hospital was deemed inadequate for his needs but he fondly remembered the man he met there, accused of being a Maoist: 'I grew up reading Mahashweta Devi's novel *Hajar Churashir*

Maa and the Naxalite movement was one I observed very closely. I was a student of law in Calcutta, and people close to Charu Mazumdar and Kanu Sanyal were there. My friend Prasenjit also became a Naxalite and their ideas were very pure – reduce differences between haves and have nots. The slogans I remember were "*Lal bazaar e laal pukar, Ranjt Gupta hoshiyar*" (Ranjit Gupta was the Calcutta police commissioner who played a controversial role in tackling the Naxal movement). All these memories were going through my head when I saw Kobad. I saw some similarities between him and me. Because he is also a Xavierian like me, I am also from a good family and he is also from a good family, he is rather from a better family. He was also suffering very badly.'

Unlike Kobad, though, Amar Singh's suffering was short-lived. Within four days, the authorities decided to shift him. As he says, they suddenly realized they couldn't risk a health crisis with him in jail. The 2G men who were a band of brothers inside, apparently asked him to stay on. 'These 2G guys were having their own group and fun. And they adjusted properly. Only Anil Ambani's executives were sad because according to them, they were not the beneficiaries, they were just paid executives. All of them said don't go to hospital as here at least we are all together, all like-minded, white-collared people are here. You will have nice company for about a year.'

It's not difficult to see that kind of proximity in just a couple of days in jail. They would all be locked up every evening by 7 p.m. and then he'd regale them with his observations, gossip and stories.

AMAR AFTER

And so Amar Singh got out of that 'situation'. A room in AIIMS was made into a jail and for three months Amar Singh stayed there. Closely tracking his health was the upright judge.

'Every day, Justice Sangita Dhingra would ask – when will he be all right. The nephrologist Dr Sanjay Gupta would say, "Maybe he is your accused and you are desperate to send him to jail but he is my patient and as long as creatinine levels and blood samples are not fine, I cannot give you the go-ahead."'

As jail insiders say, hospital is the haven for those accused. Even if you cuff someone to their oxygen tank, they'll prefer it to a room in Tihar. And here Amar Singh could meet his family whenever he chose, and the visitor list also became much longer than in jail. Even UPA's top minister, Pranab Mukherjee came to see him. Amar Singh believes Home Minister Chidambaram's tough stand towards him may be rooted to his apparent proximity with his rival, Mukherjee. But then, it could be the paranoia that's also typical of those who've been jailed. Paranoia and loyalty, the two common traits of an ex-inmate. The loyalty was towards Jaya Prada, and towards his then estranged boss, Mulayam Singh Yadav.

'Netaji gave a statement in my favour and he said the party was with me. More than that he couldn't do anything because he is not a judge.' He was an expelled man with his own party but the fact that Mulayam still called him his own, warms his heart even now. As do smaller gestures. Like Sonia and Priyanka Gandhi asking about his health. They apparently kept asking Jaya Prada in Parliament and they were 'genuinely concerned'.

As he sat, during our interviews, in his office at Kasturba Gandhi Marg in October 2016, Amar Singh was quietly watching news developments around him. Two pieces of news were of particular interest to him. One, the ongoing Enforcement Directorate (ED) probe into the Aircel–Maxis investment which got its FDI clearance on P. Chidambaram's watch and second, the ED probe into son Karti Chidambaram's business firm.

'I don't hold a grudge against Chidambaram. Now they are also facing problems, I pray for them, that they should not go to Tihar and face what I faced. He is also on a pedestal, from where he is facing ED. If he goes to Tihar, it is a bad thing. Apparently, he is a very cold person and doesn't realize other's miseries. Maybe, when he goes through it himself, he will realize.'

The other case he is interested in is the one about tax havens in Panama and the accusation that Amitabh Bachchan and Aishwarya Rai may have had offshore accounts there. 'The government is just probing that, let's see what happens.' And he then signs off, smiling with this couplet:

> *'Sitam karoge, sitam karenge.*
> *Karam karoge, karam karenge.*
> *Jo tum karoge, wo hum karenge.'*

THE AMERICAN MALLU WHO
SURVIVED JAIL

When I met JP at his office in Delhi, it was more than four years since he'd come out of jail. At 42, JP can pass off as a former model – he's relatively tall, dark and has the leanness of someone who works out regularly. From some angles, he looks like a duskier version of Milind Soman, only that he has jet black hair. And when he speaks, it's always in a charming, soft, articulate voice, with three quarters American and a quarter of Malayali accent. His Malayali accent becomes more pronounced when he speaks in Hindi, and while he always knew the language, it was only Tihar that turned it into a powerful tool and gave him a much more colourful vocabulary. As we are about to wrap up our first interview, a person walks in and JP asks him to sit while he walks me out. 'You know who that is? That's Bharti Yadav's husband.' Every journalist knows Bharti Yadav. She was the woman who had an affair with her classmate at MBA school, Nitish Katara, that led to her brother and her cousin, Vikas and Vishal Yadav, murdering him. The two were in jail serving a life sentence and JP had spent time with them while inside. 'They're good guys,' he says, seeing my expression appropriate for their notoriety. 'Bharti's husband comes to see me because I help him out with some work.'

What is the kind of universe that makes Vikas and Vishal Yadav seem like 'good guys', I couldn't comprehend. The son of another notorious politician, D.P. Yadav, Vikas and his cousin Vishal had killed Nitish by setting him on fire. And this wasn't Vikas's only claim to the criminal hall of fame. He had also helped Manu Sharma escape in the Jessica Lal murder case and so was out on bail from one murder case when he committed another. But JP, with his easy charm, was confident they weren't the real villains that populated jails. And that's when he agreed to tell me his story. The only reason he wanted his identity to be kept secret was because of his attempt at starting over. His jail backstory was compelling but wouldn't be so impressive in his current line of work.

IIII

At the time of his detention in September 2008, JP was in Dubai. As he says, he was living the good life, running an advertising agency that he had started in 2003 and living in an apartment on Palm Islands. His parents lived with him but his mother had just undergone a kidney transplant and was recuperating in India. What JP didn't know when he was coming down to see his mother was that the Americans through Interpol had put out a red corner notice for him.

'I was shocked when they stopped me at Sahar,' JP recalls the day he landed at the airport in Mumbai. Coming to India was a regular thing with an extended family in Kerala and this was totally unexpected. At the time he had no idea that this was linked to his drug-related arrest in the US. In 2003, he was detained in Virginia when the police recovered ecstasy pills from his friend's car. He was bailed out the same night, but because he left for Dubai and did not attend the trial, he didn't realize that he was entering a phase of a never-ending nightmare in his life.

Sitting at the Mumbai airport though, he started feeling that initial phase of shame that so many white-collar prisoners experience. He looked around the detention room with people who had fake visas or fake passports, and he thought about his family – a family well respected all over Kerala and in the expat community of Dubai and where no one had ever gone to jail. 'Suddenly, an idea struck me and I looked at the medicine bag I was carrying for my mum.' At that time, his personal belongings were still with him and he thought about this one medicine for kidney patients, which he had heard could be fatal for others. 'Everyone in my family looks up to me. I have about 40 cousins, my dad has eight brothers and two sisters and I kept thinking about the embarrassment I was going to cause them all. So, I took the medicine in my hand. I thought what's the worst that could happen if I die? My mum will cry for a month, but at least there will be no embarrassment.' He juggled these thoughts in that small toilet at the Sahar airport. With the tap running, he was about to take that fatal medicine when he heard another voice inside his head. 'Ok, suppose you don't commit suicide, how would your life unfold? Let's just see what happens.' JP says that at that moment, a battle between death and life had occurred within him. And life, miserable though it was, came out triumphant.

After a few hours of being detained at the airport, he was moved to the attached police station where they handcuffed him to the table. All these developments were slowly driving the fact to him – he was under arrest. It's just that no one had bothered to tell him. JP realized much later that it was also because they weren't familiar with how to treat such cases of Interpol detainees. JP had an Indian passport but he was wanted by the all-powerful FBI.

'This was a regular police station so people were being brought in for various crimes – drunken driving and other things. I stayed cuffed to the table for 3 hours and then they realized I was harmless and they un-cuffed me.'

During the routine court appearance and medical check up, JP had his first initiation into Indian idiosyncrasies. Apparently, at that time, somebody had hurled his shoe at the judge. So, instead of keeping an eye out for such errant behaviour, the judge had passed an order that no prisoner would be brought inside the courtroom in shoes. Stripped of footwear, JP was taken to court and he remembers having to go the bathroom barefoot.

'From a rich life, I was transported to a black hole. The toilet was full of goo, so much so that when I was lifting my feet off the ground, the black peanut butter lifted off my feet.' From the description you could feel JP was still traumatized by that toilet. Having been transferred to police custody, he was taken to a different lockup by evening – a room with no lights and insects crawling everywhere. That entire night, JP just sat. The place was so dirty he could not even think of lying down. He was given something in a plastic bag to eat, and it all added up to repulsing him tremendously.

By the next day, things started looking a little better. His uncle had come in from Kerala and JP was in a position to negotiate with the police – with good old-fashioned bribery. The price worked out was a daily sum of 10,000 rupees and what it bought him was first, the freedom to use a phone.

'I owned a restaurant in Dubai, I had a business and while I was in custody, life had to go on. So, I called my brother in the US to give directions to handle everything. We couldn't actually tell anyone where I was but even in the shock, we were all trying to figure out what to do.'

The daily bribe also gave him access to better food, brought in by his uncle. The most important aspect was that he didn't have to spend the day in the lockup. All day, he could be at the police station, eat outside food, and only at night, was he taken to the filthy lockup with no lights and insects crawling all over him. That's how four days just went by – a back and forth between the holding cell and the police station. In a way, it was JP's first real interaction with India. Brought up in Dubai, studied in Connecticut University, he hadn't even interacted with the traffic police in India. He was going to have to learn things very fast. And the first big lesson he learnt was about the power of money.

JP's family hired a lawyer who was told that he had to find a solution to the cell in Mumbai. The lawyer didn't come cheap – he charged 2.5 lakh rupees per appearance but he did get the judge to pass an order that provided an option. Standing barefoot in court, JP was told he could be moved to Delhi and face extradition trial there. 'In my head, I kept thinking I would get go back to the US and just deal with my case there.' There was another option that the lawyer gave JP's uncle. If they coughed up 50 lakh rupees, then they would get him out. 'We didn't have that kind of money to spend and there was no guarantee. What would "get me out" mean? Would it be bail, or just out of the case?' So they took the transfer option. What he didn't know at that time was that he would get so involved in the politics of Tihar, he'd end up serving 10 times the amount of punishment just in Delhi.

The day after the order, JP's uncle bought train tickets in Rajdhani for him and the two policemen who'd accompany him. JP remembers them wearing civilian clothes and carrying Samsonite suitcases. 'They had spoken to my family so there was some comfort factor. However, these people or anybody else would never tell me what was going on. What would happen when I reached Delhi? What should I expect in such a case? No one said anything and maybe it was because they didn't know either.'

After their goodbyes, the three got into an auto and were on their way to the railway station when at one point, JP remembers, he asked for some water, and the cops let him get down from the auto and buy it himself. 'I remember I crossed the road, and bought the water and some gum and then slowly walked back.' Much later in the jail, whenever he recalled this story, the others told him he had basically been given an opportunity, which in his naïveté, he threw away. 'The cops, obviously, wanted me to run away. But I was innocent then.'

His chance to escape thrown away, JP settled down in the train with the two men and their friend – a bottle of Royal Stag. They asked him, '*Piyega?*', and a cozy, illicit train party began. Between the three, they finished the entire bottle and just when things were getting really friendly, they took the handcuffs out and cuffed him to the bar on the berth. 'I was shocked and embarrassed. They hid the cuffs with the sheet, and were discreet enough but being handcuffed in a public space was another wake-up call.' As the Crime Manual puts it, handcuffs should be avoided. That's why when you walk into any court in India you will see the slightly comic scene of policemen holding hands with the prisoners. The Prem Shanker Shukla vs Delhi Administration judgement of the Supreme Court says that if you feel that you have to use handcuffs because your prisoner is dangerous and may run away, you have to get special permission from a magistrate. The court held:

'It is disgusting to see the mechanical way in which callous policemen, in cavalier fashion, handcuff prisoner in their charge, indifferently keeping them company assured by the thought that the detainee is under "iron" restraint.'

Forget magistrate's permission, in JP's case it was just to ensure that they got to sleep well after getting drunk.

By next morning, they were at the New Delhi Railway Station, a place totally unfamiliar to JP, as was the entire capital. They took an auto to the CBI headquarters which was the officiating office of Interpol in India and they met an officer there. 'He was very, very civil and heard my story. He had applied for his Canadian visa and kept asking me how to go about it, figuring from my American accent that I was a foreign boy and would know how it worked.' The officer was so grateful for all the inputs that he took them in his own car to court. JP had no idea he was in the infamous Patiala House courts and all he could figure out was that they talked to a man about him. The man was apparently the judge. After that, the CBI guy suggested that they take his car and not the '*doosra gadi*' (the other vehicle). 'At that time, I didn't know that *doosra gadi* was the ferry bus for Tihar. I didn't know that I was being sent to judicial custody.'

JP's police custody phase had now ended, and on 20 September 2008 he entered the jail phase of his life.

JP only realized he was entering Tihar Jail when he saw the gate and the signboards. The word 'Tihar' had no meaning for him at the time. The gate opened, the two policemen got off to deliver him and then they turned to him to say – '*Kuch to de do* (Give us something).' JP was fast learning how it worked. Just like in Mumbai, where 10,000 rupees daily helped to get him out of the lockup during the day, these policemen wanted payback for the relative comfort they had given him during transit. JP had 12,000 rupees which his uncle had given him for travel expenses. Out of this, he gave the officers 8,000 rupees. 'They were like "*Bas, itna hi?*". Their attitude was – I gave you booze, I took care of you, only for this much!' It was 5 days in custody and JP had already spent 5 lakh rupees including his lawyers' fees.

LIFE IN A MULAIZA WARD

The first set of people you meet when you enter the Delhi Central Jail are the Tamil Nadu Special Police or TSP. The most fascinating thing about the TSP is that they are a testimony to the understanding that people from South India are less likely to be corrupt than those from the North. As JP noted, Tihar Jail wouldn't function without the TSP. These guards who don't get fazed made him wait for half hour with a polythene of food which the Mumbai police had left him with. They hadn't told him anything about what he should expect, or how long he'd be in Tihar. It was all up in the air for JP.

After the routine medical check-up where they asked if he was beaten or bore any scars on his body, JP was asked to pull his pants down and remove his shirt for a complete search. He remembers it to be the first time he was 'standing naked in front of another man. The first time after maturing and attaining an adult state.' The search of his anus over, the TSP then conducted a more physical form of search. They made him turn this way and that; they checked the lining of his clothes and the lining of his track pants. He was wearing a green and white T-shirt that he'd worn on the train and would continue to wear for many more days to come.

The next level was moving inside another gate where he met two men in white shirt and trousers. These men are convicts who also serve as semi-officials because they have been around for long. They asked JP his and his father's name. 'Giving my father's name was something I had never done abroad, it was very new to me.' It was such a common practice in jail that everyone knew everyone else's father's name.

One of the men in white had been given papers about JP and he, a convict, after seeing his Dubai and US background started speaking to him in English. It was after days that JP had a proper conversation instead of one in Hindi, which wasn't fluent. And that's when this man gave him a life-changing piece of advice. 'You are an Indian with a case in America. Do you speak Hindi?' JP nodded. 'Don't speak Hindi in jail,' he said. JP didn't know him. Didn't know if he was an inmate or some official. But he took his advice seriously.

JP was finally taken to barrack 14C in Jail Number 4. It was about 7 p.m. and was lock-in time but the first thing he witnessed was a custodial beating. There was a man being beaten mercilessly. He had no idea what was happening but the man, who by now was also bleeding was soon taken away. JP later found out that he was being beaten because he took too long to say goodbye while heading out of the *mulaiza* ward. *Mulaiza* is the ward where first-timers are kept and after the first two months, they are either bailed out or moved to another ward, and this unfortunate soul was collecting somebody's letter to the outside world. The others with him, who were also being moved, were in a hurry, and they started raining blows on him. JP's first lesson – if you upset other inmates and they beat you, no prison official will ever intervene.

'*Khana khayega*? Will you eat?' The words came from the leader of that ward and JP, even though he has had no food that day, could only manage a 'no'. The food looked as if it had been out for a long time. It was in a *balti* (bucket), and the remnants of what would have been soya chunks and potato, were staring at him. 'Even beggars get better food. There were flies everywhere and it looked disgusting.' More than food, his concern was finding a place to sleep in the barrack. It was so packed, there was barely any space between two people.

JP got some room underneath a shelf. They gave him a brown coloured material to sleep on – poky, scratchy, like a scotch brite that was about 1 mm thick. And the mosquitoes feasted on him. The man sleeping next to him said in broken English, 'Bhai, you should eat food.' Already, they were curious about him. He was dark skinned like Indians but spoke no Hindi and had an accent. '*Arre yeh to baat hi nahi karta hai* (This one doesn't speak),' they said.

As JP tried to sleep, he thought of the past week and the ordeal it had been. He didn't know what was next. His thoughts were drowned by the common TV that played some Bollywood film till 11 p.m.

The wake-up call next day came at 6 a.m. Feeling leached out by the mosquitoes, the inmates were made to line up while prayers were sung. They pulled out JP and a few others and made them squat in four lines. Then they allowed him to freshen up, use the toilet in a bathroom with piles and mountains of shit. 'You have to find an empty spot to shit or you have to shit on top of somebody else's shit. The mountains of shit were formations in different colours because people hadn't put water after they used it.' Of course, JP said, compared to Mumbai, this was heaven on earth. Here he could see the metal of the commode. There he couldn't see anything but crap.

Back outside, the chosen few were taken to a place in jail where some construction was happening. JP's task was to carry massive blocks of stone. As he carried heavy blocks, he thought this was going to be his life from now on. He noticed some people were trying to communicate with him. They would say 'USA' or monosyllables of English especially when JP again refused to eat the black chana served on newspaper strips. '*Arrey, yeh to kuch kha hi nahi raha* (He's not even eating anything).'

The construction work lasted till noon. JP couldn't get over how from owning three companies, he was reduced to doing manual labour. He cleaned his hands in a concrete tub full of algae-like substance when lunch was served, again in *baltis*. It was the same unappealing soya chunks. The man next to him asked, 'Why aren't you eating? Do you have any money?' And without waiting for an answer, he gave him a coupon worth 20 rupee. With the money shared by the Good Samaritan JP bought *pakoras* from the canteen and some soap for his use. And it wouldn't be the only act of kindness the two exchanged. Falsely accused of a dowry death, he would forever be suicidal and JP would go on to become a kind of counsellor to him.

By evening, it was shower time in jail. JP hadn't had one since he got on the train. With the soap he now had, he went to the hosepipe which everyone used as a shower. It was outdoors and everyone would shower in their underwear and then use a towel to change their underwear too. JP had no spare clothes, so he knew that he would have to go indoors to the toilet to dry his body. He saw how the others were noticing his body. There were whispers of 'bodybuilder' and his cut muscles. JP went inside the bathroom warily and was relieved to see it was shit-free. While he had been doing construction work, some unfortunate undertrial was made to clean the loo. He believed he hadn't been chosen for that job because he spoke English and apparently no Hindi, '*Is chutiya ka kya karein? Kuch samajh mein nahi aata hai isko* (What do we do with this moron? He doesn't understand a thing).'

The next day JP woke up with blisters all over his hands and feet, blisters that had ruptured too. He was spared the construction work and it was on the second day that he also gave in to hunger and had his first jail meal of two *rotis* and soya chunks and potatoes. There was no work for the next few days because of his affliction and he met some other people who seemed to know English. 'They were dressed well, were sitting with officers and seemed educated.' These were a bunch of real estate dealers who were in for some fraud and were fascinated by JP's backstory. Beguiled by his American connection, they started giving guidance about lawyers.

While JP hung out with this lot all morning, no one disturbed him, and then at around noon, after lunch, the entire jail got locked-in, which is the norm. As JP explained, they forcefully want to put you to sleep, so that even they can have some rest. During lock-in time, only those who are favoured and influential get special permissions to move around.

It was during the lock-in that JP heard the intercom going off: 'JP, son of TP, please report to *chakkar*.' Now, it was a matter of good fortune for JP that his father's name happened to be the same as the deputy superintendent (DS) of the jail. The DS happened to be from Kerala like JP, and they immediately thought that this NRI inmate is related to the jail boss. JP didn't do anything to dispel that myth.

So, he headed to the *chakkar* to figure out who was finally asking for him. 'You know how parents say "*Beta, in chakkaron mein mat par*", the jail *chakkar* comes from that phrase. You don't want to know what happens there. If the superintendent sits in the entrance area of the jail, the deputy superintendent, the assistant superintendent sit in the *chakkar* area. These officials sit there with their 'orderly', commonly called 'urtherly'. They are convicts who act as assistants to the officials and are often beyond the law. Their duty is to be the mediator between the inmates and the officials. You route all your requests through them as they are the designated persons attached to the officials and if they don't like you, they will ensure that you end up regretting it. The dirty work of asking for bribes is also done through them.

Being summoned to the *chakkar* is always stressful. The stand-alone building is often described as the nerve centre of the jail and a call from there could mean being bailed out or it could also mean that you get your bones broken. While the front area of the *chakkar* is covered by CCTV, the back area is always off the record. It's here where the torture happens. JP recalls that every day they would hear cries of someone who would be strung up on a pole, with their wrists and ankles tied to it, and the rest of their body hanging. 'It was like a chicken on a grill and they would hit you on the feet.' They would beat people till they were on the verge of dying, then they'd untie them and make them walk. In pain, the tortured man would fall, when they'd kick and say, "*Abey, bhenchod uth*". As soon as the person was on his feet and capable of walking, they'd again tie him up and repeat the process. The person would then be taken to the jail dispensary or the Deen Dayal Upadhyay hospital where the staff would do the necessary patch up without any questions asked. The reason for this torture could be anything – insolence or the jail officials being paid off to treat someone like that.

That day, the *chakkar* people told JP to go to the canteen. When JP got there, for the first time in many days, he saw proper food being prepared. The one who had summoned him was an inmate called Avtar Singh who was running the canteen. Avtar had heard from the jail grapevine that an American had arrived in Tihar. The reason for Avtar's interest was logical and was soon revealed. He was facing death penalty in the US for killing his wife. He used to be an accountant in Starbucks there and when he found out his wife had an extramarital affair, he killed her. He then tried to commit suicide but when he couldn't, he booked a flight back to India. The FBI put him on the watch list and when he landed in Germany, he was arrested. Over the next four years that he spent in Tihar, he rose to be one of the most influential people in Jail Number 4. He was extradited after that and is now on death row in the US.

Avtar's canteen on that day looked heart-breakingly tempting to JP – pakoras, bondas, bun-samosas, everything his starved eyes hadn't seen for days. Apart from selling these, if you paid 30 rupees, you could get your tasteless jail food enhanced. Those who could afford 30 rupees per meal could also afford to have an inmate as servant to do the running around. His job was to gather the jail food, run down to the canteen to get it enhanced, and then live off the leftovers. The canteen also catered to special needs. For instance, the Nigerians loved a dish that was made of *suji* (semolina). This was so tasty that it was sought after by other inmates too, for the price of 45 rupees per plate.

JP was admiring the tempting food when Avtar gave him *parathas* and *dahi*. It was his first proper meal and he wiped off the two *parathas* and wanted more, but wasn't sure whether to ask. 'I didn't know at the time that he was the owner so I didn't know if he was paying. Even though I was really hungry I couldn't ask for more food.' In exchange for the hospitality, Avtar wanted to scope out how much JP knew about prisons in America. He knew he was eventually headed there, so he wanted all the information. It was a conversation that he wouldn't tire of having so he eventually hired JP to do the accounts for the canteen.

Just hanging out with Avtar brought JP in touch with other influential people in Tihar. The only ones who could talk to him were the ones who spoke English, who were better off than the others and dressed better. There was one called Jojo who took a particular interest in his case and wanted to know which ward he had been allotted to stay. JP seemed to have made quite an impression because that evening at 7 p.m. when everyone was about to get locked-in, there was another announcement for him to report to *chakkar*.

'Everyone was looking at me and shouting "*bail ho gaya*" and "*release ho gaya*" as that was the usual time for that. As he was being taken out, he heard someone say, "*Samaan leke aa jao*. Ward change *ho gaya* (Your ward has been changed, get your stuff).'

JP had practically no *samaan*. He was wearing the same clothes he travelled in and after saying bye to Ward 14, he reached Ward Number 6.2. When he arrived, he realized that Jojo had spread the word and he'd been moved there to be a part of Kamaljeet's posse. Kamaljeet had the distinction of being the first man charged with the Maharashtra Control of Organised Crime Act for operating a high-profile prostitution racket. Ward 6.2 was like a second *mulaiza*, where you could stay for six months, and already the difference between this and where JP had come from became evident. He was soon offered food – not the inedible, puke-worthy stuff that had been served till then, but *proper* food. They also gifted JP a towel, and for the first time in jail, JP had space to sleep. It was luxury that was unimaginable. Kamaljeet had also been given that brown rag to sleep on, but he had taken many and made a mattress with it. On top, he'd laid a nice bedsheet so that the roughness of the rag wouldn't disturb him. While in the previous ward some would have had to sit and sleep because of the overcrowding, here Kamaljeet had paid people off to get extra space. 'Privilege in jail is that you got space and cleanliness. In the previous space, where 15 would have slept, now only three were sleeping. Here, instead of having everyone jump on to the food *baltis*, they had cucumber and radish salad with *subzi* that came from Avtar's canteen. It was all available because it was paid for.'

JP was quickly learning why that first man he met in white had advised him to speak in English. It, coupled with his American background, made him a showpiece for gangsters like Kamaljeet. They would also make fun of him in Hindi, thinking he couldn't understand. And, it would also allow him to escape petty jail rules and intimidate the staff. So, every day when he would go to visit Avtar at 2 in the afternoon, when everyone had been locked-in, some policemen might call out to him and say, '*Ei ei idhar kahan ja raha hai* (Hey, where are you going?)' JP figured out that pretending not to understand meant that cops just gave up. '*Saala habshi hai* (Bastard, nigger).' They bracketed him with the Nigerians but also did not bother him.

JP also figured out other systems, like how to send messages to the outside world. Through Jojo's family, and through Avtar's police contacts, he was finally able to ask his family for clothes and other things he needed. Initially it was Jojo who gave him shampoo, and he finally cleaned up. The messages he sent earlier through the inmates who got bail, seemed to have never reached his parents. So, it was completely hit and miss.

THE NEWBIE BECOMES THE BOSS

By the time six months had passed, JP was finally feeling comfortable in Tihar. Out of 2,000 people who lived in Jail Number 4, he was sure he knew 1,900 of them, at least. At first, he was able to get by only by befriending the rich and influential in the jail like Kamaljeet and Jojo. But then, slowly, he also let out that he knew Hindi and that widened his circle further – the revelation of this fact wasn't without the necessary drama in various circles.

For instance, there was one favourite ritual that many had while in jail, which was getting a massage or a shave. The chosen person for this service was Mukesh, an inmate who would charge 20 rupees per shave. He had mastered the skill so well that he was sought after for a haircut as well. It wasn't bad business – a haircut by Mukesh would get him 50 rupees per person and that was not bad earning by any means. There were other costs too – a body massage, face massage, anything really that helped the inmates kill the ample time they had.

So, one day, Mukesh was shaving JP while others were watching. He had asked for longer sideburns and seeing a crowd gather around, Mukesh decided to play to the gallery. He started cussing JP in Hindi, saying things like '*chutiya* foreigner' and making the others laugh by saying that he would slash him if he wanted, as the blade was on JP's face. Mukesh was comfortable in the knowledge that JP couldn't understand any Hindi, so he spoke with complete derision and used all kinds of expletives. As soon as he finished the shave, JP caught his hand. With the crowd still watching, he said, '*Behenchod, tu mere ko katega? Behenchod mujhe!* (Sisterfucker, you'll slash me?)' Everyone's eyes popped out since they couldn't believe that this man, who many believed was black, knew no Hindi. Mukesh was terrified. He still believed that JP was the deputy DS's son, who he had angered terribly. He kept going to JP's ward and apologizing but a line had been crossed. JP went to the *chakkar* and ensured that the master barber could no longer earn from this skill.

The DS who had the same name as JP's father, too, never busted the myth of JP's parentage. This had given him so much unwritten power in jail. He would never talk to JP when he saw him around *chakkar* but would always be kind to him. When he finally retired, JP's parents went and met him. 'What happened to the boy?' That's how his father figure always referred to him. JP's family was grateful for whatever kindness they could get. They spent close to rupees 50 lakh in four years with the promise of release. One lawyer told them he could get JP out for 6 lakh rupees as some judge's son was their friend. JP's mum paid up and kept waiting for the release that never came. The scam was detected months after when the messages finally got through and JP realized his parents had been taken for a ride.

Perhaps, it's the number of cheats in and around jail that drives many to people of faith. If Sushil Sharma (tandoor murderer) spent his time getting havans performed, JP found his biggest support in nuns. They met him as part of their job to counsel prison inmates. As JP had no friends in Delhi, these nuns became family and friends to him. They also became the communication channel between his parents and him. And of course, they were the people he celebrated Christmas with. Arun Fareira in his book *Colours of the Cage* talks about how elaborate festivals become in prison. JP describes how 100 churchgoers from outside would come to Tihar and mingle with prisoners. It was also special because the police officials would allow Christian inmates like JP to buy almonds, cashew nuts, cheese and other goodies. So, JP would really stock up and use them as food supplements for months after Christmas. They could also order some fruit cake to cheer up their otherwise dull fare.

As JP was in the seventh month of prison stay, the news came that they were all going to be moved to Ward Number 1. This wasn't very bad news because it was newly renovated and had amenities like standing showers. JP was looking forward to the shift as by now he'd also moved out of the shadow of people like Kamaljeet, after having learnt all their tricks. He basically took over about 25 per cent space of that barrack and made it his own. Thanks to his PR skills, he hired someone to use phenyl and clean that regularly and it was the area that had his protection. JP would charge 2,000 rupees per month from inmates who wanted to stay in the space. What were they paying for? Well, JP had an understanding with the *munshi* or undertrial in-charge of that ward. JP would give some of the collection to the *munshi* who would share it with officials like the DS, the ASP and the SP of the jail. In return for the money, JP and those who were part of the space were never woken up at 6 in the morning for the daily head count. 'I didn't ill-treat people and neither did we take money from those who couldn't afford it but we just created this system for things to be smooth.'

But this system didn't flourish for long. Almost within three months, JP was again moved to Ward Number 14(2). Here too, JP marked out an area for himself but it was much smaller and cramped than the previous one. He was trying to make himself comfortable when an incident happened that would turn his life upside down again, in jail. JP would indulge in charas now and then. As he confessed, he had got into the habit when he would hang out with Kamaljeet and his gang. Some people would do ganja, some heroin and coke, but JP would smoke charas like many other inmates. The DS of that ward received a complaint about this charas smoking. So, one day, when JP had gone for *mulakat*, they raided his berth. They looked around his sleeping area, and JP claims they planted some charas in his jeans. The DS filed a complaint and as a result he was moved to the back or the *Kasuri* wards, which are specifically meant to punish people or have the really rotten inmates. 'We tried to come to a settlement but they wanted 50,000 rupees and I only had 10,000, so the punishment came through and I was moved.'

This was the real hell, as JP had never experienced before. He was allotted a spot to sleep which was next to the gutter. 'I smelt shit day and night and this was really upsetting.' From one hit of charas a day, he was now smoking charas all the time. In fact, JP said, the back wards had people light up charas when they woke up instead of having a cigarette in the morning. This was where the real criminals came to stay and no one bothered about the inmates here, no officials, no cleaning staff, nobody at all. 'I was back to seeing shits of different colour every morning again.' In two months, JP couldn't take it anymore and when on the verge of a breakdown, he moved an application in court. He had spoken to all his influential friends like Avtar but no one could help him move from the back ward. The court application said that JP was not an undertrial but on detention; that he was a foreigner and the conditions were too unhygienic for him to survive. While rules suggest that inquiry in case of extraditions cannot go on for more than 60 days, no one seemed to be bothered that JP had already spent a lot more than that in custody.

The court approved for JP to move but it wasn't going to be so easy. The DS had to sign off and implement the court order. Days and then weeks went by and the orderly would keep saying 'Wait *karo*'. Finally, one day, the orderly said, '*Paise de de, kaam ho jayega* (If you pay up, your work will be done).' The money he wanted was 50,000 rupees – the same amount that he wanted when JP was busted for charas. He still didn't have the money but by now he'd had a taste of the back ward and he couldn't take it anymore. 'I wrote to my parents and asked for money. It took several weeks but they sent it and very soon I was shifted.'

MOVE TO VIP WARD WHERE SANJEEV NANDA STAYED

There was a specific reason that JP asked for a move to 4B. That's where his friend Jose Vargas, a Canadian, stayed and that's where he saw the facilities that he and the other inmates like Sanjeev Nanda got. Sanjeev Nanda, the Wharton Business School graduate and son of a powerful arms dealer, grandson of a Navy admiral, got drunk and killed six people while driving his BMW. He was serving the last of his two-year sentence when JP was in jail. They would walk in the park every evening since they shared a common American education. 'He studied in Philadelphia and I lived there, so we talked about all the places he had gone to. I wasn't his buddy but we used to hang out together.'

Ward 4B had all the high-profile prisoners. Jose had been convicted for 10 years in a heroin related crime. He saw someone having gay sex in prison and started crying, which is why officials put him in the VIP ward. There were Vikas and Vishal Yadav, Avtar, and also members of the President's Bodyguards involved in the Buddha Jayanti Park rape case.

Sanjeev Nanda kept to himself but everyone could see that his relationship with the jail authorities was excellent. While other convicts wore cream coloured pants and top, he would always be in his white kurta–pyjama. Other inmates talked about the special food he got including non-vegetarian food, but JP couldn't vouch for it. What he did have was an entire cell big enough for four people, just allotted to him. He had got some construction work done to make it better. The floor in his room was tiled and even outside, where there was a peepal and a jamun tree, he had made a seating space using blocks of stone. His cell certainly had a Western commode. 'The thing about Sanjeev Nanda was that he never showed arrogance about these privileges. He wouldn't show off and in fact, no one had ever been inside his cell.' It was only when he left jail that people realized how he had transformed his living area in the jail. 'There was no air-conditioner in his room but he had made it comfortable by adding a wash basin. He had also put in a rack so that he could have a library of books on the wall. It felt plush inside but only relative to the others.'

Soon after JP moved to ward 4B, Sanjeev Nanda was gone. JP was sharing a cell with Jose and the other inmates convinced him to start giving Spanish lessons to others like Vikas and Vishal Yadav. He was so relieved he was out of the muck of the back wards that he relished all the time that he had and made the most of it.

There was a gym in that area where he started working out, he took Vipassana classes and started studying law. 'I find people who go to jail dying to come out. The mind plays games but it took a couple of Vipassana classes for me to make the most of it.' JP realized the fact that his cordial relations with foreigners and Indians as well was an asset. So, suppose the Africans got into a fight, he would always get called in to mediate. He was the one that many trusted.

The study of law got JP to really focus on his case. It had been one and a half years and he had lost a lot of money with bad lawyers. He started paying more attention and then he got what he calls the dream team. This dream team consisted of a blind lawyer and a nun, who too, was a lawyer. They were inexpensive because no one else would hire them, but JP had learnt enough law to direct the case himself. So, he filed an appeal in the High Court for a daily hearing and every time he came to court, he had five nuns accompany him. The nuns would sit and pray while the proceedings were on, and all this along with the blind lawyer made quite an impact on the judge. 'It worked very well and I would whisper in his ears whenever I thought he could add an extra point.'

As the Human Rights Law Network got involved, JP started seeing results from the dream team. The first one was that he got custody parole for 12 days to visit his mother who wasn't well. The judge said he could go from Delhi to Kerala and stay with his family but he had to take 14 policemen with him. This parole visit would cost him 1.5 lakh rupees.

JP was undeterred and got all their IDs to buy their tickets but his parents refused. They calculated that they couldn't show their face around their home if JP turned up guarded by 14 policemen. 'I was very disappointed; I wanted to come out like a child. I was so angry. But today, as I look around their neighbourhood – everyone knows my grandparents. If I came with 14 cops, and would have to report daily to the beat cop, my parents would have been shamed. I understood where they came from.'

JP moved another application, and finally the judge amended the order to allow him to be released on parole in Delhi if his parents travelled there. JP's friend Vijender, who was an inmate at 4B, made arrangements for all of them to stay with his wife and children at their Vasant Kunj home. The day of the reunion was quite dramatic as JP still had the 14 policemen accompanying him. Before they let him in to see his parents, they went and searched the house. So, when JP entered, his mother cried out while beating her chest, 'Son, who would have thought I would even have to see this day!' JP still can't believe that she said this before giving him a hug.

On 24 February 2012, JP was finally acquitted by Patiala House courts. The order dismissed the extradition plea and ruled that JP would not have to go back to the US to face trial. 'If I went back as soon as I was arrested, it would have been fine. But I had gotten so involved in Tihar that I didn't realize how much of my life it had eaten up.'

However, the period of acquittal was short-lived. In just two months, the FBI and the MEA appealed against the order, which means that the trial is still going on. 'It still feels like I am in a mortuary but being kept alive.' The friend who got busted for ecstasy served three months in jail and is now living his life. JP is still running around courts, moving between Delhi and Kerala every two months. The appeal hasn't moved at all, the judge is never there. His mum died in October 2015 without seeing his case resolved.

'Today, I know how to escape a red corner notice. My years in jail taught me that; it teaches you to commit a crime. From rape to theft to murder – you make a circle of friends and network for that. How to commit a crime is all you talk about – how someone killed 35 times and only got caught once – how to hide a dead body, how to escape.'

JP says that like many others, he will never be normal again. Other friends like him, middle class and respectable, who were in jail because of bad luck or unusual circumstances, never worked again, scarred by the prospect of what others thought of them. JP, always thinking out of the box, has managed to set up a firm again where he works online and has others working with him. But the woman he's seeing, the only one who's accepted him with all his past, will never be allowed to marry someone who once lived in Tihar Jail.

THE TANDOOR MURDERER

'No man is born a criminal. I read that somewhere. Can you please write that when you write about me?' Sushil Sharma says in our last meeting before he goes back to jail after completing his furlough, which is vacation time for every convict after they've completed a minimum of three years behind bars. We are sitting at American Diner at the India Habitat Centre and it is a bit too noisy for my interview, but the last time we met, Sushil told me that he enjoys drinking coffee and this was the most convenient place for him, being next to the Sai Baba temple, which he visits regularly while out of Tihar.

'I'll have an espresso,' he says and accepts a side order of French fries. When I see the waiter bringing his short cup of the strong brew, I'm a little worried if he'll like what he's ordered or if it'll be too bitter for him. After all, being in jail for the last 20 years meant that he hadn't been exposed to the Barista culture that made coffee shops and fine brews regular for all of us. Sushil has been at Delhi's Tihar Jail since July 1995, after being accused and then convicted of the murder and disposing the body of his wife Naina Sahni. Sushil's image of a bearded man staring blankly while being led by police officers is familiar to all, and yet as he sits with me, enjoying his espresso, hardly anyone gives him a second look. He is clean shaven with close cropped hair, and each time I meet him he has an ash *teeka* on his forehead.

The coffee takes him back to another time, a time that was mostly spent at the coffee shop of the Taj Mahal Hotel called Machan. It was the time when he was with the National Students' Union of India (NSUI) and the Youth Congress, and was fighting elections against Akhil Bharatiya Vidyarthi Parishad's (ABVP) Pinky Anand, who's now a well-known lawyer working as additional solicitor general for the NDA government. His seniors at the Delhi University Students' Union were well-known journalists Rajat Sharma and Pankaj Vohra, and he would hang out with Congress members at member of Parliament G.K. Moopanar's flat at the Western Court in Janpath. His friends in the Congress were all upcoming leaders who now occupy influential positions, and you could sense the lifetime worth of regrets Sushil experiences for being left out of any kind of career. He went back to Machan the first time he was on parole, but this time there were none of his friends from the Congress or other hangers-on but just his loyal cousin, Vaibhav, which didn't feel the same.

'I feel terrible that I let all of them down. All of them who believed that I would go far in the Congress Party.' Sushil Sharma broods a lot, but he also answers my questions because he believes in coincidences. He believes it isn't sheer chance that we first met in 2003 in the jail while I was filming an innocuous story about the recreational activities of inmates. Our camera was panning for a shot, and it stopped dead when Sushil came into the frame. He wore a sparkling white shirt, black jeans and a shiny belt and it struck me that he looked like any other man who may be out for a regular evening of socializing.

We asked him if he would like to talk to us. He, very politely, refused but didn't object to us taking some shots. 'Yes, it is him,' said another inmate, noticing our astonished expressions at encountering the 'Tandoor murderer'. '*Bhale aadmi hain*,' they said. You know Tihar is a parallel universe when someone who has more or less accepted killing his wife, and then disposing of her body in a tandoor (clay oven), is described as a 'decent' man.

This was soon followed by another coincidence when the news of his conviction by the lower court came in. '*Arrey*, didn't you meet him in Tihar?' The producers at Star News hollered and rejoiced in playing his smiling shots in the black jeans and white ensemble juxtaposed in another window with the live pictures of his worried face as a dead man walking.

I left Star News, Sushil Sharma went from an undertrial to a convict, swapped his own clothes with the jail outfit, but apparently kept a tab on those who had captured him on film inside jail. 'Didn't you go to the border once?' he asked about a July 2015 assignment. 'I liked how you politely asked questions from people. I told others too. So they would all say to me – Look Sushil, your Sunitra (sic) is on TV.'

He said this at our next meeting, 13 years later, and coincidentally, it was just a day before the 21st anniversary of the murder. By now, Sushil Sharma had had enough time to tally all the coincidences of his life and attribute meaning to where all those invisible lines intersected with each other. Those lines always ended or could be traced back to the one event in his life – the one that unfolded on the evening of 2 July 1995.

THE NIGHT THAT CHANGED IT ALL

'I keep thinking what if I had arrived 2 minutes later. That's all. Just 2 minutes. I would not have done this.' It was again a coincidence and a chance that Sushil Sharma came home to his Mandir Marg flat and found his wife, Naina Sahni, on phone. He was the Delhi Youth Congress State president and she, a qualified pilot, was the general secretary of the Youth Congress' Girls' wing. Their relationship seems a complicated one, which comes across even from various court documents. Their work brought them together and after living in for a while, they got married in 1992. But Naina seems to have had a lingering connection with another Youth Congress member, Matloob Karim. They knew each other much before Sushil came into her life, and according to Matloob, they were to get married but couldn't because it was a Hindu–Muslim affair. Matloob married someone else in 1988 but he and Naina kept in touch. In fact, Naina gave him regular updates, on Sushil's proposal, their wedding and even on their fights. When Sushil came home that night, it was during one such update.

'I asked her who she was talking to and she said to her family. I pressed redial and realized it wasn't her family, but someone else.' Sushil had heard about Naina's affair with Matloob and it had resulted in terrible discord in their marriage. But that night, the violence went to some other level altogether.

'We started fighting and it was so bad that she tried to commit suicide. That's when out of anger, I reached for my gun and shot her twice.'

When you have 20 years to chew on 2 minutes that changed your life, like Sushil Sharma, you keep envisaging different scenarios and the what ifs. What if he had come just 2 minutes later? He would not have heard her on phone, and then asked who she was talking to, which meant he would have never had a breakdown of rage and slaughtered his wife. And what if he wasn't an influential youth leader of the Congress party? He would never have had a licenced gun at home. It was just one of the perks of being in that power circle of Delhi, and now it had led to this, just like a soothsayer in Amethi had predicted in 1984, just before he'd met Naina Sahni.

Sushil distinctly remembers how he was part of a Congress pep rally in the Gandhi bastion for an inauguration of the Bharat Heavy Electricals Limited (BHEL) unit in Jagdishpur. While the big Congress boys including Rajiv Gandhi, Arun Singh were all there, Sushil had taken 60 party workers to put up posters and work for its publicity. At the Jagdishpur guesthouse where everyone was staying, there was a seer-like person from South India who everyone sought out for a spot of palm reading. Everyone insisted Sushil show his palm. Apparently, the pandit told him – 'Everything seems to be okay for you but be warned. A woman will bring you tremendous infamy (*badnami*).' Sushil keeps going back to that episode, as if relying on the seer's words takes away his guilt. 'I brushed it off then. How was I to know it would come true 11 years later?'

▌ ▌ ▌ ▌

Sushil at no point denies that he killed Naina Sahni. What he does deny is that he chopped her body into pieces so that it could be cooked in the tandoor to become the perfect murder. The tandoor was at his new restaurant, Bagiya barbeque at the Ashok Yatri Niwas Hotel in Connaught Place, close to their home as well as to his old hangout of Western Court. It was an investment he had made with five other shareholders, but this incident ensured that it shut down just eight months after it was started. After all, the goriest details emerged from there, as the post-mortem report reveals – 'intestines exposed to outside with portions of other internal organs in the abdomen', 'thigh was chopped off, 28 cms below left', 'leg was chopped off 23 cm below the knee', 'distal phalanges in the hand missing (chopped off)'.

Sitting across Sushil Sharma and knowing these details brings the awe-inspiring realization that human beings are capable of the most unimaginable things. Sushil, however, cites the 2013 Supreme Court judgement which said 'no opinion could be given as to whether the dead body was cut as dislocation could be due to burning of the dead body. There is no recovery of any weapon like chopper which could suggest that the appellant had cut the dead body.' In other words, if he did indeed chop her up, the police didn't find the weapon that was used and so this wasn't conclusively proved. Sushil claims that it was the impact of the heat that made her limbs fall apart.

After getting his staff's help to put her body inside Bagiya restaurant's tandoor, Sushil made his getaway. Someone raised an alarm about a fire in the restaurant and the beat constables were already on the scene, while Sushil made his way to the Gujarat Bhawan where he spent the night. The next day he went to Jaipur, from where he moved on to Tirupati. 'I did *prayaschit* (penance) there,' he said, getting his head tonsured in an apparent act of 'atonement' for this sin. But while he was atoning, he also got in touch with a lawyer friend and managed to get 14 days' anticipatory bail from the Madras High Court. Even in that era of limited media outlets, the outrage was tremendous. How could the judiciary give this privilege to such a sadistic killer? 'The press was waiting in huge numbers for my lawyer to emerge in Chennai,' he recalled. And so on 10 July 1995, exactly a week after he'd killed his wife, Sharma was shown being arrested in Bengaluru. 'After consulting my lawyer, I approached the police and so they made it look like an arrest,' he said. IPS officer Maxwell Pereira led the Delhi Police team which landed with great fanfare to take Sushil Sharma back to the Capital so he could stand trial. But the moment was so intense that it seems to have made everyone go overboard. Sharma hadn't even been cuffed yet and Pereira announced – 'I will ensure that he is hanged.'

'Maybe, at that very moment, my fate was sealed. My case was open and shut,' he said to me.

OF LOVE & OTHER SURVIVAL THEORIES

When you talk to Sushil Sharma he's full of mythological stories from collections like the Panchatantra. He'd read them earlier in life but they all came back to him in Tihar and started meaning a lot more. 'R. Kumaramangalam (former NDA minister who died in 2000) gave me Panchatantra stories when I just joined politics because he said it would teach me strategy.' He didn't get to practise those lessons in strategy but he found stories that were parallel to his own story. Many of these tales have the common theme of passion and love, because in Sushil's eyes, Naina's killing is a 'crime of passion'. 'I went home not knowing I was going to kill,' he tells me. 'It wasn't cold-blooded at all.' There is no mention of being influenced by alcohol anywhere in the court orders. Sushil confirms that he'd given up drinking after some Congress session in 1984. So as an explanation to why he did what he did, he offers two stories.

The first is that of the King of Ujjain, Raja Bharat Hari. As the story goes, Bharat Hari was besotted by his youngest wife. So when someone brought him a fruit of immortality, he immediately gifted it to his favourite queen. But the queen had a lover and she gave it to him, who in turn passed it on to one of the royal maids who he truly loved. She, as it turned out, was actually in love with the king and the same gift of love came back to him. He not only discovered his wife's infidelity, but also how blinded he was in love. He immediately ordered her beheading, but also abdicated his throne and all his worldly belongings.

'The king loved her a lot and the main element of love is sacrifice,' said Sushil.

The second story he relates is that of Parikshit. Parikshit went hunting in the forest to tackle animals that were being pests. Exhausted after this exercise, he landed up at the ashram of a maharishi or holy man. But the maharishi was in a state of meditation, which was impenetrable. That enraged Parikshit. In his fit of anger, he threw a dead snake on the holy man who was still in a deep trance. That single act led to a curse that Parikshit would also die of a snake bite, and despite his immediate remorse, he still had to pay the price.

'I cried when I heard this story. Because it perfectly illustrated the difference a *lamha*, a moment, can make in your life. What would have happened if Parikshit didn't throw that snake? What would have happened if Yudhishthira had not agreed to gamble? These are all just moments which changed the course of life.'

The preoccupation with the concept of time is perhaps expected. Sushil Sharma has spent the last 21 years killing time for killing his wife. He was first sentenced to death by the trial court, a decision that was upheld by the High Court too. That meant, from 1995 to 2013 when the Supreme Court overturned the decision, Sharma stayed in solitary confinement. 'Do I look like someone who has spent so much time in confinement? Do I look depressed in any way? I don't think you can make out,' he asks me rhetorically. It's a rainy afternoon in the Capital, and while it's all dark and gloomy outside, Sharma seems to have retained a degree of cheer. He has an easy smile and he tells me it's the result of a carefully cultivated strategy – the strategy of breaking time into units that he could understand.

Sharma's unit of time is based on the presumption that each man is allotted 100 years in his lifetime, which means 36,500 days in total. According to him, God gives man a rupee per day to spend, and Sharma's strategy was just to plan how to spend that one rupee. That's all he had to do, spend a rupee, and that's what he carefully mapped out every morning in captivity. 'This really helped me avoid depression,' he said. 'If you don't prepare for it, then you die every moment you spend there.'

When Sushil arrived in Tihar towards the end of July 1995, Kiran Bedi had recently finished her tenure in May. Her Magsaysay award-winning work – introducing Vipassana, yoga and educational courses for inmates in Tihar – is personified in Sushil Sharma who took one course after another, including computer science. Without that, he said, he wouldn't have the coping mechanism to survive.

'They wake you up between 5.30 and 6 a.m. with abuses – *Khare ho jao, oye, bahar aao* (stand up, come out) – so that they can take the roll call. It's a terrible beginning to the day. After you have been marked, a line of 200 people is formed for the 10 toilets.' As a Brahmin, he showered every time he used the toilet, and so in winter. It was brutal. 'From morning until lights out, it is a battle, and free will is taken away, can't even talk of own volition,' he said. While he struggled to cope with this, he was constantly told by others how much tougher it was just a few years ago. For instance, before Kiran Bedi's diktat banning smoking in jail, the cells would be full of men aggrieved with coughing fits. 'The jail guards told me, they'd find it difficult to open the locks in the morning because the area outside the cells would be full of phlegm and spit.' Some inmates still smoked, but it was surreptitious and invited penalties of no family visits for a month or more or no letters. That wasn't really a deterrent; people would use carriers or 'Godrejs' to transport contraband items like cigarettes. The term 'Godrej' was used for those who would transport illicit items by stuffing it inside their anal cavity. The cost of hiring a Godrej was not too much, sometimes even just a few cigarettes was enough. As a non-smoker, Sushil had no tolerance for such means. 'Do you know that in America, they have full cavity search every time somebody comes back inside prison? That means they'd make them bend forward naked, and search every cavity. If we had that here, we wouldn't have any such problem and things would be much cleaner.'

From the comfort of an upcoming politician's life in Delhi to indefinite incarceration was too much for Sushil to accept and he toyed with the idea of suicide. The idea consumed him in his initial days in jail until he met a Delhi Development Authority (DDA) officer in jail who was implicated in a dowry case. The officer's entire family, including his daughter, were in jail, and their home had also been sealed, after their daughter-in-law had made allegations against them. Seeing someone worse off than him, Sushil heard him out. The officer offered him only one piece of advice – chant the Gayatri Mantra. He told him he'd heard that if this sacred Hindu prayer was repeated 1.25 crore times, then the gods would hear his prayers. 'I took to it fervently, counting 40 malas with 108 beads. This took me around three hours daily.' Taking care of three hours of a day took a huge burden off his shoulders, and it gave a kind of objective to his life behind bars.

The other activities worked themselves around it. He'd

wake up, do his puja, do yoga, then have breakfast of tea and biscuits. When Sushil was in solitary confinement, he'd also spend time cleaning his toilet. The day would then go in planning court visits, which would entail all those with court appointments being taken in a jail vehicle and then spending the day in the courtroom lockup till their turn came. Then everyone would come back to the jail complex together. After that, those that were employed would do their tasks. Sushil first took computer lessons and then was employed to teach it for a daily wage of 90 rupees, which was then credited to his PP or Prisoner's Personal account. The PP account could earlier be used to obtain coupons with which prisoners could buy snacks from the canteen or other provisions like toiletries, but now it works as a smart card. Sushil, for instance, would skip most of the jail meals and have a mid-morning snack like a parantha at the canteen. That explained his considerable girth. 'I'm trying to lose weight now,' he said, adding, 'I wouldn't like to walk around for exercise as you'd have to waste time talking to a lot of useless people. So, I improvised. I would take my bucket of water and keep lifting weights with it.'

In between working with others, he'd keep writing his own notes and printing it all out. These notes were like his mission statements which he kept next to his bed at night – 'I'd wake up some nights and just start writing. You never have complete darkness in jail, so when I couldn't sleep, I did this.'

Sharma spent considerable time describing these notes in detail to me. They were his theories on various themes – love and child rearing and sometimes political issues like the Lok Pal Bill. The one on marriage seemed completely inspired by his own circumstances. His big idea was to start a diploma course for couples planning to get married. The course would be of three months' duration and taught by a psychologist. 'It will have everything in the course, it will teach the girl how to deal with her mother-in-law, teach the boy how to handle a girl's family and how he will now have two sets of parents. And also teach the boy that instead of just loving his wife, he should respect her.' I asked him what was wrong in loving one's wife. 'Problem is that when a husband loves the wife, then, because of the physical intimacy, it leads to high expectations. A man should love his children and just respect the wife.' In a way it was the story of Raja Bharat Hari yet again – the consequences of what he saw as too much love, leading to too much rage after being disappointed. 'That's what my Art of Living course taught me,' he said, 'expectations kill marriage.' The strangest aspect is that these ideas of love and marriage are mirrored even in the Supreme Court Chief Justice Sathasivam's 2013 order commuting Sushil Sharma's death sentence to life. The order says that Sharma 'was deeply in love with the deceased (Naina) knowing full well that the deceased was very close to Matloob Karim. He married her hoping that the deceased would settle down with him and lead a happy life.' At another place, the order says, 'Despite knowing her intimate relations with Matloob Karim, he did not turn her out of the house. He only restricted her movements as he wanted to stop her from her wayward ways.' The order goes on to conclude: 'It appears that the appellant was extremely possessive of the deceased... the appellant (Sushil) suspected her fidelity and the murder was the result of this possessiveness' and was not an offence against society.

It's unclear why Sushil Sharma wrote a note on child rearing, and whether it was a way of dealing with his own childhood. He was born on 24 January 1959 to Inder Mani Sharma, a bank employee, and Premlata. They are now 82 and 79 years old respectively, and most of the time away from jail, he spends looking after them in their Pitampura home. He is the oldest of four siblings, his two sisters are married and live away, and his younger brother, a student of Hindu college, died in an accident in 1980. Sushil studied at Satyawati College of Delhi University and went to the Ludlow Castle School around the university area. He didn't do particularly well in school, usually scoring a 3rd division.

'I think what's important to do for a child's training is to take them to an old age home so *daya* (compassion) gets ingrained in them,' he gives out some details from his note. 'This will ensure that they not only look after their parents when they're old but also people around them. If a father comes home tired and his child is crying out of hunger or his tummy is hurting, he hits or snaps at him to stop. But that's not good as the child learns fear and just suppresses his emotions. If there are grandparents at home, they can handle it much better. They could distract the child.' I tried to ask Sushil if his father was like that, but he avoided my question. I kept wondering if he propagated this kind of child rearing so that people wouldn't grow up to have latent anger or aggression built into them, which he felt he did. Perhaps he felt he was just a victim of his father's aggression, and then getting trapped in a cycle of violence which resulted in killing his wife. It's something I prodded him on but Sushil shut down, instead focussing on how just like marriage, couples needed training in child rearing too. Sushil certainly didn't need any training in looking after his parents. His cousin Vaibhav tells the story of how Sushil would massage his parents' feet every night until they slept off.

Even Naina Sahni's parents testified in favour of Sushil Sharma. As the Supreme Court order notes, Naina's brother and sister-in-law even said that they were 'indebted' to him for all that he'd done for them. 'I think they took the moral position,' said Sushil. 'They thought I'd been wronged by their daughter and so they supported me. Twice they came to court and I'd always touch their feet.' The overt suggestion is that he had everyone's sympathy, from the Supreme Court to his peers in jail to even Naina's parents – his wife cheated on him, so he lost his mind and killed her. Of course, Sushil never says that Naina cheated on him. 'She's now passed away so it's not good to talk about those who have died.'

The other significant note that Sushil wrote in jail was about the need to return to a jury system. An inspiration for that note is not too hard to find. Very soon after Sushil Sharma went to jail, in October 1995, the OJ Simpson verdict came out which made headlines across the world. The cases of former National Football League player and actor (OJ Simpson) and Sushil Sharma had several things in common. OJ was also accused of murdering his wife because she was now with someone else. OJ, like Sushil Sharma had a history of domestic violence and both the men recorded their suicidal feelings after reportedly killing the love of their lives. But where the OJ story differs from Sushil's is that OJ was acquitted by the jury for lack of credible evidence that he'd killed his wife and her friend.

'Did you know that most of the jury members were black and that helped his case?' Sushil may have been in jail but he followed these nuances closely. Maybe he thought that he too would have had a more sympathetic order if there was a jury deciding his fate. Just like the black jurors felt OJ was being set up by a predominantly white police force, or that OJ was representative of all the wrongs that black men face in the hands of the law, maybe an Indian jury would have taken a moralistic position on the nature of the crime and been sympathetic to the cuckolded husband. In a way, the Supreme Court certainly was.

ENCOUNTERS OF A JAILED KIND

When Sushil Sharma first came to Tihar, he stayed at the high-security ward that was relegated for high-profile prisoners. It was where Indira Gandhi had been kept when she was jailed by the Morarji Desai government in 1978. It was also where IPS officer R.K. Sharma, accused of ordering the murder of journalist Shivani Bhatnagar, stayed. It wasn't just a cushy spot carved out of Jail Number 1 with five cells. It was a place where those who could be harmed by others were kept. For instance, IPS R.K. Sharma had been DG Prisons and so may be threatened or harmed by a fellow prisoner who he had put in jail as a cop. These high-security areas were always manned by TSP personnel. The logic was that there were fewer prisoners who would bond with them or chat with them in their language.

The high-security area was one of relative space and ease, but soon it was time for solitary confinement, which involved being closer to the real bad boys like gangsters Babloo Shrivastava and Subhash Thakur. Solitary confinement involved being in a cell that was barely larger than oneself and one was only let out for just an hour a day. 'The idea was to put the hardened criminals in one space so that they didn't manipulate or harm the ones who weren't like them,' explained Sushil. And there he stayed till 2003.

The first letter he got in jail was from the notorious bikini killer Charles Sobhraj. Accused of more than 20 murders, Sobhraj was serving the last three years of his jail term in India when Sushil Sharma arrived.

'Dear Sushilji, you have no reason to worry. Tell me if you need anything. CS'

Sushil asked around and found that 'CS' stood for the man who was practically the most infamous person in Tihar, the man who had thrown a party inside the jail, drugged the staffers and then escaped. He was captured a month later and now wanted to make friends. Sushil treated the letter with a certain degree of distrust. 'He was like that, speaking sweetly and making overtures at whoever he thought could be of use.' Sushil believes Charles Sobhraj even killed some people inside jail, although in the guise of food poisoning. For example there was a 'numberdar', a convict who also doubles up as a jail staffer because he has spent 12 years or more in jail, who had been assigned to live in Sobhraj's cell. Sobhraj didn't like this and objected to sharing the cell with him, but the jail authorities went ahead. The man died of a stomach bug soon after, and according to Sushil, this was Sobhraj's handiwork as poisoning was his specialty.

The one other person who he is grateful for in jail is R.K. Sharma. The former DG Prisons fought to have phone booths in jail and so, in 2010, fancy phone booths were installed with each prisoner's biometric data fed into them. The prisoner uses his fingerprint to log on and then two numbers of his choice pop up on the screen. The numbers are previously screened and cleared by the authorities; for Sushil it was his parents' landline. This way, each prisoner is guaranteed five minutes of talk time daily – a huge booster for those who would only have the twice a week *mulakat* with families. For Sushil, it couldn't have come at a better time, since his mother had a heart attack in 2009 and she wasn't strong enough to regularly visit him in jail.

There were many Congressmen who were in jail while Sushil was there. Kalpnath Rai, Godman Chandraswami, Shibu Soren and, more recently, Abhishek Verma, the son of a Congress MP and arms dealer. They would all mingle but Sushil liked the reputation of being a loner in jail. 'A lot of people were professional cheats and so I didn't want to associate with them,' he said. Instead, he cultivated an image of turning around his life.

For instance, a Right to Information application in 2010 revealed that Vikas Yadav (of the Nitish Katara murder case) went out of jail on the pretext of visiting hospital OPD 66 times in 2 years. The same RTI application revealed that Sushil Sharma never did. 'The young boys had a clever technique. They would have an understanding with the jail doctor to send them to a specialist outside. This meant they'd leave jail in the morning with the police escort and head to town. There again, another understanding with the doctor would be that they would see them after 2 p.m. This meant that they could come and see the doctor even just before closing time at 5 p.m.,' he explained. That day out would sometimes mean hotel room visits, meetings with family and friends and a general good time out. The police guards accompanying the prisoners would tag along or trust them to get back at appointed times. This explains why so many prisoners routinely run away enroute to court or hospital in various parts of the country. It's purely a case of the prisoner making a deal and duping them.

So, Sushil Sharma knows all the tricks but kept his record clean because he's hoping for an early release. He believes he has earned it because he has reformed himself and been an exemplary inmate. 'So many people came and went, but I am the one who was stuck there. How much of a price can I pay?' From the man who wanted to commit suicide when he entered prison to the man who told the reporters after the High Court upheld his death sentence that he didn't want to appeal, Sushil Sharma has come a long away. He is now fighting to live outside jail.

THE PLATINUM BLONDE WHO
WORE LV IN JAIL

If there is ever a possibility that you might be going to jail, what you may try and do as soon as you get over the initial shock is to start working on your classification. Just as there's a Type A and a Type B personality, as popularized by American sitcoms and self-help books, the Delhi jail manual makes a clear distinction between types of inmates. Once upon a time, there used to be Classes A, B and C. Class A was for politicians and senior bureaucrats, Class B for income tax evaders and high net-worth businessmen and Class C, as a wise insider described it, was cattle class.

When Kiran Bedi came in as Director General of Prisons in 1993, she issued a notification that suspended this class system, but by 2000 classification was back again. However, rather arbitrarily, the new system banished Class A (perhaps under the assumption that if you're in prison, you can't be an A1 person).

The current classification that the jail manual sets out for both convicts and undertrials is Class B and C, and however you manage to do it, you have to get yourself classified as a B-Class person and not C. And to get classified in this section, some of the basic requirements are:

- to be of good character;
- to convince authorities that you are educated, have a 'social status' and are used to a 'superior mode of living';
- that you haven't been convicted or charged of crimes that have elements of 'cruelty', 'moral degradation' or 'personal greed'; and also were not involved in any premeditated violence, serious property scam or arms related offences.

Now by any standards, all of these provisions are subjective. For instance, the very first yardstick of being of good character in official language infers that you have no previous criminal record. However, the truth is that all first-time offenders are not classified as prisoner B. Putting in qualitative terms like 'moral degradation' ensures that the classification process is dependent on the whims of the jail superintendent. Being a B-Class prisoner gets you these basic benefits:

- they stay in cells instead of barracks, and if lucky they even get a cot with a wooden stool;
- they can get storage space as a shelf, cupboard or box;
- and become eligible to get washing and sanitary appliances.

There are also dietary differences between the two classes. Class B means you get 400 ml of milk every day.

It may not sound like much but the difference between a cell and a barrack would mean sharing your toilet with three or thirty! And if there's one thing everyone is desperate about, it is to avoid sleeping on the floor, and in that too, classification can help. But what if you could be in jail and continue to look the same? What if you could walk around the jail compound in your favourite LV boots? What if you continued to have your own television set with your favourite channels set in? That's what Anca Verma achieved while living in Tihar Jail Number 6 from 2012 to 2016 and this is her story.

||||

THE BLONDE WHO CAME TO COURT

There is a certain degree of lasciviousness that's attached to crime or investigative reporting. Because the police force is predominantly male and while there are women crime reporters, men outnumber them easily; stories that emerge from the CBI or from the police have an undeniable male gaze. And so the first reports of Anca Neacsu being arrested along with controversial arms dealer Abhishek Verma were almost greeted with wolf whistles.

The pictures of her walking into the court when they were produced soon after the arrest, showed a platinum blonde in a white Western suit and aviator sunglasses. As cameras clicked photos of her at Patiala House Court, striking at 5 feet 11 inches, stories of the 'mysterious' Anca and her modelling past surfaced all over. Reporters hungry for details were fed titbits about how Abhishek Verma, who was previously jailed for bribing officials and obtaining information in the Navy War room leak case in 2006, used her as a front to again get sensitive information out of the Ministry of Defence. The biggest story about her was that she managed a meeting with the minister of state for defence, Congress' N.M. Pallam Raju.

I was covering the agency and even though the investigating officer was much more guarded with me, I clearly remember him describing the relationship between Anca and Abhishek: 'They are partners and living together, but now he says they are also married. We don't know what their status is.'

The CBI's case against the two was straightforward. A Swiss firm called Rheinmettal Air Defence (RAD) was blacklisted by the Ministry of Defence in 2012 for bribing the then director general of the Kolkata Ordnance Factory Board in connection with a deal to supply revolver systems. Anca and Abhishek had set up a firm called Ganton India in 2005 and, according to the CBI, they got in touch with RAD and offered to lobby on their behalf to get them off the blacklist. Abhishek's father Shrikant Verma was a Congress MP and so was his mother Veena, and so his connections with those in power at the time were well established. The CBI suggested that because Abhishek was already tainted at the time due to his Navy leak case and his run-ins about Foreign Exchange Regulation Act (FERA) violations, he used Anca to contact and meet the Congress minister and also several key officials.

For their lobbying services, RAD paid them 530,000 US dollars through their affiliate company in the US, which was handled by Edmund Allen. While the payment went through by 2011 to their New York account, the deal with Allen went sour and he complained against them to the Indian authorities. That's when CBI and the Enforcement Directorate (ED) slapped charges of bribery and money laundering on Anca and Abhishek, raided their Vasant Kunj farmhouse on 7 June 2012, and arrested them soon after. It was just four days after they'd got married.

Recalling that time four years later when she was out on bail, Anca displays a great sense of humour: 'Tihar was my honeymoon,' she said in her distinct East European accent. Maybe it's because she was already seeing Abhishek when he went to jail in the Navy war room case in 2006, so she knew what to expect. Their daughter was also born when he was behind bars. The two met in 2003 when she was working with Atlas group of companies in Bucharest. Abhishek had already been in trouble with ED about his foreign bank accounts in the US, but that never stopped his business prospects. 'He would keep calling me using some work as an excuse.' By 2008, they were already working together and she was spending almost half her time in India. During those visits, she would leave her daughter with her parents back in Romania. Since 2012, Anca has only seen her daughter, now eight, on Skype as she's no longer allowed to leave the country till she's on trial. They did try and protect her parents from the news of their arrest by pretending to be stuck with work in the US. 'When I got my first phone call after the arrest, I called my father and tried to make some story but he was like, your arrest is front page news everywhere in Romania!'

Making headlines from rural India to Romania, Anca and Abhishek were a big catch for the agency. While the CBI boasted to media how they had busted the Bonnie- and Clyde-like duo in the midst of their failed bribery attempts, it turns out the agency was making familiar bloopers. The Indian Criminal Procedure code lays down very clear and strict guidelines about the standard operating procedure to follow while arresting a woman. One of the key guidelines is that a woman cannot be arrested after sunset. When CBI started the raid, they miscalculated and decided too late that an immediate arrest was necessary. By the time the paperwork was complete, it was almost evening, so what actually happened was that instead of spending the first night of their arrest in lockup, they spent it at home with some members of the CBI team also staying there so they couldn't run away!

The next day they were brought to the swank, new building that makes up the CBI headquarters. By that time, the agency had already sealed all the designer items that characterize Abhishek Verma's flamboyant lifestyle. When he'd first hit headlines in the 1990s, he appeared on the *India Today* cover wearing Versace. This time again, the press lapped up the list of his 14 designer watches and 40 expensive paintings that were termed 'proceeds of crime' by the agency. The list had all the high-end labels – Bulgari, Omega, Hublot Geneve, Louis Vuitton and many others. The subtext of these stories is always that those with conspicuous consumption and little regard for the law are at one point or another made accountable. In Abhishek and Anca's case, they weren't even separated from their fancy labels for too long. For now, Anca was left pleading with the CBI to retain her gold Rolex watch. She told them that it had nothing to do with her husband, it was her mother's watch and meant for her daughter. The story was effective enough for the agency to allow her to retain it. She handed it over to her lawyer because if she took it with her in the lockup then again it would get stored away in the CBI's *maalkhana* or storehouse of alleged evidence.

The court had allowed CBI custody, which meant that they would be interrogated and kept at the Lodhi Road office for a few days before they were sent to Tihar. At the CBI headquarters, Abhishek was put in a separate lockup, and for lack of any other appropriate space, Anca was kept in a guest room meant for officers. The CBI building, which has terrace gardens attached to senior officials' rooms and airy atriums, left quite an impression on its well-heeled accused. 'It was really like a five-star hotel with AC and a fancy TV but I still had to show some attitude.' Apparently, then Anca demanded to be taken to her husband. She felt that it was part of some ploy of the CBI to keep them in separate spaces, so she insisted that she be taken to him immediately. The officers relented and when she went there, she found Abhishek lying on the floor. 'I immediately changed my mind and told him, "Sorry baby, but I can't sleep on the floor." The officers and my husband were all very amused.'

But these lighter moments aside, the CBI meant serious business. Not only were they booking Anca for bribery along with her husband, they were also pushing for the very stringent Official Secrets Act after it emerged that she had met the minister of state for defence, Pallam Raju. Anca looked towards her embassy for help and the ambassador who was supposed to meet them socially for dinner, turned up to see what consular help she could provide to them while in custody. The options were limited. Anca recalls how her husband, with a couple of years in jail behind him, prepared her for life in Tihar. 'I told him, *theek hai*. I am okay. Whatever will happen will happen.' Unlike many other foreigners, she understood Hindi perfectly well and would often pepper her speech with 'Haanji' like other North Indians.

Though Anca was mentally prepared, Abhishek warned her. One, she should not trust anyone too much inside jail. Second, if she was offered the services of a cell phone by someone, she should desist from giving in to such temptation. 'We will get everything through proper channels,' he promised her. And so the relative comfort of CBI custody ended to take her to Tihar Jail after about two weeks. The five-star comfort of the new CBI office would now be taken away and also the easy dealings of socially awkward but refined CBI officers. The deputy superintendent of police in the agency, Ram Singh reportedly told Anca that if she hadn't been an accused, she was smart enough to have joined their force.

TIHAR: THE NAKED TRUTH

The biggest advantage for Anca in Tihar was that she was

Mrs Abhishek Verma, well-networked in the government and, due to his previous stints, also familiar with all jail officials. So when she arrived on 21 June 2012, apparently there was quite a welcome party, as he had ensured that all the right calls had been made for her living arrangements. And yet, it is the small humiliations that can add up to greater hurt.

The entry to Tihar Jail Number 6 is through a large room where various guards sit to carry out frisking and checks. On one side there is a partition that is typical of all checking areas. It resembles one that is used in hospitals to separate various wards or beds but doesn't fully hide what's behind.

In this exposed space, Anca like all women prisoners entering jail was asked to strip all her clothes, including her underwear. She was then asked to walk up and down while at least five women security guards scrutinized her. The walk to and fro is to apparently check whether the prisoner has tried to hide something by inserting it in their anus or their vagina. In the past, prisoners have been caught trying to smuggle in cell phones like this, and DMK leader Kanimozhi told me that she even witnessed someone getting caught doing this while she was getting frisked herself.

'With one hand I covered my lower area, the other hand my breasts. They were also looking because I was a foreigner,' said Anca. When she told her husband about this later, he was enraged that they had the audacity to do this. Apparently, once the TSP (are considered unbiased as they aren't very fluent in Hindi) asked him to do the same when he was entering jail. Verma threw the rule book at them and asked for the superintendent. The rule book makes it clear that one should only be stripped if the security buzzer goes off. Most other prisoners, like Anca, have no knowledge of this clause and so they quietly undergo this humiliation.

Once inside though, Anca soon forgot, finding some adoring fans who were taken in by her exotic, foreign looks. They sat her down on a mat and apparently one said, 'An angel has come from the sky,' while another asked, 'Are you a princess?' Perhaps this kind of fawning went a long way in mentally adjusting to incarceration. The ones that really suffer talk about how they are welcomed with abuse, harassment, and even physical violence that instills an atmosphere of fear from the very beginning. One of these fawning women that Anca encountered was a woman named Archana Datta. Archana Aunty, as Anca called her, was in jail because she got embroiled in a murder case. What happened was that her son got into a physical fight with someone and the tussle led to his opponent's death. When the police questioned a witness, they said that Archana and her husband were also present at the scene of crime. So Archana was taken into custody too, even though she had apparently not done anything. When the court finally set her free, she'd already spent two years in jail.

The stories of inmates like Archana are examples of those that make up the 600 women that fill Tihar's women section of Jail Number 6. The jail is only meant for 400 but overcrowding is the least of its problems. Many of the women that Anca introduced me to were in jail for years for abetting rape. Yes, rape. After languishing in jail for three or more years, they'd either get acquitted or get bail. They are economically backward and say that their cases are actually cases of personal fights. For instance, Anu Rajen is originally from Nepal and had to spend three years in jail in a rape case before being acquitted. A widow, she's a mother of three and was charged with illegally trafficking women who were exploited.

Or there is the story of the chirpy Farida Siddiqui who is still an undertrial accused of kidnapping, having spent five years in jail. Farida is about five feet tall and maybe it's her exuberance at finally getting bail or she's just of an extremely sunny disposition, that she's always cheerful. She tells me that she's accused of kidnapping someone who's double her size! In reality, her neighbour eloped and they accused her of having a hand in that. 'I still don't understand how I ended up over here,' she says.

Farida and Anu Rajen represent the majority in Tihar who have no legal aid. The government data states that almost 40 per cent of the women who are lodged there are illiterate, which means they have no knowledge of their rights. The jail manual says if they are unable to read, someone ought to read it to them, but this is hardly ever done. In fact, another reason for Anca's popularity among the women was her writing applications on their behalf which led to them getting bail.

But all that was still some time later. In the beginning, it was about getting acquainted with life in jail at the *mulaiza* ward meant for first-timers. Because of Abhishek's lobbying, Anca was even asked whether she would stay in a cell, which would be a room for three or four, or a barrack with 20 people; of course, her choice was obvious.

'The people in the barracks looked very poor and the condition there was pathetic,' she recalled. When they were served dinner of rice and *subzi*, they had no choice but to eat with their hands – not because it was an Indian tradition, but because in jail, a spoon becomes a weapon of attack after inmates sharpen it.

So her island of privacy was cell number 17 at ward 8, and her cellmates were Sridevi, accused of cheating; Manisha, accused in a cheque-bounce case; and Archana Aunty, who soon became her 'jail mum'. While Archana spoilt her and mollycoddled her needs, it was useful to have Sridevi in the cell as she was the official *munshi*. The *munshi* is tasked with locking up all the other cells, which meant their cell was always the last one to get locked.

The thing that strikes you most about the routine is that it all seems to be part of the punishment. Inmates are woken up at 5 in the morning and their breakfast of tea and biscuits is at 6.45 am. They sometimes got bread but it wasn't regularly served. Lunch is at 10.30 am everyday and then dinner by 4.30–5 p.m. The only variation was that sometimes with lunch they would be served lassi. The men in contrast had some breathing space, getting their dinner between 6 and 7 p.m. It's a routine that some never got used to, and the only ones who were okay with it were those who had special permission from court to get home food during their *mulakats*. *Mulakats* are the times allotted for families to meet the inmates, which was twice a week, and a legal *mulakat* with a lawyer was once a week. Special permission again meant that you have to be well-off enough to hire a lawyer who would keep renewing your permissions.

For instance, the district judge allows Anca to eat home meals during court hearings where she would step out of prison. This was almost every day with the three ongoing cases against her, and so it was fairly effective. But the legal application has to cite the permissions that the judges of the Saket, Patiala House and the Tis Hazari courts have all given her for the same in the past. It also includes doctor's reports suggesting that the jail's spicy food was harming her health. It is not humanly possible for a regular inmate to make such an application without any legal help. And the problem isn't just that.

There is an option of a 'wet' canteen in jail which serves snacks. As each prisoner is allowed to keep 6,000 rupees on their card to spend every month, they can supplement the jail meals if they want. But the problem is that for a lot of women, there was no family to get even this amount. Almost 80 per cent of the inmates in jail are those from the income bracket of less than 8,000 rupees a month, so if they were sitting in jail instead of working, no one was there to supplement that income. For instance, nobody ever came to meet Anuara, no lawyer or family, so she had no money at all. In order to earn some money, she worked as a maid for other inmates inside jail. She would get paid 200 rupees per month to clean their cell and sometimes also for giving a massage to them.

Where someone paid 200 rupees, Anca gave a lavish 2,000 rupees or more, and so they jumped to do cleaning and other odd jobs for her. It's not something anyone admits to because it is clearly illegal, but Anca perhaps rightly saw it as doing the other women a favour. 'Only the convicts are allowed to work inside jail, for which they get paid about 90 rupees per day. So how are these women going to survive?' When she wouldn't go to court and get home food, someone would give her the food that is served to the children at the crèche, much more bland and palatable than what was served to adults.

The obsession with food manifested itself in strange ways, as Anca pointed out. Like her and Abhishek, there were other married couples in jail who were allowed a meeting of 30 minutes every week. 'It was the most bizarre thing,' recalled Anca. 'The first time I experienced the meeting, I also got dressed up like the other women. Then they all got food for their husbands from the canteen. And when their husbands came, they kept eating and the women would keep talking. Is that what this *mulakat* was meant for?'

A *Hindustan Times* article of January 2014 had a headline that read 'Arms dealer, wife have a jailhouse romance', which cites jail sources on these weekly dinner meetings. The jail spokesperson is quoted as saying that there was nothing special and all couples get this time together, but anonymous sources cite how Anca dressed up for the meetings. Perhaps the most romantic aspect is that they decided to never eat at these meetings. They didn't need to because unlike the other inmates, they never needed to worry about their next meal, even in jail; they never went hungry.

'YOU HAVE THE RIGHT TO REMAIN IN YOUR VERSACE'

When Abhishek met Anca for the first time inside jail during their *mulakat* slot, he apparently turned up in tracksuit bottoms. The sight of him in that shocked her more than a lot of other things she had seen in jail. 'I told him to burn that tracksuit forever,' she said. And so their lawyers and their family members brought in items from their regular wardrobe, which got not just Tihar Jail but also the legal community talking. 'Have you seen Abhishek? He wears Hermes to court,' that's how one lawyer described him to me. It's not that Patiala House or Tis Hazari haven't seen rich people appear, it's just that very few had flaunted their lifestyle like this before. Tis Hazari with its narrow lanes, its corridors with dogs lazing around, and open urinals, provides a contrast to such visitors that is almost surreal. It's the kind of place where my colleague who was a legal journalist got hollered at for wearing a sleeveless top: '*Nangi ho ke kyon ghoom rahi hai*? (Why are you walking around naked?)'

In that dreary atmosphere, there's a picture of Anca and Abhishek waiting for their court hearing. They are both seated very close to each other on one of those iron benches outside the courtroom. She's in a peach shift dress that ends mid-thigh with black peep-toe heels, and he's in jeans and shirt. Their labels are indeterminate from a distance, but tucked between his legs is an easily identifiable Louis Vuitton office bag.

Anca tells me that she likes to dress up for work when

she comes to court. 'Judges are not looking at my clothes, they are looking at my case,' she claimed, and she even asserts her position with a clause in the jail manual. Chapter 6 para 31 of the manual says: 'Maintenance of certain prisoners from private sources – A Civil prisoner shall be permitted to maintain himself, and to purchase, or receive from private sources at proper hours and days foods, clothing, bedding or other necessaries, but subject to examination and to such rules as may be approved by the Inspector General.'

It is this simple rule that empowered Anca to 'maintain' her designer wardrobe in jail. Photographs taken by the jail photographer show her on Christmas day with her Versace couture sunglasses and Louis Vuitton wedges in real 24 carat gold leaf work. She tells me that they are from the 2015 winter collection. Yet another photograph shows her wearing a leopard print dress, and another in a black shift dress in the Tihar Jail library. In fact, for two years she even kept her stilettos in prison, but there was one jail superintendent who came and declared her heels to be too dangerous especially after a physical altercation with another jail inmate.

Anca claims it all started because one jail official wanted too many bribes. When the demand wasn't fulfilled, she got a convict called Sonia to pick a fight with her. It started with abuse but led to a physical fight where she broke Anca's thumb. Not one to let it go, Anca's lawyers and mother-in-law didn't just file a police FIR, they also wrote to the President of India. Anca's thumb stayed in plaster for two months, but the jail official was transferred and a departmental inquiry was initiated against her. But Anca's stiletto heels were now called too dangerous, and so on 16 April 2014, she wrote to the superintendent:

Dear Madam,

I am a European national and an undertrial lodged in Jail number 6 for two cases of CBI and Enforcement Directorate. Besides my mother-in-law who is 73 years old, there is no relative here in India. My husband is also lodged in Tihar Jail for the same cases as mine.

The sandals I have been wearing since June 2012 have got worn out, torn and tattered. I do not have any relatives outside to procure a pair of footwear for me. It is therefore humbly submitted, that I may be allowed to procure a pair of footwear through *mulakat* from the open market.

The details of my article to be procured are given below:

Brand: Mochi (wedges sandals)
Size: 38
Colour: beige
Price: ₹2500-3500
Available at: Mochi, South Ext store

She then again cites the same clause and attaches pictures taken by her aides of the shop's window to point out the style of shoes. The application is soon accepted according to jail rules, and so are a series of amenities that she applies for to 'maintain' herself in jail. Some applications could be seen as personal indulgences, like the electric brush to give a groomed look to her blond hair, but other items, she said, were absolutely vital. For instance, the fight for a Western commode. Usually, the 'loo' is just a urinal within the cell, which has no privacy. Anca and the other women would use their own clothes or a sheet to create some kind of privacy. But the lack of a pot was a battle Anca wasn't willing to give up on. She built her case with letters from the jail doctor. S.S. Rathi gave a letter saying that she 'should avoid squatting' as she was suffering from inflammation of the joints. And so finally, besides all her legal battles, she also won the battle to defecate comfortably. For this, it wasn't just the jail authorities or the district court, but she had to file repeated pleas in the Delhi High Court. It took her two years but she finally won, and the added advantage was that no one wanted to share that commode with her and so it was almost exclusive.

In that space of 8 feet by 10 feet cell, was Anca's prized possession – an LCD 14-inch TV with 27 satellite channels including Star World Premiere. In her handwritten note dated just a month after coming to prison, Anca promises that she would donate that television set to the jail when she leaves. The permission is quickly granted, and in my interviews with other high-profile prisoners, it is clear that it's not very unusual. If you can afford it, then it can be yours. 'I always say it, jail is hell for poor people,' says Anca.

One of the side notes written in the permission letter allowing Anca to buy an electric hair brush was by the deputy superintendent who said that it should be kept in the 'beauty parlour'. It's strange to think of inmates being allowed to indulge in a parlour, but it was essentially a space where the convicts could work and also pick up skills they could use for employment after leaving jail. Inmates like Anca, who had also got a court permission to use her cosmetics, would store and use them all here – shampoos, shower gels, hair colour and anything else which they could charge to the prisoner's personal account.

One of the women working there was the one who made Abhishek's premonition come true. Madam Zora was the wife of a known gangster and she came to visit Anca soon after she arrived in Tihar with the promised use of a cell phone or anything else she may need. She had been in Tihar for more than eight years for a conspiracy case. 'I folded my hands and told her I don't need anything,' said Anca. But she remembered that for all her organized crime inside the jail, Zora was also terribly troubled and conflicted. Her arms were patterned with marks of self-inflicted injuries.

For most of the women who didn't have means like Anca, no influential husband in the next lockup who dictated terms to jail officials, no battery of lawyers, Tihar's loneliness seemed to drive them towards each other. In an anecdote reminiscent of Ismat Chughtai's *The Quilt*, Anca talks about the 'joridaars' or couples in the women's jail. The superintendent apparently had a list of 22 women who had paired up. The list was prepared because the matron had caught one girl, and she ratted out the names of all the other couples. Some of them shared short moments of intimacy that had been caught and shared with all. As lights were never turned off in jail, these women would use newspapers to dim them.

For instance, the two women who shared Anca's ward for sometime were 45 and 20 odd years old, and Anca caught them fondling each other early one morning. When she suspected something another day, she asked them to shift to another cell if they wanted to carry on. 'They told me I had a dirty mind. I said I may have a dirty mind but it is not visible. What they were doing was visible!' One of them was shifted out after Anca complained, but apparently she would sneak into the other's cell as soon as the locks were opened each morning.

The incident was obviously viewed quite seriously because one afternoon the superintendent called out the names of all the joridaars on the intercom. At a meeting in the office, she asked rather bluntly, 'Is she your girlfriend?' One of the suggestions, that was seriously considered, was to move all 22 of them to one barrack – not to humiliate them by singling them out, apparently. The intention was to stop the others from complaining about them. The other options included discouraging them during weekly checks of the cell. They would make sure there were no sleeping spaces together in the cells.

'I don't think they were all lesbians, many of them were just bored.'

Few months later, in October 2016, Anca's husband Abhishek was again out of jail. During the time that she was bailed out and he was still inside, he'd call her regularly from the superintendent's office. It was just one of the perks that he had as someone with lots of influential friends. On the night he was released, the couple were joined for a celebratory dinner at Maurya Sheraton's Bukhara restaurant by Bollywood actor Rajpal Yadav. Rajpal had spent 10 days in jail because he couldn't repay a loan of 5 crore rupees he had borrowed from a businessman. Even though he didn't have to spend too long in jail, Abhishek obviously made his stay comfortable, which is why he flew down to greet him after being released. That's the thing about incarceration – the bonds and memories you make, stay with you for life.

THE TERRORIST'S BRIDE

*Sunni girl with BA, Shahnaz Diploma & computer
knowledge smart slim 32/5'3" respectable upper caste.
Western UP based family. Early marriage. Widowers may
also apply.*
*Dowry seekers excuse. Require respectable well settled
caring loving teetotaller Godfearing person.*
Call Safia (011 XXXX223)/ Write Box No DEB145C
Times of India, New Delhi – 110002.

This matrimonial ad appeared in the *Times of India* in
October 2000 and when Rehmana reads it out today, she
doesn't even have to look down at the yellowed piece of
paper she has so carefully retained. She knows all the words
and she especially stresses on 'Godfearing'. She hasn't just
retained the newspaper where it appeared, but has the receipt
from the classified section that proves that they paid 3,380
rupees for it to get published in the matrimonial supplement
that comes every Sunday. It's been 16 years, but Rehmana
will never throw away these pieces of paper. It's what got her

out of jail and acquitted in 2007. It's also what got her there in the first place.

At her home near Qadri Masjid in Delhi's Jamia Nagar, Rehmana has many such scraps of paper carefully tucked away in all kinds of folders and notebooks. She's been in this second floor, one-room tenement for more than three years but it still looks like she's just arrived. There's a saucepan of milk that's been put to cool after boiling, on the floor. And a bed that also doubles up as a work station with all her folders laid out on it. Over it is a rack containing more such notebooks and papers. Rehmana is still 'slim' as the ad described her all those years ago but she looks much older than the 48 years she is. And when she speaks, her frail voice is like one who has been recently crying. As you get to know her, you realize that's because Rehmana is constantly crying, her large eyes always brimming over. Her room may be slightly bigger than her jail cell, but she's still trapped mourning those years she spent in captivity.

'We got a lot of response for that ad. For three weeks we kept getting calls and letters.' With her eyes brimming, she manages a weak smile now and then. Fate has a strange way of bringing people together, the way this BA (Pass) from Maharaja Harish Chandra College, Moradabad, met Arif, a Pakistani from Abottabad who's on death row for firing at Delhi's Red Fort and killing two soldiers and a civilian. This is one of those fateful accidents where if only one small event would have altered, things would have turned out totally different. As Rehmana sits rocking back and forth, since it helps her cope with her back problem, she can't help going over and over saying, *if only*.

THE JOURNEY FROM MORADABAD TO JAIL

Maybe it all started in 1997 when Rehmana after graduation

moved to Delhi to stay with her sister. You couldn't tell by looking at her life now, but she comes from a family with four other siblings, three sisters and one brother. 'Everyone's well off in my family, other than me.' When she went to jail for harbouring, concealing and assisting her Lashkar-operative husband, in a way, she lost them all. But in 1997, she had her life ahead of her and she moved in with her sister, who was a career woman working at the Sofitel Hotel in south Delhi.

'Don't write their names,' Rehmana's aware that she's already created considerable problems for everyone associated with her. One of her sisters, a government school teacher in Bhopal, is afraid that Rehmana has spoilt her daughter's chances of getting a good match. Her brother, a year younger than Rehmana, is still mentally disturbed by all that happened. Rehmana may have married Arif but they were all hauled to the police station for one night in December. And that night's nightmare is still too scary for them to emerge from.

'I wanted to do the Shahnaz Husain course and that's what I immersed myself in completely.' Sharing her sister's flat in Ghazipur in east Delhi, Rehmana soon learnt to move around Delhi. She'd make her way to Malcha Marg, the diplomatic enclave by bus daily and work non-stop, starting at 9 in the morning and working till early evening. She loved it, but other than learning a beautician's skills she also developed a major back problem. It was an important factor for her because that's what went on to decide who she could marry, or the fact that she may have to settle for less since she wasn't completely healthy.

'I would work on Sundays too, and the work involved long hours of standing. I tried to keep myself busy but I ignored my health.' One customer harangued her into getting her back examined and Rehmana found out that she had a slipped disc. She reaches out for her stash of papers, and displays all her medical records. There are some from the Spinal Injuries Centre in south Delhi where she went first.

'When they saw me, they asked how did I manage to walk there?' It was serious but apparently, the doctor also promised her if she had surgery, she'd be fine in six months' time. Fine enough to be married too. 'You can have 12 children, he said,' she stresses on this because when the police tried to prove a case against Rehmana, they said that she was part of the conspiracy because why else would a younger man like Arif marry a woman who was not even healthy enough to bear babies. The prosecution case was that he paid her 2.8 lakh rupees to become a wife and a co-conspirator in the Red Fort attack. An ortho walking stick is still in her one-room flat, and looking at that, Rehmana recalls how the future terrorist came to be her husband.

The *ToI* ad happened soon after Rehmana's recovery. Her health situation prompted the family to make a few concessions. They wouldn't have welcomed 'widowers' before but they did because Rehmana had undergone a major surgery and they wanted to be honest about it from the word go. The ad was published on 8 October and Ashfaq, as he called himself, at that time was one of the respondents. When he called at the phone number that they'd given out, he said he lived in Okhla, not too far from where she lives now. 'We actually thought we would see the others first and meet him later, because he was close by.'

And so after almost a month of meeting others, Arif, aka Ashfaq, came over. Rehmana remembers that her sister went to receive him at the bus stop and brought him home. And she also remembers there was something about this clean-shaven man she really liked. 'He sat on the floor and looked down. I brought tea and he never looked up even then.' Rehmana couldn't even make out that he was the prospective groom.

'He looked nice and *sharif*.' Her sister did the background check and his neighbour also said that he was a nice enough man. Arif told them that he owned a computer centre, was originally from Jammu, his father had died and his mother was the stepmother. As they say, fate plays strange games. As a matter of coincidence, Rehmana also had a stepmother and so she felt even more connected with him. But he left out a key piece of information. 'He never said he was a Pakistani.'

The imperfect background checks done, the two got married in the first week of December. And before her *rukhsat* could happen, Rehmana's world turned upside down. On 22 December 2000, there was firing at the historic Red Fort in Delhi where a contingent of the Indian Army was stationed. After a call to the BBC office was reported, the police declared it to be an attack by terrorist group Lashkar-e Taiba (LeT). A scrap piece of paper found just outside the Red Fort with a mobile number led them to Arif. The defence claimed that he never owned a mobile phone, but that's what the court upheld and that's how the police landed up in Ghazipur on the night of 25 December.

'My *rukhsat* hadn't happened yet. In a way, my *vidai* happened in jail. Not *mehendi*, they put *kalik* in my hands.'

As Rehmana remembers it was the holy month of Ramzan and her new husband and she were yet to consummate their union. They were yet to settle down and move into Ashfaq's house, so in her sister's tiny flat that still had the post-wedding air and food that had been delivered by some relative, they waited for the groom to come back from work. Rehmana's aunt from Preet Vihar also had some prospective match for her brother, so it was a happy time and even though Ashfaq and Rehmana were strangers, there was a bit of intimacy in the air.

'I remember that he would follow me around the house. And even on that day, he followed me to tell that he'd eaten and come.' It was 10.30 in the evening and when Rehmana came out of the toilet and glanced outside, she saw three men in jackets looking towards their flat. She thought they were robbers, so she quickly bolted the door, and once she told the others, they were all very scared. As they cowered, they saw the men jump into their compound and start shouting, 'Open the door!' Now it was a house that had recently hosted a wedding, a *shaadi ka ghar*, so there was naturally some cash and jewellery around. The first thought they had was that the '*Sariya maar gang*' had come. This gang, as the name suggests, is one known by their signature rods that they use to beat their victims with, before robbing homes. Active in the outskirts of the capital and western UP, they have spinoffs like the '*Kaccha Banyan gang*', and their modus operandi is to come in bare undergarments, beat the family members of the house they are robbing. Sometimes, they also rape the women of the household.

Rehmana and her aunt were terrified. They dialled 100 but couldn't get through. They tried to call Rehmana's sister at the Sofitel Hotel but then realized their phone was disconnected. By then their door had almost been bashed in. 'I opened the latch of the door because I knew they would have shot us if I hadn't. Looking back, I think they would have done an encounter.'

What Rehmana didn't know was that they weren't some stick-wielding goons. It was the Delhi Police's special cell. They instantly grabbed Arif and Rehmana's brother and took them away. The women in the house – Rehmana and her aunt – were told not to utter a word. They were taken away separately. If you look at any police manual, and read any basic handbook, it informs you about the D.K. Basu guidelines laid down by the Supreme Court regarding fundamental principles that have to be respected while making an arrest.

The police officers have to make their identity known and have to have witnesses to establish and record the time and place of arrest. This isn't always followed and in Rehmana's case it certainly wasn't.

What's even more shocking is that while the above methods are routinely flouted, police officers are now careful to at least ensure proper guidelines are followed for questioning or arresting women. In Rehmana's case, no woman constable was present and so it was in complete violation of the rule of law. Though it is not allowed that women be taken into custody after sunset till sunrise, Rehmana and her aunt, and later her sister were picked up and detained at the police station.

At the Lodhi Road police station, they met the infamous encounter specialist ACP Rajbir Singh. Now just like there was a breed of encounter policemen in Mumbai who dealt with the underworld, Delhi too had its own crop. ACP Rajbir Singh was the one leading them. Whether it was the encounter at Delhi's Ansal Plaza or any other alleged Lashkar operatives being shot down, Rajbir was always there to take credit. Unfortunately, in March 2008, Rajbir was shot dead by his own associate apparently because he was tired of Rajbir's demands for money.

Rehmana's interrogation started with a smack on her head. 'How do you know Arif?' They hit her sister on the head too. At this point Rehmana had no idea what was happening, why was her entire family being detained. All she knew was that she was a new bride and for some reason, she'd been dragged to the police station. 'If I knew nothing, what could I say?' Slowly, however, the police let her in on the bad news – that her life partner wasn't from Jammu as he'd said he was, but from Pakistan. The cash and jewellery that had been picked up from their home wasn't being looted by some gangsters but was going to be presented as 'sources of terror funding'. And if she wanted to protect herself and her family, she quickly needed to take sides. Rajbir apparently told her: 'I sympathize with you as you are an Indian.' To prove she was an Indian and not waging war against her country, he wanted her to give a statement against her husband and also dissociate herself. The new bride hadn't even gone to her marital home and she was being asked to divorce him. When she relates what happened that day, Rehmana tries to explain her dilemma and what made it extra tough. 'They said that he was behind the attack, but he was with me that day of the attack. It was Friday and even the Qazi saw him at the prayers.'

This explanation is so ingrained in Rehmana's heart and soul, it has stayed with her ever since. It was what she felt that night being smacked around by some police officers, when she learnt that her husband wasn't from Jammu as he had claimed. And it still stands true even now that she's free outside, but fighting for Arif to be spared the death sentence. When she chose to stick by her new husband, she was also alienating herself from her family – from the brother who was tortured for this.

Rehmana cries just talking about her brother who was looking forward to getting married when she was, but still remains a bachelor, 16 years after. '*Peshab ki jagah par torture kiya* (He was tortured in his private parts).' That entire night, this went on. They were all kept in custody. But 24 hours later, the family was released and Rehmana realized that she was going to be held back and formally arrested. Right then she knew her family was terribly angry with Arif for putting them through this ordeal. They were open to doing anything to rid themselves of him, but Rehmana says, 'I didn't care what happened to all.' Much, much later, when her sister had recovered enough, she came and related to her their horror stories and what they individually went through. Stories of how her sister was threatened with a pistol. Like Rehmana was asked to give a statement against Arif on a blank paper, her sister was made to sign too. 'She said I'll sign whatever you say.' The guidelines for arrest and the movies always show how the accused are offered legal aid but at this stage, no one was. You had to stand by and do what the police told you to or face the consequences.

IN JAIL FOR WAGING A WAR

When you read the case documents and judgements in Arif and Rehmana's case, there are several questions that still remain unanswered, even though Arif's conviction as a Lashkar operative has been upheld by a higher court and so the police story has been justified. The police say that Arif was trained in Pakistan to fight against Indian occupation of Kashmir. He came to India a year before the Red Fort attack in 1999, and stayed in Srinagar with other associates where they plotted against India. Police also made a case, which the High Court didn't buy, that Rehmana married Arif knowing that he was a Pakistani who was going to carry out that terrorist attack. She did this apparently because he paid her a good amount of money and then let him stay in her flat.

This, according to the police, is hawala money for 'waging war' against the country. The police doubted their entire marriage and called it 'alleged' marriage in every document. However, what's really strange is that to counter this story, Arif gives a very detailed account with real people and names. He claimed that he was an agent working for R&AW (Research and Analysis Wing). He went to Karachi to meet another R&AW operative called Sanjay Gupta who then suggested to him to travel to India and meet Nain Singh. In his statement to court, Arif claims it was Nain Singh who told him to take on the identity of someone from Jammu and he set him up with the computer shop in Okhla. Now this would have all sounded like an elaborate story of a terrorist, only that Nain Singh did turn up in court as a witness and did admit to being a Cabinet Secretariat official, which is a euphemism for R&AW! What human rights organizations point out is that instead of probing this further, because Arif's story had elements of truth, the judge chose not to follow it any further. The judge didn't think it was necessary to probe Arif's allegations that Nain Singh and he had a difference over money, and that he conspired with the police to make him a scapegoat in a case.

Of course, this was all in the course of the trial. In jail, Rehmana was learning a lot more about her husband. They'd hardly talked before but now they were experiencing the Special Cell's confrontation methods – at 2.30 a.m. The police always hope that it is used to trip up the different versions given by the accused, but Rehmana actually wanted answers for herself.

'Why did you do nikah?' Rehmana remembers how he looked as if he was trapped. He couldn't say much. There were officers who were all standing around, listening to this couple, allegedly terrorists, talk about their union. After a long time, Arif only had one line to say, '*Mere bhi jasbad hain* (Even I have feelings).' For some reason, this really upset the interrogators. They hit him hard on the nose, and he started bleeding. 'I couldn't take it anymore.' The tears that had been glistening in her eyes fell over, overwhelmed as she was. Apparently, Arif tried to tell her that he was home when the attack happened and at Friday prayers, but the police were already dragging him away. The confrontation had only served one purpose. Rehmana remembered some other witnesses other than the Imam. She remembered that they'd had visitors on the day of the attack. There were two women who had come home and they'd met her new husband too.

This just strengthened her resolve further – her husband may indeed be a Pakistani and not an Indian but he was not behind the killing at Red Fort that day. She held on to it, even though there were other confrontations before which the police made the usual noises about turning her into an approver. They told her that they would also release her. But she never said what they wanted to hear, and so they never did release her. When they presented them in front of a lady judge, Rehmana remembers Arif's efforts at dissociating her from the entire thing. He told the judge, 'My wife is innocent.' The judge simply sent them both to custody.

'In jail, the suffering I went through – even if someone were to leave one crore rupees under my bed, it wouldn't make up for it, I wouldn't want it.'

Of all the different shades of pain that one experiences in jail, the torture that one goes through as a terror accused comes in a different category altogether. There may be bonhomie between all other inmates, but perhaps nationalistic feelings are heightened in small spaces leaving no room for the alleged traitors in jail. It was perhaps this that made even little things difficult for Rehmana, like getting her right to meet her incarcerated husband in a weekly *mulakat*.

Till they were in police custody, they were brought together for 'confrontations' for investigation purposes. In jail, they could only meet according to laid down procedures. However, this was contested by the jail officials. The police case which stated that they were 'allegedly married' or 'to be husband' gave them enough leeway to do away with the jail manual, which says you have to facilitate a weekly meeting between husband and wife. But just as Rehmana, despite her bad back, stood up to the Special Cell in refusing to testify against Arif, she also decided to fight against the jail authorities.

So, in court she told the judge how the jail was denying her right to meet her husband. The judge was convinced and gave an order in her favour. When Rehmana flashed the document in jail, the assistant superintendent tore up the court order allowing her to meet her husband. This is something which jail inmates repeatedly point out – the law or rules are how the person in charge in jail sees them. Nothing else really matters.

For 17 months, this fight continued. Rehmana wanted to support her husband but they could only meet when there were joint hearings in the courtroom, which meant that their conversations were according to how much time their accompanying guard allowed them to interact. Finally, a year and a half in jail later, when the National Human Rights Commission accepted their plea, the jail *mulakats* were allowed. Rehmana learnt an important lesson – you cannot give up fighting. She was educated and she had to ensure that she used it to fight for her rights. At every point in jail, this was going to be challenged.

During the first *mulakat*, instead of the usual time of 30 minutes they were given just five. As soon as these five minutes had lapsed, the jail official cried out, 'You said you didn't want to meet, you said he's not your husband. How come you are meeting him now?' Rehmana couldn't believe that she was hearing such a lie. The ridiculousness of the situation, where she was meeting her husband after a long fight and was being accused in front of him of not being interested in meeting him, just threw her off.

The jail official then said, 'I'll tell everyone, Rehmana's husband is a Pakistani.' Perhaps smarting over the NHRC direction to allow the couple to meet despite her orders not allowing it, this was an easy way to make matters tough for Rehmana. Till now, everyone had left this frail looking, quiet, and obviously unwell woman alone. But would they not attack or try to hurt her when they get to know that she had harboured a Pakistani? And she couldn't deny being married to him either because that would mean taking away her rights to these weekly meetings.

The fear of such intimidation heavy in her heart, she went back to her cell crying. It just so happened that the Director General (DG) of Prisons was visiting the women's jail that day because of some event. Fresh from her victory on the *mulakat* issue, she managed to get the DG's attention and told him everything. 'He said don't worry, we'll ensure there's no threat to you.' If nothing, these words were a warning to the official who threatened her.

These small victories hadn't made her stay in jail all comfortable. Her back which was supposed to be all healed after the surgery was undergoing a phenomenal pressure test – the test of jail life with no beds and no one to help around. As soon as she entered the *mulaiza* ward, Rehmana realized just what a mammoth challenge it was going to be when the warden asked her to pick up a blanket from the floor. 'I simply couldn't do it. I tried to explain my surgery, I showed them my back but no one seemed impressed.'

And so, terror accused and harbourer Rehmana Farooqui spent two weeks in jail without even taking a shower. All she would do initially was to cry because she couldn't get herself to pour cold water on herself. Then someone suggested she do something about it, like officially getting help and showing herself to the jail doctor. Rehmana remembers her as an extremely tough person, Dr Kakkar. 'I would keep crying to her, but in all my written applications, she would reject by saying that I was physically fine.' It all made sense now why Rehmana was hoarding her medical papers so carefully. These were medical records signed by the doctors at the Spinal Injuries Centre before she knew she'd be marrying a terrorist.

When the jail doctor didn't relent, Rehmana took

it to the judge and this time the judge took note of her complaint. She instructed the doctor to get her examined at the government's Bara Hindu Rao hospital. When Rehmana went to that hospital, the doctor there said that it was an All India Institute of Medical Sciences (AIIMS) case because they didn't have the facilities. At some point, it seems, Rehmana's X-rays which showed the real condition of her back were also swapped. And imagine all this back and forth to just determine whether Rehmana actually deserved medical care in jail or not. What they didn't factor in was that Rehmana may have looked frail, and she was sick as the police had so vehemently argued against in court, but she wasn't going to give up without a fight.

She again complained to the judge that they had swapped her X-rays and were trying to mislead the court about her health status. The judge, at that point, just tired of it all, summoned the doctor and told her off. She asked for an immediate report. 'I think that was the turning point for Dr Kakkar of Tihar Jail. Of her own volition, she also allowed hot water for my use.' The doctor finally allowed her to go for further treatment to AIIMS.

This, to some extent paved the way for other forms of relief. Rehmana was being treated poorly by the other inmates who expected her to help with the cleaning chores. While the jail manual says that undertrials don't have to indulge in such labour, it is routinely done by inmates, supervised by long-term convicts. Rehmana was finding this excruciatingly difficult and that's where Dr Kakkar stepped in again. She gave her a certificate that said she was not fit to do all these chores.

GUILTY AS PRONOUNCED

There's never a dull moment in jail and just when Rehmana was settling down to her miserable but monotonous life behind bars, there was an incident that added to the already dramatic cases against her. It all started at a *mulakat* session. Since these were harrowing for all parties involved – fighting for time, screaming to hear your relatives, aching to reach out to them and resenting the lack of privacy, it led to a fight between two women inmates. In order to tackle the fight, one was kicked by the police. This physical altercation was followed by the sudden death of the woman involved two days later. The sequence of events led many in the jail to instantly start questioning and protesting against the jail staff. They were all locked in and as the news spread, the protests became louder and more violent. There was one cell with women from GB Road, facing solicitation charges of sex-work and trafficking, who started shaking the cell gate so hard that the lock and the latches broke. Rehmana found herself with these women and when they started chanting 'Zohra was killed,' so did she. This didn't go down well with the vengeful jail authorities. The police booked a case of breaking jail property against six women including Rehmana. Even after she had been acquitted by the High Court, Rehmana was still fighting in this case and it took a cash payment to finally settle it once and for all.

However, what this side case did do was provide Rehmana an opportunity to bond with the other inmates. The quiet woman from Moradabad who was usually seen crying in one corner, made a few friends. The sex-workers told her that they were even willing to vouch for her innocence. That they were going to tell the court that she didn't do anything. This kind of support couldn't have come any quicker because in October 2005, five years since she'd been in jail, Rehmana Farooqui learnt that her stay in jail was no longer a temporary thing. She'd now been pronounced guilty of 'concealment' of a terrorist. The judge said Rehmana should have been 'suspicious to know the reality of her would-be husband. But she ignored all these things as she was willing to harbour accused Md. Arif @ Ashfaq knowing his reality that he was a LeT militant and a Pakistani national and who entered India illegally to carry out militant activities.'

When the judgement was announced, Rehmana had screamed out loud in the courtroom. She'd forced the judge to record what she had to say about the charges. She'd made this emotional plea to judge O.P. Saini in the courtroom:

I am innocent. I have been falsely implicated in this case. Police wanted me to become a witness against Mohammed Arif which I refused. They also wanted me to divorce him, which also I refused. My sister, my aunt [*mausi*] and my brother H. Farukhi were tortured in police custody. They were kept in detention without authorization. My relations referred to above were also tortured to become witnesses against Mohammed Arif for the facts which my relations and I did not know. Since we refused to become witnesses against Mohammed Arif, I have been falsely implicated in this case. Mohammed Arif did not tell us that he is a Pakistani national. He told us that he is a resident of Jammu.

All the screaming and objections came to nothing. Rehmana was now a convicted terrorist along with her husband, sentenced to seven years' rigorous imprisonment. Groups like People's Union for Democratic Rights (PUDR), among others, wrote extensively about her case and how the evidence didn't add up, but at that time, it didn't hold for much.

'I'd taken a piece of paper to court on which I'd written "*main bekasoor hoon*" in Urdu so I could show it to the waiting media. But even this I wasn't allowed to take in by the police.' They called it a security threat. They tried to snatch it, and in that scuffle Rehmana hit her head on the lockup wall.

So, even this small rejection of her conviction she couldn't air publicly. It really hit her hard that she was now relegated to spend her time in that and all the charges that ACP Rajbir and his gang had levelled against her, the world held it to be true too. She was bedridden for days. She couldn't speak and was on a wheelchair and couldn't move, literally immobilized by the shock. It kept going on in her head – 'I'm now a convicted terrorist.' When she refused to eat and even reduced her water intake, a Kashmiri doctor lodged in the jail warned her that she may be force fed.

'She said to me, I feel your pain, we feel that in the valley.' That did something for Rehmana and she looked around at the other friends she had made in jail. There was an African woman called Elizabeth who used to make fun of her and make her laugh. Elizabeth had once thrown a *matka* or a pot at a superintendent of the jail because she was angry, and they had an argument. The police stripped her naked and beat her in front of everyone. She was an accused in a minor drugs case but had been languishing in jail for years. Rehmana said she realized she should be thankful for little things like she'd never been physically tortured in that manner.

In jail, when she looked around, there was just desperation. Like this cellmate who along with her mother had been arrested in a dowry case. They had spent so much time in jail even though she claimed she was innocent that she attempted to commit suicide, but was saved last minute. She was then kept in the medical cell but even there she tried to hang herself in the toilet, with her own dupatta!

Rehmana got up and began fighting again. Within a year she was granted bail, and finally a year later, in 2007, came the Delhi High Court order that she'd been waiting for:

We are, therefore, of the view that the prosecution could not be said to have established that accused Rehmana Yusuf Farooqui had married accused Mohd. Arif @ Ashfaq in order to provide a shelter to him in Delhi so that he could go ahead with his terrorist activities without being suspected because of his living with Rehmana Yusuf Farooqui, her mother, her sister and brother in their house in Ghazipur from where Mohd. Arif was arrested. So, she was not rightly convicted by the learned trial Court and there being no evidence whatsoever adduced by the prosecution from which it could be inferred that she was either a party to the conspiracy to attack the army camp inside Lal Quila or that she had some knowledge about that plan she cannot be convicted for the offence under Section 120-B IPC for which the learned trial Court has acquitted her. The appeal filed by the State seeking her conviction under Section 120-B IPC is, therefore, liable to be dismissed and the appeal filed by Rehmana Yusuf Farooqui deserves to be allowed.

In other words, neither was she part of any conspiracy, nor did she do anything wrong by marrying Arif. Rehmana had finally succeeded in clearing her name.

| | | |

The thing about being freed after spending years in jail is that your life never becomes normal. Rehmana still lives in that one-room tenement. She may have got her name cleared but she can't go back to Moradabad anymore. It was Arif's family in Pakistan that paid for her lawyer, along with Arif's, and so there are multiple bonds she now shares with him. She'd always stood by her husband with whom she was yet to share her bed, and now she was determined to continue to do so: 'He's innocent. I know he is.'

It's not easy fighting for someone who's on death row for a famous case like the Red Fort attack. When she has fights with unscrupulous lawyers, they abuse her even now and call her a terrorist even though she has a High Court order saying that she's not. That's why when she went back to live with her sister, it wasn't the same anymore. They didn't want Arif, the man who led to them spending a torturous night in custody, to have anything to do with their lives. While Rehmana was spending every Friday, the entire day, running to jail to meet Arif and collect his notes and coordinate with his lawyers.

There were other injuries too. While Rehmana was in jail, her sister had a major accident due to which she was bed-ridden for almost a year. At that time, when she had no one to look after her, she resented Rehmana for landing up in jail. And Rehmana resented her for not visiting her in jail for so long, not knowing that she was seriously hurt.

She moved out of her sister's home. 'I just left home and I kept walking.' She walked out and ended up at the home of a man who her friend in jail had described as kind. Rehman Bhai would come to jail to meet another cellmate, and he appeared to be a generous man. She didn't know where else to go but to his house. 'Of course I didn't think that his family and wife would find it odd to see some strange woman land up at his house.' Fortunately for Rehmana, they didn't find it too strange. They helped her out and now are a major part of her support system. Her life post-jail is thanks to the help she received from her friends from jail. She sometimes goes to Moradabad when she misses her family or they reach out to her. But otherwise she stays put in Jamia Nagar. The terrorist's bride has a mission in life – to rid him off the 'terrorist' tag. Or at least get him off death row.

THE RAJA WHO WAS BANISHED

From the autumn of 2010 until 2012, if there is one story that dominated all headlines, it was the 2G spectrum story, and as the reporter on the CBI beat, it was the only story I followed. When the winter session of Parliament started, the Comptroller and Auditor General (CAG) report on spectrum allocation was tabled, blaming the Ministry of Telecom and its minister, A. Raja, for losses up to rupees 1.76 lakh crore in granting telecom licences.

A. Raja, an upcoming star of the Dravida Munnetra Kazhagam (DMK), a Dalit leader from the Nilgiris, was being accused of manipulating the process of giving 2G licences to a favoured few, and Anil Ambani-led ADAG was accused of using a front company to get a telecom licence. While most people, including the CBI investigators, as Raja claims, didn't understand anything about this case because of its technical nature, what they did understand was that it was a case that involved the who's who of the country – the Ambanis, the Ruias, Ratan Tata, the Goenkas, Chandras of Unitech and top politicians – and they were all under scrutiny. Apart from Raja, his party and the government's southern ally DMK chief M. Karunanidhi's daughter, K. Kanimozhi, was also charged because she was part of Kalaignar TV, the party's mouthpiece, which apparently received the kickback of 200 crore rupees. To complicate matters even further, Kanimozhi's stepmother and Karunanidhi's wife, Dayaluammal who was over 70, was the majority stakeholder in that bribe-receiving company! What these high-profile people had going against them was the optics of time. As the CBI closed in on them, a body called India Against Corruption, with Magsaysay awardees like Arvind Kejriwal, Kiran Bedi, activist Anna Hazare and Prashant Bhushan, was preparing to begin a moral war against corruption. With all these iconic figures sitting at Jantar Mantar calling politicians and industrialists 'thieves', the CBI, the government and the courts knew that the VIPs couldn't get away this time.

I remember the period as one just after I'd come back from my maternity leave in October 2010. One vivid memory that I associate with that time is when the news broke of Anil Ambani being summoned by the CBI. The Supreme Court was monitoring the probe on a regular basis and guiding investigations, and they would keep nudging the CBI to call the 'high and mighty' involved in the case – after all, there wasn't a dearth of them. Raja had given licences to several operators – Unitech or Uninor owned by Sanjay Chandra, Swan Telecom owned by Shahid Balwa (but accused of being a front company of Anil Ambani's Reliance), Tata Telecom, Loop Telecom owned by Khaitans, and the Ruias-owned Essar. The CBI had to question them all to figure out which one of them had received special favours from the minister who helped them get 2G licences.

We knew they would all be summoned, but the CBI being CBI, nothing would be disclosed in advance and no one was going to confirm anything. So for a new mother, it was a nightmare as I always had to be ready to rush to the agency because I couldn't miss precious pictures of these people being questioned in dingy *sarkari* settings. It so happened that I was in the car with my seven-month-old baby when Anil Ambani was rumoured to have stepped into the building. My sources inside confirmed the news and I could immediately do a phone-in report. But that posed another challenge – my son Neel had a unique problem of crying whenever the car would stop in traffic, and I couldn't guarantee if the background noise to my phone report would be a crying baby. So, if I didn't have my hands full already, trying to confirm a piece of news from very cagey officials and explaining a very technical story to my audiences, I also had a peculiar problem of being a new mother. Fortunately, I discovered a packet of Gems' chocolate buttons in my bag, and although it is totally not advisable, in the line of duty I came up with the plan that as soon as my report would start, I would keep popping them one after another into Neel's mouth. This was a calculated risk because the news of a powerful industrialist being summoned at an investigation agency was likely to be a long phone report that would last over several minutes, at that time there was no other choice. As my driver hurtled the car towards the agency's headquarters, I reported on the phone with faint interruptions of my son's 'goo-goo gagas' to indicate he was through with the chocolate button and was ready for the next one. Despite my best efforts, Neel's exclamations did make it on air, because a viewer tweeted to tell me that my baby had made his on-air debut!

Anyway, just like you'd never expect to see an infant like Neel at a CBI office, there were several people who no one had ever imagined encountering there. The headquarters was one of those old government offices where corridors smell of urine. This was the time when CBI was just about to abandon this horrendous building and move to a swanky new one with glass exteriors, but A. Raja and A. Ambani were destined to meet in this old one that was brown and rotting around the edges. As our sources told us and as I reported that night, it was one of those dramatic confrontations which crime reporters are often told about. Whenever a CBI officer leaks this information, my mind always drifts to a movie where the two subjects are about to duel and the CBI sleuths wait on the side to see who draws first and who kills. The CBI wanted us to believe that Anil Ambani was sweating under pressure of being summoned to such a location, and when he left they gave him the courtesy of leaving from a back exit. It may have been a courtesy, but it was also another symbolically loaded move for a man who would proudly be seen at the North Block of Ministry of Finance as an honourable captain of industry or jogging down Raisina Hill having to sneak out in the shadows hoping the waiting press wouldn't pounce on him.

But they did. It was a chase where cameramen fell over each other and almost knocked him out too. He looked stoic, walking briskly, as if this was the most normal thing in the world. The pictures were soon flashed across TV screens, with reporters using phrases like 'grilled', 'under pressure', 'CBI turns on the heat', 'top industrialist under the scanner'.

However, these impressions are rather delusional. The CBI may be the best investigative police unit in the country but neither their appearance at the time (the new office is much more modern) nor their practices would put anyone 'under pressure'. The main reception of the CBI office consisted of a small room adjacent to a regular door. When you entered, you encountered a cop who would double up as a *chowkidar*, sitting with a register and an old iron rod heater to warm himself in those cold December nights. On the sofa, you'd have reporters like us who could go no further and would hang around here waiting for all those who emerged. Sometimes in this reception area, you'd also meet people like Raja's doctor and his nephew, who was a spitting image of him. Every time he'd make a move, camera crews would start rolling, or start following him to the toilet, mistaking him for the minister.

That's what the appearance was and the CBI's practices, too, seemed quite contrary to the impressions reporters had. Their leaks suggested that the CBI investigators were putting the fear of god into VIPs' hearts, but indoors it was an entirely different scene. The first day that Raja was summoned for questioning was on Christmas Eve 2010. Now this was more than a year after CBI had first registered the case into spectrum allocation and it was days after they had raided him. To say that he was expecting to be summoned was an understatement. In fact, when your house gets raided a year after the case has been registered it can only be a source of nuisance and not a stress situation where you are scared of what the investigators will find. The only thing Raja found irritating about those days was the intrusive media that followed him around everywhere till he got arrested two months later.

'My daughter would go to school at 6 a.m., and the camera would follow her. My wife was putting the *alpana* outside the door and she came out in her night gown. The camera started filming her again so there is no privacy at all! This would begin at 6 in the morning. Can you imagine?'

The media circus trail would be from his house at 2, Moti Lal Nehru Marg to the CBI office on Lodhi Road. The OB (Outside Broadcasting) vans outside his home and, of course, the CBI office, were waiting everyday for a word of A. Raja's arrest. To us, the waiting media outside, it looked like he was being cooked over a slow flame, pressurized to confess, but apparently it was all just an attempt to mollify the Supreme Court. The top court was overseeing the investigations and the investigation agency was only following their instructions. That's why they initially registered the FIR against unknown people instead of the minister and didn't do anything for a year. And then the top bench saw the CAG report, which said that 1.76 lakh crore rupees of taxpayers' money had been stolen, and that's when they shouted out 'It's a loot, it's a loot!' This is what finally got the ball rolling and the CBI, who would later be called 'caged parrots' by the same court, decided they couldn't avoid but move on this minister. The top court had to give an order to A. Raja – please join investigations.

'I would go there in the morning. Then they had a total of one or two files. They would keep going over that and nobody really understood what the 2G scam or the telecom policy was all about. All we did was eat biryani and drink tea and coffee while the CBI guys tried to understand what the 2G case was all about. They hadn't read the documents that were all there – the TRAI recommendations, the National Telecom Policy, nothing, and they didn't understand it so they were all dithering. They just knew that something had to be done.'

Raja said that the file-searching would be on for a couple of hours in the morning. Then, lunch would arrive from his home. He would eat that, and while the media assumed that he was being grilled, he would have a nap in the officer's room. Then there would be more going over the files to understand what Raja was being accused of in the CAG report, and then he would be sent home. This revelation finally explained why he was arrested in February, a month and a half after they first started questioning him – it probably took them that much time to comprehend what the case was all about!

Looking back, Raja knew his arrest was inevitable. In

his Gulmohar Park house, which he had rented so he could attend the daily 2G hearings, there is a stack of papers next to a screen showing Press Trust of India (PTI) news tickers. He waved a thick folder, just one of the four fat files, towards me: 'I have every record of what the Supreme Court bench has said in the matter.' Anyone would think that he could have just kept a record of all the news clippings. But Raja knew that PTI also gave real-time updates of what the judges were observing in court – their off-the-cuff remarks about 'loot', for example, which sometimes never made it to the news reports. For the sake of his legal cases, he wanted to make sure that he had a record of everything. He only had to glance through them to know that the courts were pushing towards an arrest.

'Parliament hadn't functioned for the last 45 days because the Opposition kept demanding a JPC (Joint Parliamentary Committee) probe in the matter. The government said that they'd rather the government fall than agree to a JPC, and so the pressure had to be relieved. That could only be through me.'

And so, on 2 February, when Raja was making his daily appearance at the CBI, it became clear that he wasn't going to get his usual afternoon nap. Of course, CBI being the kind of political organization that it is, the news first emerged not from inside the building but a few kilometres away, from Parliament. His doctor and his nephew were both called in to meet him and his nephew, realizing what was about to happen, started crying.

Raja, who never looked uncomfortable through it all, coolly sat for the medical examination that is part of the process during an arrest. It was the CBI Investigating Officer Rajesh Chahal who was sweating it. 'The doctor was taking my blood pressure which was perfectly normal. Chahal looked bothered and asked if the doctor could also check him. It turned out that his was as high as 180/120. I was joking with him – "Who is the crook here?"'

'I CAME FROM DUST, FLEW UP HIGH BUT I WENT BACK INTO DUST'

Raja's arrest was a watershed moment. It was unprecedented that a sitting minister was arrested for corruption and he was threatening to take down many more with him. Behind the jargon of 'first-come-first-served-policy' of 'UAS licences', of allocating the precious commodity of spectrum, was a very simple investigation – when Raja claimed in his defence that the entire band of UPA ministers supported him for not auctioning licences, was he in fact right? And what kind of bribery is a 200-crore-rupee loan that is given by cheque to his party's mouthpiece, Kalaignar TV? This personal benefit is the one that CBI was trying to convince everyone about, but it looked weak. The CBI in its charge sheet claimed that as soon as they summoned Raja for questioning, Kalaignar TV started returning the 200-crore loan as kickback to DB realty (a Mumbai based real estate development company), which had got the 2G licence but had failed to convince most politicians that bribe can be given by cheque, and that too to a third party. Off the record, the CBI did explain that the pay offs may have happened by other means too, but they were never able to get any hint of evidence on this.

So, while Raja's arrest along with all the top industrialists, like Sanjay Chandra (Unitech) and Shahid Balwa (DB realty), created a kind of political turmoil which eventually led to the exit of DMK from the central government, at CBI, things carried on as usual. Raja's police lockup was actually Deputy Inspector General S.K. Palsania's room. Palsania, an amiable officer who died tragically of cancer during the course of the investigation, had the usual set up which included an attached toilet to his air-conditioned room. 'During the day, I would be with the other officers going through files etcetera and by evening, I would sleep in the DIG's room.' This fine treatment was a trademark of CBI's premier status – the roughing up, second or third degree was only for other police agencies to use. Not that anyone would use it on A. Raja in any case. Even as the accused, he claimed to be forever explaining the technical details which once when the investigating officer finally understood, he apparently exclaimed: 'Mr Raja, you are acquitted!'

But the legal steps, or what officers like to call 'due process', still had to be followed. And so from Lutyens' Delhi they moved to the West Delhi complex called Tihar Jail. Raja moved into his own cell in Jail Number 1, and for his next-door neighbours he had his associates – his telecom secretary Sidharth Behura and his private secretary R.K. Chandolia. If Raja was the first minister to go to jail, Behura was also one of the first from the powerful Indian Administrative Service to be charged, and who the CBI had sanction to prosecute. The charge against him and Chandolia was that they had connived with Raja ever since Raja was the environment minister. The friendship with businessmen Sanjay Chandra and Shahid Balwa went back to those days and they all got together to ensure that Chandra and Balwa got the precious 2G licences, which they then sold to foreign investors like Etisalat and Telenor at huge profits. Behura and Chandolia as senior bureaucrats were accused of manipulating public notices, helping Raja bring forward cut-off dates surreptitiously, so that only a favoured few would qualify. From Paryavaran Bhawan to Sanchar Bhawan, they were all now left to confabulate in Jail Number 1.

'It was the high-security ward, and so apart from us there was also IPS officer R.K. Sharma. I was the only one with a separate cell, a fan and a Western toilet. It was very comfortable.'

The jail experience of a regular inmate and a VIP is never comparable. Ward Number 9 in which he was staying was the very same one that Indira Gandhi was also kept in 1978. There were only five cells in that ward and a separate kitchen to cater to them. Each cell had two rooms, one sitting room and one bedroom. The bedroom had an attached bathroom with shower, washbasin and a mirror. The other occupants of this plush setting included Subrata Roy or Saharasri and a former minister from Haryana, Gopal Kanda. Of course, Subrata Roy also spent some of the time in a special jail which was the old court complex of Tihar. The complex had been converted into meeting rooms and conference rooms for Roy and his associates to conduct their business, and that was with the permission of the Supreme Court. Of course, the fact that these meeting and conference rooms were air-conditioned and had a telephone connection and internet facilities, caused a lot of heartburn among all the other high-profile inmates. As one said, 'Subrata Roy is perhaps the only one in the history of Indian jails to have an air-conditioner. Moral of the story: If you steal 1,000 rupees, the hawaldar will beat the shit out of you and lock you up in a dungeon with no ventilation. But if you steal rupees 55,000 crore, then you get to stay in a 40-foot cell which has four split air-conditioning units, internet, fax, mobile phones and a staff of 10 to clean your shoes and cook your food (in case it is not delivered from Hyatt Regency that day)!'

Raja may not have had the court-sanctioned digs that Saharasri enjoyed, but he too had the entire jail staff at his beck and call. The only luxury they couldn't have was an air-conditioner in their cells, but as Raja was a high-security prisoner, he could spend his day in the jail superintendent's office which was air-conditioned. At any rate, their cells were privy to the luxury of a cooler. According to their security assessment, the 1.76 lakh crore tag meant that some common criminal could attack him in jail, and so if he needed to go around jail, he needed security. So they preferred him sitting in the superintendent's office. If others were woken up at 5 a.m. and were served breakfast at 6.30 a.m., Raja had a jail orderly asking what they could get him from the canteen.

'Only non-vegetarian food wasn't allowed, but the food was delicious and we also had sweets and *nariyal paani* (coconut water). It all came from the canteen. Every day, someone would come and ask: "Sir, what would you like today?"'

Even if he ventured towards the library, Raja would have about five policemen following him. That is why the DG of Prisons and other officials gave him the provision to get all the 2G documents in his own cell. Not just that, he could also have the other 2G accused come into his cell, so that they could all work on it. Now, if you want to know why that is a big deal, you have to remember that when the CBI filed the charge sheet in court, they had to bring in seven trunk-loads of paper. So the jail permission meant that a rickshaw had to make several trips to jail to carry all the papers that were needed for these accused. And they were all stacked up along the corridors of their cells.

'You have to understand. If they threw the jail book at me, then each and every paper would have to be cleared by the jail authorities, but they were very kind. I also never asked for unreasonable things, but this allowed us all to work together on the case even from inside.' The most limiting thing about jail life is that you have to be locked up at particular times, like in the afternoons from 2 p.m. to 4 p.m. and by 7 p.m. in the evening. But this allowed the entire

2G gang to be together as Raja had asked for all of them to be able to legally work on their cases. Raja is a trained lawyer who would cross question the prosecution witnesses in court. In jail, as the charges of cheating and conspiracy were common to all of the accused, they divided the papers and prepared together. The CBI alleged that they all knew each other and conspired to loot the country together, but this close proximity brought about a different kind of bonding. For instance, Vinod Goenka and Shahid Balwa's hotel Grand Hyatt in Goa has become a kind of second home for the other accused. That's where R.K. Chandolia can often be found when the court is not in session. When Goenka comes to Delhi, he has stopped staying at hotels and only stays with Sanjay Chandra. And when Goenka's father died in Mumbai in August 2016, all the other accused including A. Raja rushed to be with him.

Maybe the loyalty or kindness that is shown in jail matters much more than anything of its kind in the outside world. That's why some of the orderlies or inmates who help VIP undertrials like Raja have now become permanently attached to them. Raja and the others helped ten people get bail just by writing applications to court. People like Sudhir had been forgotten and had been in jail for years without even a charge sheet in his case. After being freed, Sudhir started working for Shahid Balwa and his wife now works as a cook in Raja's house.

'I know that tomorrow if my daughter, Mayuri, needs any kind of help there are these friends who will do everything in their power to help.' It's a bond that formed over the 15 months he spent inside jail, but as Raja himself admits, it wasn't a regular jail life.

THE JAILED MINISTER

If the Supreme Court forced the CBI to arrest Raja, then they were also the reason he had a comfortable life inside, although it was totally unintended. The top court wanted a thorough investigation and they wanted it done as soon as possible. So, in a regular case one would see court hearings every 15 days, at best. But in the 2G case, there were daily hearings, and this provided unlimited advantages.

For instance, it meant that they were out of the drudgery, the sheer nothingness of jail life that drives so many into depression and addiction to some kind of narcotics. For the 2G accused, every morning a special Tata vehicle would take them to court at 8.30 a.m. Once they reached Patiala House courts, they would have to bear the lockup, but soon the courtroom of O.P. Saini with its air-conditioned coolness would welcome them. They would then spend the entire day, some with their wives and families attending court proceedings, and some extra time till 4.30 p.m. or so and then go back to jail for the rest of the evening. 'It was only public holidays and the weekends that we would experience jail life, otherwise there was nothing to it.'

They had also moved an application which allowed them to eat food that their families brought from home in the court complex. This meant that unlike other inmates, they had access to non-vegetarian food, too. There were hiccups though, and Raja loves telling this one story when a new sub-inspector came into Patiala House courts. Now, for whatever reason, the new cop in town wasn't very impressed with the airs of all his high-profile inmates in the court lockup, and he said that he couldn't allow them to eat the food that their families had brought for them.

'It created a major outrage and we all protested, but that inspector didn't budge from his position at all. So everyone went without lunch and all these rich people, they all experienced for the very first time what real hunger was.' Raja couldn't stop chuckling, 'As a politician, we go to different places so are used to everything. But for one day, these people felt what it was like to go hungry. Their families were very upset.' Of course, unlike the daily pangs of hunger that many in jails endure, the group of dozen-odd 2G accused found a solution the very next day. The jailer sent a message to the court lockup that they must not be stopped from eating their home food and the special status was restored again.

There is another story about going to court that Raja likes to tell. The Tata van, or the 2G bus, was once on its way back to Tihar Jail after a day of legal proceedings, when its dozen or so occupants felt a little wistful. 'The windows of that bus had grills and we couldn't even look out properly. It had been 5–6 months in jail, and we were all saying, "When will we be able to walk the streets of Delhi freely again." All we did was to stay inside Tihar, get into the bus and then back inside a lockup and then courtroom and then jail again. You won't believe it – just when we were talking like this, the bus broke down.' Raja, a man who otherwise doesn't display too many emotions, had his face all lit up just thinking about that day. The breakdown apparently happened in the salubrious environs of the diplomatic enclave where the roads are clean and wide and there is no dearth of trees around. The police escort with them asked for a vehicle but they were informed it would take at least an hour to arrive. So, just as they were wishing for, they were allowed to get off the bus and smell the fresh, free air.

'There was also a dhaba nearby, and we were all walking around and we asked for tea. We were happy.' Apparently, the spectrum bunch was also spotted by some passersby who stopped their cars and scooters. 'Some just said "Hi", some said, "You will come out of it, don't worry", and some said, "*Arrey*, A. Raja – 1.76 lakh crore!"' Very soon, the replacement bus arrived and they were all back in their cells, but that one hour and few minutes at Chanakyapuri gave them quite a story to talk about for sometime.

The 1.76 lakh crore rupee figure had obviously become Raja's catchphrase, even though when CBI calculated the extent of damage he had caused, they put it at a relatively modest 22,000 crore rupees in his charge sheet. But politics is a game of perception and there had been so much noise in Parliament and media about the CAG's figure of 1.76 lakh crore that it stuck with him – from the convicted murderer of Jessica Lal, Manu Sharma, asking Raja: 'Sir, how do you keep 1.76 lakh crore?' every time they played badminton together, to the other inmates who would stare at him with exactly the same question.

For all the respect that he got from the top bosses in Tihar, Raja had one fan club that superseded all. It was the Tamil Nadu Special Police or TSP. They may have been there to dissuade everyone else from becoming too chummy, but many of them had known Raja because he was from their part of the country and their MP. 'Many of them came to me and said that they had served with me as personal security officers. Whenever I'd go to Coimbatore, the state police would give me protection during my official trips so some of them who were now posted in Tihar, remembered spending time with me. They were thrilled and so even in jail they would come and salute me every day. My friends said, "Even in jail, you are a minister!"'

There was one allowance that Raja got in jail that he appreciated above all. In 2011, his daughter was a 13-year-old student at Mater Dei Convent. If there's one person who was severely affected by his incarceration, it was she, because of the media's incessant reporting about his case. Her school performance was severely affected, and from being a student who always got above 85 per cent, her marks dropped significantly. It was at that time that the Tihar Jail officials relaxed all *mulakat* rules for her. They allowed Mayuri to visit her father at whatever time she liked after school and on any given day. The superintendent of police would give them space in his office to talk. The regular Tihar visitors would otherwise be waiting for their weekly meetings, which would take place over a glass partition with the help of headphones. Raja was grateful for these VIP allowances.

'I am also grateful to the teachers of Mater Dei. They kept encouraging my daughter and telling her that this was a part of politics and that I would come out of it soon. They issued instructions to everyone in school that no one would say anything about me.' The teachers may have succeeded but salacious members of the press had a field day in speculating about the link between Raja and co-accused Kanimozhi. It was part of the gossip circles but their reported intimacy also made it to print, which hurt Raja the most.

'Kani's son was 14 at the time. How do you think they felt reading "Raja is going to marry Kanimozhi"? What is going through their head?' There were a lot of unsubstantiated reports. When one is an accused, and especially when a woman is involved, it gives everyone a field day to put unnamed sources and rumours into print. Whether it is shepherding by the staff of the school or good fortune, Mayuri is now a confident student of law, just like her father.

AFTER JAIL, RAJA TELLS HIS TALE

When you go to Raja's office, right on his desk are two copies of B.R. Ambedkar's *Annihilation of Caste* – one in English and the other in Tamil. And yet, you never hear him speaking or citing his Dalit identity. 'Many people suggested that I was made the fall guy because I am a Dalit, but I will never say so, I will never play the caste card.' Maybe it's the philosophy that he's picked up from his favourite sixth-century poet Thiruvalluvar, who he is always quoting from. Philosophy and legal arguments, that's all that Raja was counting on. Unlike most others in prison, he was an atheist and so he couldn't do the elaborate *havans* and *pujas* that others organized. He didn't even swear on God while giving his testimony in court. 'I noticed all jails have a temple and you find people who have life sentences praying in those temples. I don't understand – why are they going there?'

All he can understand is the code of loyalty which makes him bow down to his leader M. Karunanidhi, and also command the following of the people of the Nilgiris, hundreds of whom took trains to receive him the day he was freed on bail. He's proud that his loyalty to his team meant that he never applied for bail till all of the accused – Sanjay Chandra, Behura, Goenka, Hari Nair, Kanimozhi – had been freed.

The deepest cut has been the one that was inflicted by his former boss and colleagues. Since Raja always maintained that all his actions were collective decisions, his colleagues cut him out for political reasons. They indicated that the CBI's case was that he misled Prime Minister Manmohan Singh into believing that he was doing the right thing when he went with the first-come-first-served policy instead of auctioning 2G licences. For political reasons, they isolated Raja and it wasn't something he appreciated. 'Whenever I was in the Central Hall afterwards and the prime minister would come in, I would immediately walk out. I met P. Chidambaram also on the flight to Chennai so many times after coming out, but we would just turn our faces away. But I have the deepest regard for Mrs Gandhi. When she met me in the corridor once while she was with Shashi Tharoor, she asked me how I was and we spoke.' There were some former allies he couldn't turn away from but had to face in court. Like the former Attorney General G.E. Vahanwati. Vahanwati plays a key role in the 2G case because it says that Raja forged and manipulated a note to which Vahanwati gave his approval. Raja says it was cleared by the country's top law officer, but he contests it by saying Raja added a paragraph later and forged it.

Vahanwati is no more, but when he was testifying in court, Raja decided to question him himself. 'We used to go for a drink at the bar in Taj Hotel before all this but I didn't want to show my proximity in court before everyone. After the questioning was over, he asked the judge, "Can I please talk to my friend?" The judge announced a tea-break.' As Raja tells the story, Vahanwati held his hand and apologized for all that had happened. Raja said all that he could tell him was 'ok'.

It is unclear whether A. Raja has accepted this as rapprochement. He's now written his own tell-all about the 2G case, and he promises it will expose many of those who were in power at the time. Most people who have been to jail have written their memoirs while they were in jail or, like Raja, once they've been released. It's not always for publication. Sometimes, it's just a means of catharsis.

THE HIPSTER JUVENILE
WHO WENT TO JAIL

If you were to judge YB from his Facebook profile, which is what other 19-year-olds like him do, you might think he's quite precocious for his age. His profile photo shows him sprawled topless on a hotel room bed as if he was posing as a model for Teen Cosmo. As he's looking at his smart phone away from whoever took the photo, his chest shorn of any hair, his bedside is decorated with a bottle of scotch and a can of beer. The comments section with 169 likes is full of adoration, with YB replying to many with the heart emoticon and warding off queries about who he's with. His photo album is full of such uninhibited exhibitions of teenage rebellion, with champagne and beer bottles, hookahs and cigarettes, smiling confidently at the camera, and it's perhaps no different from other teenage boys acting out while growing up in the city.

The only difference is that this Facebook profile and YB were at the centre of a gang rape case at Bindapur police station of Uttam Nagar in Delhi. And it was only on

12 July 2016, after almost two years of proceedings and after spending a month at the Mukherjee Nagar juvenile home, that YB was finally acquitted of rape. As the judges who are members of the Juvenile Justice Board, Punam Singh, V.K. Pandey and M.P. Singh, ruled that they found 'the deposition of the prosecutrix not of sterling quality and unblemished... on the basis of uncorroborated testimony of the prosecutrix, no verdict can be returned in favour of the prosecutrix. For the reasons recorded, the juvenile is acquitted of 376 D (gang rape), 328 (causing hurt by means of poison), 356 (assault or criminal force to commit theft), 379 (theft), 34 (acts done by several persons for a common intention), section 6 of the POCSO Act (aggravated penetrative sexual assault punishable by not less than 10 years).' At the time of the offence, the prosecutrix was aged 15 and YB was 17 and they had been going out for almost six months.

It's a long list of charges for YB, who is just a young boy. And when you meet him, it's even harder to believe that this shy, young student of Bachelor of Computer Application is that exhibitionist character from Facebook. 'My brother almost deleted my account,' he says. But then it was social media and the profiles of all key players that provided key evidence to the courts. Perhaps that's why YB stays on and hasn't lost his personality on FB. And the prosecutrix, as she is legally called, SS continues to diligently post updates on Instagram and Snapchat. If his profile picture shows off his topless chest, hers shows her as a fashion-conscious teen. Sporting sunglasses here, over-sized glasses there, sharing a chocolate sundae in one to selfies in the mirror, SS comes across as another pretty, supposedly popular, preening teenager of Delhi.

BOY MEETS GIRL

The court documents state their story goes back to February

2014, just a week after Valentine's Day. As YB sits with me in the Connaught Place coffee shop, with other millennial couples all around us, his narration of events has only minor diversions from the documents. These differences point out how YB saw things differently from SS, and how the court arrived at a sequence of events.

As YB and SS tell their story, they met through a common friend. SS went to the state-run government school in Vikaspuri where YB's best friend also studied. The best friend, Kunal, lived next door to YB, and having grown up together they often came back from school together (even though YB went to a public school) in YB's Santro car. He was driving before 18? 'Yes. Actually it wasn't my car but no one in my family knew how to drive at that time, so I'd drive.' YB was the youngest of three children, with a stay-at-home mum. SS was the older of two siblings, with her grandparents also staying with the family.

'Both our schools were in Vikaspuri. So I would often go to pick up Kunal, and sometimes, I'd meet his friend SS. She asked about me one day and then that very evening, she sent me a FB request.'

In her 164 statement or the statement given on record to a magistrate, SS's version is slightly different and says that he sent her a Facebook request, not the other way round. The court documents show how the authorities tried to recreate and understand this world of teenagers and their initial experiments with social interactions. Their flirtations, their flip remarks were all now reproduced and scrutinized to make a judgement about who was at fault; was the 17-year-old guilty of rape? The court writes: 'She told him that she does not speak to boys; that he asked for her mobile number and was curious to know whether she was on WhatsApp, that she told him that she was on WhatsApp, but she maintains contact with limited persons only; that he asked whether he was an unlimited person (sic); that she told him that she would remain in touch with him only on Facebook; that she shared her number with him; that on 10.04.14 she met the juvenile for the first time, and that to his query whether she would be his girlfriend, she replied in the affirmative' – the boy-meets-girl story as investigated and reproduced in front of the juvenile justice board.

It's a version that YB more or less agrees with, of course in his narration she appears as the keener party. 'I had another friend Gaurav who said, "Stay away from that girl, she's had lots of boyfriends." I said I have nothing to do with all this and so I accepted her friend request. After that we'd chat now and then on FB. Once she called me even though I didn't have her number. Randomly she said: "I'm waiting for you at Arya Samaj Road." I said why are you waiting for me, we never even spoke. This was 3–4 days after we became friends on FB. I told her that I was getting ready and ended the call, but she again called two days later. The second time she called, she fixed a date. She said let's meet at PVR next to our house. I called Gaurav too. Very soon after meeting, she said, "I want to drink." There was a wine shop just next to PVR so they both drank. Now, Gaurav being a guy maybe had more capacity but she, even though she'd probably had just 2 pints, was totally drunk. Because she couldn't stand, we gave her a lemon drink and fixed her and got her home.'

After that eventful date, their meetings became more regular. YB also acknowledges that they became an official couple – going for regular afternoon clubbing sessions, a fixture for school kids with conservative parents. The afternoon jam sessions or parties are organized by local clubs that cater to teenagers who might be bunking classes, changing out of their school uniforms in the club's toilets.

The one that YB and his friends spent most of the time in was the Keeva Club in West Gate Mall of Rajouri Garden. Their website says they are open from 12 noon to 1 a.m. and boasts of a full bar and smoking area. What is taken for granted is that these clubs are quite relaxed on the law of no drinking for under 25. At 200 rupees for a glass of beer, it wasn't too expensive either. YB and his friends would often organize parties there and when they gave out passes, SS and her friends were always on the guest list.

In her statement SS told the authorities how it would also get quite intense for what was basically a teeny-bopper love affair. In fact, while the court only looks at one day's assault, she reports a sexually abusive relationship: 'On 22.04.14 she met him again at his friend's house where he made physical relations with her against her wishes; that on 23.04.14, he gave her a pill, that on 12.05.14 he gave her a pill, that on 12.05.14 he called her and asked her to prove her love for him, that she told him that she would get a tattoo of his name done below her breasts; that the next day she got the tattoo done.'

The tattoo's image was shown in the children's court and the tattoo artist was also called. However, the other parts of her allegations were never proved. According to YB, they weren't in a sexual relationship, just the usual kissing and making out. YB also has his own set of allegations which were never proved. He alleges that when he was seeing SS, the real problem was her mother.

There were problems in SS's parents' marriage which led her mother to take an unhealthy interest in him. 'Her mum is a bit different. SS would tell me that her dad had some mental problems. That's one of the reasons he acted out in court which got him thrown out too. One day, her mum called me and asked what's the deal between us. I said it's normal. So she asked: "*Tum logon ne sex-wex to nahin ki.* Tell me the truth (I hope you haven't had sex, tell me the truth)." I said, "*Nahi, nahi aunty, bilkul normal hai* (No, aunty, we have a regular relationship)." So she asked to meet me.'

This meeting between YB and SS's mother took place when SS had gone for her English class. According to YB, her mother dropped her to the class and called him. She suggested they meet near Uttam Nagar and when he went to pick her up, she suggested driving to Dwarka. 'We went there and sat at McDonalds and spoke, and after a bit, we left.'

This meeting didn't stay hidden from SS and a few days later, she apparently warned YB not to meet her mum. He agreed. It just so happened that a few days later, he was driving by the same area in Uttam Nagar when SS's mother saw him. She called him immediately, and they met again. She wanted to drive towards Dwarka again. 'While we were driving, there is a metro station in Sector 10, and there's a big park where people learn to drive. She started some *harkat* (antics). So I immediately stopped the car near this hawker who sells *nariyal paani* (coconut water). She came on to me, and so I spoke to her and took her home.'

YB clarifies that nothing happened between SS's mother and him. He initially didn't tell SS about what had happened – 'How could I say this about someone's mother?' However, when she invited him over and he didn't feel very welcome, it became a little difficult to hide. SS told him that her mother had advised her not to see him as he wasn't the right company. That's when he decided to come out and share the entire story with SS. 'I told SS what her mother had done too. She had started telling me that her mother didn't approve of me so I told her all. How once her mom had called me to their home in the afternoon. When SS's mother heard, she was very upset with me for telling her all. She wanted to blame me for everything.'

Now, the rules of the Juvenile Justice Act say that because these matters concern children, they are never called a 'trial' but an 'inquiry'; that the child is not supposed to attend to 'adversarial proceedings' to hear evidence. However, when a case is so complicated, it is difficult to avoid that. For instance, in this case, the witnesses were all the family members of the two children, and other young friends who implicated the two in damaging ways. For instance, YB's friend's on-record deposition stated that 'the prosecutrix was in friendship with many other boys and she had affair with some other boys. He further stated that she had consumed alcohol with him and that to his knowledge there were no physical relationship between the prosecutrix and the juvenile.' Fortunately, the operational part of the judgement didn't seem to give too much weight to this character testimonial.

THE THREE VERSIONS OF WHAT HAPPENED

Young love isn't easy as it is, but throw in parents with marital problems, alcohol and peer pressure and it becomes even more complicated. YB's counsellors are bound by confidentiality but they say that he is a good kid who landed up in jail due to unfortunate circumstances. There are three versions of what happened that day. While one is of the accused, YB, the other two are of SS, which finally failed to withstand scrutiny. Essentially, the JJ board felt that her statement before the initial FIR and then her statement under 164 were too conflicting to be relied on. But first, here's how YB recalled the night of 6 August 2014.

YB says that by that time, they were already fighting a lot. They would have personality clashes and she would share it all on Facebook. Their arguments were mainly about going out all the time – 'anything to avoid going home'. Sometimes the fights would also lead to SS inflicting some self-harm, and so YB started withdrawing from the relationship. 'When I'd fight, she'd cut her hand. Then people from school would say: she's crying, she wants to commit suicide, do something.' And then, it would all become public. Just a day before the incident, her mother also got embroiled in the fight. Her disapproval of YB's relationship with her daughter was out in the open and so the bitterness between them was fresh.

'Kunal said please speak to her, she's really bitched you out. So we planned to go for a party. She wanted me to buy her a dress, and I did, and sent it through friends. Kunal said all the kids from school are coming, so we agreed to go. When we went to the club, SS was there and she was already drunk.'

YB recalls how he initially tried to avoid her. He and his friends had paid a 1,000 rupees cover charge which got them a private room and unlimited drinks. This area was inaccessible for SS and so she kept calling him on his mobile. He then went outside the private room and danced with her. 'I must have danced with her for about 15 minutes, when she said, "I want to drink more." So I said, drink then. She said she didn't have her wallet. I said, that's fine, I'll pay for it. She and her 3–4 friends drank so much; the bill came to more than 7,500 rupees. I didn't have that much money. I had only 3,500 rupees. Anyway, somehow we all pooled in money and we paid the bill, after which I left.'

On his way home, YB said he got a call from Kunal. It was an SOS call about SS: '*Bhai*, she is vomiting lots and her clothes are fully in vomit!' YB said that he didn't really want to get into that but Kunal begged him, so he agreed to go back. When he saw her, she was quite a sight. 'We took about 15–20 water bottles and literally bathed her but she was still covered in vomit. So we took curtains and put them all over the car. We took her and she had a bag with regular clothes in. I asked her to change as she was stinking.' SS changed her clothes in the car, but there was more drama in store for that evening. When she stepped out, she left the keys locked in the car. They were all stressed and it was early evening, when they should all have been home, but now they didn't even have the car keys. And YB was most worried about the stink in the car with her dirty clothes still inside.

Finally, a man offered to help and open the car door for just 100 rupees. They succeeded, but when they got into the car SS gave them the news that she had switched off her phone so her family didn't know where she was. They must have tried calling her and couldn't get through, so now because she didn't want to immediately face a set of angry parents, SS said that they should go somewhere else. It was an idea which everyone loved, including Kunal and another boy who was with them, Prateek. So they decided to go to Buddha Jayanti Park. Now, for anyone familiar with Delhi, the Buddha Jayanti Park sends off ominous signals. First of all, like any other park in Delhi, it serves as a meeting point for couples desperate for some privacy. It's also got imprinted on our collective memory as the place where in 2003 a college student was raped by four members of the President's Bodyguards. In fact, even before that in 1978, two school children Geeta and Sanjay Chopra's dead bodies were found in this park. Geeta was also raped by the killer duo, Billa and Ranga. So it was this Buddha Jayanti Park where they all headed. YB said that they decided to go to the park because he had taken a few pictures there and posted them on Instagram, and they had been a talking point ever since.

'It was 6.30 or so in the evening. She was totally drunk, so she just sat there, while Kunal and Prateek were taking pictures. We stayed there for 20 minutes and then came back.' YB said that as they drove back home, SS wanted to be dropped off at a Mother Dairy outlet a short distance away from her home. She apparently told them that she wanted to hide her phone and tell her parents that it had been stolen. YB told her it was a terrible idea, but they did drop her off at the outlet, and the next time they'd see each other it would be the next morning when the police came to arrest him.

But before that, here's the first version given by SS that led to the FIR:

> I had gone to my friend Kanika's house at Shukra Bazaar Chowk to do my schoolwork. My grandmother dropped me there. I had gone there on 5.08.2014 and 6.08.2014. At about 5.45 p.m. after completing the homework, when I was on my way back home on foot, three boys came on an orange colour motorcycle from behind. I could not notice the registration number of the motorcycle. The boy who was sitting in the middle pulled my hair. The boy sitting in front pulled my neck and he pulled away my gold ring and my Apple iPhone 4S. Those boys dragged me inside a *gali* [lane]. They made me drink something due to which I became intoxicated. I do not know what happened with me as I was unconscious. When I regained my consciousness I found myself in the very same *gali*. I was feeling pain in my stomach and in my back. I think that the assailants committed rape upon me after making me consume some intoxicating substance. I do not know where they took me.

After the FIR was registered, the medical examination report stated:

> 15-year-old unmarried brought to casualty with history of sexual contact with her boyfriend (juvenile name not being disclosed). Patient had sexual intercourse in car on 6.08.14 at 5.30 p.m. She had it on her own will. No history of

physical assault or drug addiction was given by the patient. Patient had sexual intercourse multiple times since April 2014. The hymen was found torn. No injury was found on her person.

YB also had to undergo a potency test, which is routine in all cases of sexual assault, but the report wasn't made part of the court documents. YB denies any sexual contact with her but the real contradictions about what happened on 6 August actually emerge from SS's second statement, which was given to the magistrate. Here, she's no longer attacked by three strangers on a bike but she actually discloses her relationship with YB and claims it to be a sexually abusive, violent one where he also forced her to steal. YB claims this was after being coached by her family.

The statement further says:

On 21.05.14, he demanded ₹50,000 from her on the pretext that he had lost money in betting and threatened her that in case she did not give money he would shoot her; that the next day she went to juvenile's house with her grandmother's bracelet and chain; that on 24.5.14, on juvenile's birthday she went out with him; that the juvenile told her that he had sold the gold and cleared the debts; that on 12.06.14, he demanded ₹30,000–40,000 from her on the pretext that his friend's car had met with an accident; that she then stole 3–4 pairs of earrings and a gold set from her house and handed over the same to him on 13.06.14; that whenever she used to go out with him, he used to demand money from her... that the juvenile used to call her at his house while his mother used to be away under the threat that he would leak her photos; that on 6.08.14, she went with the juvenile for a party at Rajouri Garden;

that he made her drink beer; that he then went to drop his friends and returned at 4 am; that she vomited; that he then took her to Buddha Garden and the juvenile made physical relations with her over there with her consent; that he then dropped her at her house.

Thus, there are three varying versions of what happened that night, and now it was up to the juvenile board to find the truth. But before that, the police said that juvenile or not, YB had to be arrested.

THE ARREST

At 6 a.m. on 7 August 2014, the police arrived at YB's house. He knew something was wrong when SS called him the night before and said: 'Scene *ho gaya hai*.' YB asked what she meant, what kind of scene. He thought that she had got into trouble at home because she'd come back late and her phone was off, but she didn't elaborate. Kunal came over and they both discussed what she could have meant: '*Bhai, kya ho gaya, scene kya ho gaya. Bhai aisa na ho ki subah hote hi police aa rahi ho hamare ghar par* (What do you think could have happened? What scene? Do you reckon the police will come to our house in the morning?).' YB didn't realize that Kunal's joke was going to turn into reality the next morning. They couldn't have even imagined that. They were however restless enough to go to her house that night. At that time the entire family was away to the police station registering their complaint, but at that time YB didn't know that. The house was dark and they thought, 'either they are all sleeping, or they are out'.

In the morning, a police posse greeted YB's family. There were two PCR vans, a couple of bikes with cops, and they all waited in anticipation outside. In one PCR, there was SS and her mother. And in the other, there were 5–6 policemen.

'I was sleeping and so were others. My brother was single at the time. We were on the first floor and on the ground floor of our house, we had tenants. The door-bell downstairs wasn't working, so for 30 minutes the police kept knocking and no one got to know. The police then came inside using the back door. As they knocked, they woke everyone up. The police asked my brother: "Are you YB?" He said no. My father asked what happened. The police said they couldn't say anything there. They produced a warrant in my name and said, "Come to the police station and we'll talk there." They said that they had to me and then they took me in the PCR. My family followed later. I learnt that they were blaming me for everything – for stealing her mobile, for raping her and taking her ring too. All three friends got blamed initially but then her family said I was the main one at fault.'

YB remembers that when he entered the police station, he had no idea what exactly he was being accused of. He realized very soon that he was in a hostile territory as SS's grandfather lurched forward to attack him. The police had to hold him back. The investigating officer, a woman police officer, took him to another room with some other officers and they began their investigations by asking what had happened. They explained the very serious allegations that were levelled against him, including the theft of her phone. The police had already confiscated his phone at his residence. SS's family were screaming for the police to take action against him. Now, certain charges against him were resolved very quickly. For instance, the police party noticing the conflicting statements of SS and YB sent a team to SS's house.

'The mobile phone which was alleged to have been robbed, was recovered from inside the washing machine of her house' – that's what the order concluded, but the other charges of rape were going to take much longer to investigate.

'Nirmal ma'am, the police officer, was very nice and kept asking me things. Some of the other police officers would threaten and say, "We will hit you if you don't tell us".' They apparently also prepared him for the inevitable lockup. This was around the time when the terrible 16 December 2012 gang rape and eventual death of a 23-year-old paramedic was still fresh in everyone's mind, and the police could not afford to appear slacking on a sexual assault investigation.

They told YB: 'Whatever happens, you will be locked up as a minor has complained against you.' The police also suggested that he must have done something otherwise why would she have complained. 'I got so tired of it, I said ok you are not listening to me then I must have done whatever it is you are saying I have done. If you think I've had sex, ok.' After the physical examination, they took YB to Buddha Jayanti Park. They were looking for some evidence of rape. 'They said you must have used precaution. So they were looking for signs of that. I said I have not used anything.' For the next one and a half hours, the police went all over the park, pulling up the local guards. They intimidated the security men by asking why they hadn't kept an eye and raised an alarm about the couple. 'The guard was so scared, they were pushing him around. It looked like he was about to quit his job, he was so scared.' All this aside, they were unable to recover anything from the alleged scene of crime.

The next stop was the juvenile court at Delhi Gate. Located in an alley behind the Ambedkar Terminal in Central Delhi, this is just what the authorities envisioned it to be. Unlike the other courts, there are no visible touts hanging around here. The notary public officials, who are usually planted on tables and chairs in every court complex, are also missing from here. It's just a small lane leading up to an official single-storey building. There are parents with kids in trouble hanging around outside and no noticeable police presence. As YB got off the police vehicle, he spotted his family. A private lawyer asked him how old the girl was. When YB replied, the lawyer said, 'Oh, then it's decided. Go to the *bada ghar* (jail), *band ho jao* (Go to jail and get locked up).' YB smiles remembering that period. His parents don't really know he is speaking to a writer about his experiences but as a 19-year old now, he has decided to speak about them and he doesn't really need their permission. All other families and minors we spoke to weren't really willing to tell their stories. It was too traumatic.

A HOME IN MUKHERJEE NAGAR

By the time YB reached the Mukherjee Nagar home, it was early evening. It was the allocated time for outdoor and indoor recreational activities and yoga, and YB recalls feeling very strange.

'As you enter, they make you take off all your clothes so that they can check you properly. Everyone was out in the park and you can do whatever you want at that time. The security guards asked me what got me inside. The constable asked me to go and sit with all the kids. The kids were sitting in rows so I joined one such row. I noticed that there were two other boys who weren't wearing the jail uniform like me so they'd also arrived there recently.'

As YB learnt later, the home gives each inmate one school shirt, a pair of trousers, one set of kurta-pyjama, two sets of underwear and a towel, and some toiletries like a toothbrush and soap. There were separate homes for different age groups. So at Mukherjee Nagar, there were only boys from 16 to 18 years, there was a children's home for 7 to 12 year olds and a separate home for those in the age groups 12 to 14 and 14 to 16. Just like in the adult jail, the children as soon as they arrive are kept in the *mulaiza* ward. And that's where YB stayed too.

The children followed a mundane routine dictated by government guidelines. They had to wake up at 6 a.m., after which the dorms would be opened and everyone counted. YB's *mulaiza* ward had about 50 children and one toilet to be used by all of them. The children would get an hour to shower and get ready. At 7 a.m., they'd have some prayers and by quarter past 7, it was time for breakfast.

'They would do a drama of also making us exercise. For instance, the guards would double up as PT teachers. The breakfast wasn't bad – we'd get banana and milk and couple of eggs.' There was no toast.

After breakfast, the children who had to go to court would leave. The others would have vocational or life skills training until noon. 'Yes, they would have classes but they weren't serious. Sometimes, some NGOs would come to the home for counselling and they would sing songs but it didn't seem genuine.' As YB saw it, it was all an enormous exercise to kill time for everyone. Child rights groups like HAQ have given detailed advisories as to how these homes should be run, but these documents while being submitted to the relevant authorities have never been implemented.

Meal-times, whether it was 1–2 p.m. for lunch or 7–8 p.m. for dinner, were the most stressful, also when the maximum trouble would occur. 'We all formed a line for dinner. We kept standing for our turn to get food while some people would fight. They'd fight for the smallest of things.' While most of the times YB was an observer, once he did bear the brunt of this.

'I was waiting for food when someone came and hit me with a large *danda* (stick). It was one of the guards. I asked him, why did he hit me? He didn't expect me to challenge him but I kept on. So he left quietly. I told him that I would complain about him to court.' YB was aggressive so he was left alone after that, but the other children weren't so lucky.

Just as in Tihar an inmate knew who was innocent and who was guilty of the crime they were accused of, the kids also knew. And just like in Tihar, even here a majority felt that they were out of place. 'Out of 100 kids, there were 70 who were there for no reason, or for no fault of theirs. They were on the brink of suicide.'

The advisory of the observation homes says that each juvenile should be inspected by a magistrate once every two months and the report should be placed before the High Court. But this doesn't happen.

The children could meet their families twice a week, but YB told his family not to come. 'They'd keep crying and it would just upset me.' So in the course of his entire stay, they only came twice.

YB made other relationships to get him through; for instance, the two boys who had also arrived around the same time as he had. One of them was accused of attempt to murder. Apparently, it was a fight which an entire group had got into and while the others had gotten away, he was caught. The bad news was that the victim was about to testify that he wasn't the main accused, but before he could do so he died. So the question of getting a bail was slim.

There are other inmates who YB remembers. Like the three kids from Delhi Public School, RK Puram. They got into a case of fighting and were accused of stealing and snatching cell phones. This fight meant that they had to spend 23 days in juvenile correctional home.

The most awful character in Mukherjee Nagar was someone called Yadav sir, who has since been transferred. While YB can't recall any serious transgression on his part, he does talk about the everyday minor humiliations which made living with him traumatic. For instance, if someone's mother called, he'd say: 'Why is your mother calling? Seems like the *moti* (fatso) is very anxious.' He was extremely rude and would harass the children a lot. The rumour was that he wanted to be paid off. Those who paid him 30,000 rupees were left alone, but others would be harassed. If you paid, you could eat, sleep wherever you wanted.

For instance, the Gupta boy from Rohini seemed to have worked out some deal with the home authorities. He was obviously rich as the day he left Mukherjee Nagar, there were luxury cars like a Jaguar waiting to pick him up. And he was allowed to sleep in the air-conditioned office. 'People like him were fine but others weren't.'

When asked whether YB was tempted to ask his parents to pay for some comfort, he said: 'I didn't want my parents to pay a single paisa because I didn't deserve to be there.'

And so the torment of 'Yadav sir' continued with the kids. Even though he would spend just a couple of hours in office daily, he'd spend it hitting someone or mentally harassing another, before leaving.

'The only nice man was Vikas sir, the computer teacher. He was the only human being there. Once a judge came and asked what have you all learnt, so Vikas sir put me up. He was the only man who would tell the kids, "Don't worry, you'll be out soon." The other ones would say you will rot here, you are criminals. He would give and get respect. The others would only speak in *ma behen gaalis* (mother sister abuses).'

Just like the bathing area was a large hall with shower stalls, the sleeping area was also one with horrible mattresses. YB recalls how all their belongings were constantly threatened by theft. 'People would tear the mattresses to hide their clothes. I had to make a cloth bag which had all my stuff which I would keep with me. I would wash my clothes and then wear them again the next day. Wear the jail clothes while they dried. Wore the same T-shirt and jeans 20 days of the 28 days. Theirs weren't comfortable at all but I got used to it.'

Life is full of strange coincidences and one of the strangest one was how while YB was there, a friend of his also landed up at the same place. His name was A and he was a wrestler and they had a common friend. 'He had a fight with some people on the bus who accused him of stealing the bus conductor's money. It was a personal fight which they made into a theft case.'

Unlike YB, he had paid off the authorities, so his family would send food from home to save him from the watery dal. 'He would go downstairs to eat that food. He couldn't share the food with us.' The privilege meant that he could also perhaps meet his family more often than the others.

THE RELEASE AND THE LIFE AFTER

If YB had been sent to jail on 7 August, his next date of hearing was a week after. After that hearing the judge posted the matter for 21 August. At this hearing, YB's lawyer pointed out the inconsistencies in the statements of the prosecutrix. 'He argued how the story kept changing. She first said three bikers had raped her, then she said in Buddha Jayanti Park, so it is an unreliable testimony.'

Meanwhile, the police had also managed to find gaps in another allegation that he forced her to buy him an iPhone. 'It just so happened that my mother had given 10,000 rupees by cheque to add to the money to buy the phone. Rest of it I had saved. The police went to the shop and took out the CCTV camera footage. It showed me paying for it and the bill was also in my name and my mother's cheque also added up.'

YB recalls how his lawyer was late on 28 August, the date of his last hearing from custody. The court adjourned the matter and gave a date which was at least a month away. But suddenly his lawyer appeared and managed to convince the judge to have the hearing. That very day, YB was granted bail. By the time the police took him back to Mukherjee Nagar, his parents were there to receive him.

The court proceedings to decide the case would continue, but YB was back home. It may have been a relief, but it was also very strange.

'Everyone stared as I was the first person to ever go to jail from my family. I only met Kunal who was most bothered about me. It took a long time for things to get normal.' YB also realized what had happened while he was away. While SS had put up a post on Facebook regretting the way things had turned out soon after his arrest and that she wasn't responsible for it, she later also went on social media to protest his bail. 'My brother took screen shots of all of this and it was shown in court.'

At one point, her family reached out to YB's for an out-of-court settlement. 'If you pay us, we can close the case. My parents said no because I had already been to jail. They said the worst that could have happened had already happened so they didn't want any settlement.'

For a 17 year old, being accused of rape wasn't going to make him acceptable in school and so he never went back. 'Everyone knew and had seen all the charges and she had spread the word. I couldn't go back to my school and couldn't face the shame. I had to drop that year.' The next year he applied through open school, and even though he went back to studying, the infamy stayed. 'Everyone would stop and ask what happened. How many people could I explain the rape charges to? I too got irritated. Everyone knew us in Uttam Nagar and they would all ask questions. I stopped going to my relatives' place too.' For a while, his parents considered selling their house and moving somewhere else.

It took a long time, more than a year to be precise, but at some point, things started getting better. People started getting bored discussing YB's case. He had also passed his board exams and had fortunately got through a college in Bengaluru. Then in July 2016, just before he was to leave for Bengaluru, YB was finally acquitted.

To begin with, the prosecutrix has given an absolutely false account in the FIR. There is no explanation as to why such a false and a fabricated account was set up in the FIR. The mobile phone which was alleged to have been snatched... was found in the house of the prosecutrix. The prosecutrix in her statement under 164 stated that the alleged sexual assault that had taken place on 6.8.2014 was with her consent. According to oral evidence, the incident was not with her consent in as much as she was not in her proper senses. There is nothing on record to substantiate the assertion of the prosecutrix that she used to steal jewellery and cash and hand it over to the juvenile... We find this assertion of the prosecutrix to be not at all a credible one. The allegations of the prosecutrix that the juvenile had been blackmailing her and had been threatening her are also not believable... For the reasons recorded, the juvenile is acquitted.

As we walk out into a warm, sunny day in Delhi, when you know that winter is coming because the sun is no longer unwelcome, YB smiles shyly as I ask him if he has a girlfriend now and at what point will he tell her about all that's happened to him. He looks at me as if to say that it was a ludicrous suggestion – why would anyone want to tell that story again? He still follows SS on Instagram though, and shows me that she's got another boyfriend now. He smiles easily and it's hard to detect a tinge of pain.

THE CEO IN JAIL

When Peter Mukerjea launched Star News in early 2003, there was one trademark show that could be viewed as his contribution to news television. The show, called 'Sansani', focused on crime and its anchor Shrivardhan Trivedi became quite a talking point because he wasn't a journalist but an actor from the National School of Drama. As media columns critiqued the show with disdain and horror, at the way the pony-tailed and bearded anchor with angry, red eyes simplified crime stories into voyeuristic C-grade film scripts, it became a template for other channels to follow. They all started their own versions of the successful series that had catchphrases like '*Chain se Sona Hai toh Jaag Jao*' (If you want to sleep in peace, you better wake up) with little regard for follow-ups or legal nuances. And in a strange twist of fate, it would be this genre of TV news that Peter would later blame for sending him to prison – a genre that stopped presenting the story with known facts, and instead merged it with a moral voice playing the juror.

When his wife and business partner, Indrani Mukerjea was arrested more than a decade later on 25 August 2015 for murdering her daughter Sheena Bora, Peter Mukerjea still didn't think that the media could be dangerous. He was no longer the boss of Star News, in fact Star had become ABP News where 'Sansani' was still the longest running crime news show. He was also not the boss of NewsX any more, another start-up news channel the Mukerjeas had launched. And even though the way he and Indrani exit NewsX in 2009 was a bit unsavoury, hitting some news columns about their fight with journalists, Peter had no reason to think media was their enemy. That's why as the police were drawing up charges of murder, kidnapping and poisoning against his wife, Peter gave an interview to Arnab Goswami (then with Times Now). He talked about getting the news of Indrani's arrest after his return from a golf session, about being 'horrified' by the thought that his wife killed her own daughter, who everyone thought was her sister, and most crucially, he tried to convince Arnab why he didn't suspect anything when his step-daughter and his son's fiancé Sheena went missing in 2012. 'You can call me stupid or maybe, I was blindsided, but I trusted my wife,' is what he said to Arnab then. In the second of their charge sheets against Peter, aka Pratim Mukerjea, the CBI informed the court that they had obtained the original copies of this interview and were using it as evidence. This time, it wasn't Peter trying to convince a loud TV anchor who called him a liar on air, but his lawyers seeking time to defend him against charges of conspiracy to murder and destruction of evidence. Peter by then was already in jail, having been arrested three months after his wife. Standing in court for the first time, he was confronted with the beast that the news machinery had become.

'[It was] Almost a surreal experience. I'd only ever seen this in movies so I was taken by the experience than of the situation I found myself in. There were a lot of known faces in the room full of journalists who were all giving me knowing looks and nodding in acknowledgement as if to say "we know what you're feeling", but it was more to do with them doing their job and reporting on court proceedings. My days of Star News would constantly flash across my mind and I hated Arnab for having done this to me so needlessly.'

Of all the impacts that Arnab Goswami had claimed on his news channel, this was perhaps one which was most personal for both parties. At least, that's what the UK-born and British passport-holder, Doon School alumnus and MBA from London claimed. When I asked him why he 'hated Arnab', he said it could be the other way round – that there was history between the two.

'I don't hate Arnab and I'm sorry if I implied that. I don't particularly like his style of journalism and maybe at some point in the past I may have turned him down when he applied for a job at Star – so it could be some sort of vendetta – but that is silly and childish on his part if that is so – let alone grossly irresponsible. To call me a liar is incorrect – particularly when he doesn't have the facts. It's also defamatory apart from being unfair to me, knowing that I'm in judicial custody and unable to respond.'

Arnab didn't just call Peter a 'liar'. He said, '...he comes across as a scheming liar who can state untruths with a poker face. And let me tell you about some of them. In his interview to me, he said he didn't know she was his daughter. Presumption is Indrani never told him but in tape 10, he listens quietly as Indrani calls Sheena her daughter. This means in his interview to me, Peter Mukerjea lied with a capital L... a lie so cold that one begins to wonder who the real conspiracy master is – Indrani or Peter? Who is the real kingpin here? It could well be Peter. Indrani is being painted as a Machiavellian murderer which she is. But Peter, Peter has much more to hide. He's done much more than what he wants us to believe. We won't because these tapes prove that this rightly fallen and disgraced and dangerous ex-TV tycoon is masterminding the cover-up with the ease of a hardened, professional criminal. With the cockiness of a Charles Sobhraj, Peter is covering his tracks – he's creating a false story, he's trying to throw his son, the media, the police, everyone off his trail. Only a professional criminal behaves like that. We have just started uncovering the blood stains that they left behind. And Peter Mukerjea is at the epicentre, the heart, the fulcrum, of this murky murder cover-up. Will the CBI consider all the evidence or pretend to be blind?' It was as if the theatrical character hired by his channel had morphed into one speaking in English, only this one was filled with considerably more vitriol. And the worst part was that the CBI seemed to be listening to this anchor.

THE BACKSTORY

When I joined Star News in November 2002 in a run-up to their launch, there was lots of office gossip about the CEO Peter Mukerjea getting married to a young, beautiful co-worker. Indrani was at that time not yet 31, and there was the usual curiosity about the HR professional who was marrying the top boss. I was in the Delhi office and so away from the main scene of action in Mumbai, but his wedding just a few days after I joined, to the woman he was living with for the past one year, was of much interest among the social set.

I wasn't really acquainted with Peter Mukerjea though, as Ravina Raj Kohli was more involved with news operations. As he said when I first wrote to him, 'I recall your name from the Star News time although it's been a while, I'm struggling to put a face to it. Hope you won't be offended by my candid response but lots of water has flown under the bridge since the Star News version 2 days!'

There are many stories, many versions of the backstory of Peter and Indrani, but perhaps it's safest to go with what CBI found out and put on record in their multiple charge sheets. According to them, both Indrani and Peter have Shillong as their common ground. She studied there for a bit and so did he at St Edmund's when his parents were posted there for two years as Army doctors. This was years before they met.

When Indrani was only 15, she became intimate with another student called Siddharth Das. Their relationship led to the birth, in nearby Guwahati, of Sheena in 1987, and Mikhail, just a year later in 1988. So, by the time Indrani was 16, she was a mother of two. The CBI doesn't go into details of how that must have gone down in the relatively conservative town of Assam. They just say that her parents, Durga Rani Bora and Upendra Kumar Bora, adopted both the children. This was legitimized with an affidavit in 1992 which declared them parents of Sheena and Mikhail.

According to the CBI, after taking care of this legal adoption Indrani left for Kolkata. There, she met a businessman called Sanjeev Khanna who was a cable operator, and in 1993 they got married. In the next three years, Indrani set up an HR firm called M/S INX Services and they bought a flat in Howrah. In 1997, at 25, Indrani had her third child, a girl she named Vidhie. It was in Kolkata that Indrani met adman Alyque Padamsee and the CBI says that he 'offered her help for starting a business' in Mumbai. At this point, the CBI seems to have suspended its investigating skills and gone by moral judgement and general impressions, because the charge sheet then mentions that Indrani 'a lady of highly ambitious nature immediately shifted to Mumbai'. The agency wasn't sexist though because they've also used Peter's ex-wife Shabnam Singh's statement to prove that he always had 'a fascination for young women', which is why she left him. In Indrani's case, they also mention her husband's friend, a Balwinder Dhami providing a joint venture and giving her a place to stay in Mumbai.

But apparently, Indrani didn't really need that because by then, she'd been introduced to the Star News CEO, Peter Mukerjea. They met at the Library Bar of Hotel President, introduced by Alyque. Peter at the time was almost divorced from his wife and mother of two sons, Shabnam. It didn't take them long to hit it off and they started living together in 2000, planning to marry as soon as they both got their divorce. Indrani also got Vidhie to Mumbai and when the marriage took place, all of them got British citizenship.

Now, these were heady times for the Mukerjeas – Star News had replaced NDTV as Rupert Murdoch's production house in India, and so there was considerable media interest. As Vir Sanghvi, a colleague from both Star and NewsX noted, Indrani was an attractive, charming woman and so as a power couple, they featured regularly in social pages of newspapers. It was one such photo that Upendra Bora saw in the Guwahati edition of the *Telegraph* when he decided to reach out to his daughter. He told her that they were hard up for money and so couldn't really afford Sheena and Mikhail's education, and asked if she could help out. According to the investigation, Indrani agreed to meet the kids in Kolkata and paid for their tickets.

Indrani had taken along her daughter Vidhie and this meeting took place at the Oberoi. There, as the CBI says, she made her two kids an offer. She would pay for their education and their maintenance, but they must keep up pretences that she was their sister. They had no choice but to agree and they took some pictures, which the CBI has submitted as evidence.

'Indrani informed Peter Mukerjea about her younger siblings Sheena and Mikhail. She also informed that since their financial condition was pathetic, in order to continue her education, Sheena Bora was coming to Mumbai.'

This sets the stage for the romance that led to murder and arrests. In 2005, Sheena was admitted to St Xavier's College, Mumbai, and while she stayed as a paying guest, she'd come over to the Mukerjeas' Marlow Building apartment in Worli on weekends. In some time, Rahul, Peter's younger son, moved in with them and the two young people met and hit it off. This was more than what can be said for Rahul and his step-mum Indrani's relationship. Writing to me from jail, Peter acknowledges his wife and son's relationship was so stressful, he had to meet Rahul behind her back at times.

'My relationship with my younger son Rahul is a perfectly normal father–son relationship. Things went astray along the way for certain reasons. Indrani, my wife and Rahul didn't see eye to eye virtually from their first interaction many years ago, which was then further eroded when Sheena and Rahul got into a relationship and then got engaged.

'As father and son we continue to share a normal relationship now, once again, after a hiatus of 2–3 years when I had to communicate with Rahul "secretly". While I was in Mumbai and he was a student in the UK, we would meet during college term holidays; then when he was in Mumbai, we'd meet all the time – until I left for the UK and then our contact was limited to telephone conversations. I share a free, happy and perfectly normal father–son bond and of course we have our differences but that's what makes it normal.'

So, it was in 2008, three years after she moved to Mumbai that Sheena told Rahul that Indrani was actually her mother. The CBI says Rahul told his father immediately. How Peter took it is unclear but he does say in interviews after Indrani's arrest, it was his son's word against his wife's. What the CBI does put on record is that the Mukerjeas actively worked to separate the couple. Indrani first sent Sheena away to Guwahati, and then to Delhi, where she allegedly spiked her daughter's medication with some that are for mental illness. The CBI believes she was able to do this with the careful manipulation of her own employees and acquaintances in Delhi and Bengaluru who she made her daughter stay with, and who she could manipulate. When Sheena was taken to Bengaluru and became ill, Rahul came and took her away to his grandparents' home in Dehradun. That's where on Diwali of 2011, the couple got engaged supported by Rahul's mother and Sheena's grandparents.

The CBI builds a case that from 2009 onwards, the Mukerjeas conspired to separate the two using financial, physical and other threats. The Mukerjeas had little contact with Rahul and Sheena for two years and open acrimony. For instance, in 2010, Indrani sold a property in Delhi's South Extension that was registered in her and Sheena's name. The CBI says Peter signed it too, but Rahul disputes that. Indrani also sent an email to Sheena via Mikhail (she would send it to Mikhail and ask him to forward it to Sheena) threatening to disinherit her from their Guwahati property. Indrani's email in March 2012 reads:

> This is to confirm that we have changed the will and disinherited you from our property and assets as a sign of our disapproval of your relationship with Rahul. I hope we have made our stand clear and you will be wise enough not to cause any more problem than you already have. Please don't contact us till relationship with Rahul (sic).

Sheena responded to this email the next day by writing:

Again at the same time, what I fail to comprehend is that why do you threaten to cut off financial aid to your own parent (sic). If I go to Ghy with Rahul, if I get married to Rahul, why do all of that? Why pressurize Aita/Kaka into whatever, till I suddenly got bombarded with text messages today from Kaka saying this: "This SMS is a confirmation that we have decided to change our will and disinherited you from our property as a sign of disapproval of your relationship with Rahul. We hope that we have made our stand very clear. Do not try and contact us till you are in a relationship with Rahul etc., etc.

After quoting from her grandparent's SMS, Sheena then asks her mother:

I am confused, I don't know who is lying, who is being truthful... Pls be straight. Is this from you or your parents? And why suddenly all this? Is it all because of those text msgs? You should have either not given birth to me or not left me with your parents. Why didn't you take me with you? What and where have all of this left me now? All of this has left me really hurt and devastated once again. I am very happy and safe with Rahul. Shouldn't that be the most important thing for parents/loved ones? You did whatever gave you happiness in life. Even I deserve the same. Why are you upset because of it? I am your daughter. I have some of you in me. I will find my way through and just be fine.

If this affair strained mother and daughter relationship, CBI says the father and son relationship was equally strained.

They've produced emails by Rahul to suggest his father was pressurizing him to end the affair by asking them not to come for a relative's wedding in Goa in 2011. In another email of April 2011 to Sheena, which the CBI cites, Peter says:

> I feel particularly disturbed because I had called Rahul back to India from England so he could have started work, live independently and make a life of his own. Instead I find that he is in a relationship, not living independently and is yet to make a life of his own but also that he has wasted valuable time in getting engaged with matters that don't concern him as they are your personal family issues. All was well until he got into a relationship with you. We would spend time together as a family and do holidays together but all of that came to an end after he got involved with you.

The reason CBI cites for booking Peter Mukerjea as part of the conspiracy is because they feel these emails clearly show that he felt exactly like Indrani did. They also cite other emails to show that Peter knew Indrani was now threatening physical harm.

For instance, an email in April 2011 by Rahul to Peter reads:

> On several occasions, we have received threats from Indrani, which we have taken seriously, and therefore I have protected myself and Sheena by documenting this situation, with dates, events, history, conversations and messages included. These have been given to several third parties for safekeeping. Should anything happen to either Sheena or me, the authorities both in India and the UK will be made aware.

The entire murder plot may have seemed too unbelievable to be true, but Rahul's email showed that it wasn't totally incomprehensible to him. Investigators say that the motive was clear: 'Indrani was afraid that the entire property might go to Sheena Bora and Rahul, as Peter liked his son Rahul. In this context, she planned a conspiracy with Sanjeev Khanna' – her ex-husband, who the CBI notes did not remarry after Indrani left him. They also say that he got involved in this because of the understanding that Sheena's death would leave all the property for his daughter, Vidhie. And so the plotting began, including with her driver Shyamwar Rai who was initially paid 1.25 lakh rupees and promised more later.

The rest of the gory details are legendary. After not speaking for 2–3 years, Indrani first reached out to Sheena in April 2012 to win her and Rahul's trust back. They fixed up to meet later that month, when Indrani would fly down from London and the ex-husband Sanjeev from Kolkata. Peter was only supposed to come a few days later. They hired a car, taught Shyamwar how to communicate through Skype in which he was given instructions. And then after she landed on 23 April, they bought alcohol, sedatives, and also recced places to dispose of the body. Indrani then invited her daughter to dinner the next day to celebrate her engagement and give her some presents. What Sheena didn't know was that Indrani had also enticed Mikhail to come to Mumbai on the same day and asked him to meet her at their Marlow Building residence.

Sheena took half the day off and Rahul dropped her at 6.40 in the evening at the decided place. The mother and daughter hugged each other, after which Indrani gave Sheena the drugged bottle of water. Sanjeev Khanna was in the front seat but as Sheena became drowsy, he got into the back. The CBI says he pulled her hair back while Indrani strangled her. Sheena resisted by biting the driver's hand that covered her mouth, and it started bleeding. Shyamwar told the CBI that Sanjeev came back to the front as soon as Sheena stopped moving. He got off soon after and Indrani told the driver to go to Taj Land's End. Rahul, meanwhile, kept calling Sheena's mobile, and it was Indrani who answered all his messages. As Sheena's body stayed in the car, Indrani first went to the hotel and then to Marlow Building to meet Mikhail along with Sanjeev.

There she offered him alcohol mixed with sedatives, but Mikhail told the CBI he was a little suspicious of his mother because the last time this happened, he found himself in a de-addiction centre admitted there by his mother against his own volition. So he kept throwing the drinks. There are records to prove that Indrani called a Dr Yusuf Machiswala on the pretext that her son was an addict and asked at 1 a.m. why those medicines hadn't knocked him out by then. At that time, Mikhail had no idea that his sister was dead but he did tell the CBI that Sanjeev and Indrani were not behaving normally.

Unable to knock out Mikhail, Indrani and Sanjeev left early morning of 25 April and disposed Sheena's dead body at Gagode Khind, Raigad by burning it. The evidence against Peter for being part of the conspiracy is that he and Indrani were constantly in touch through it all. She spoke to him for 1329 seconds, or 22 minutes soon after fixing their meeting, then again twice in the afternoon before meeting Sheena, in between calls to Sanjeev Khanna and then, according to the CBI, the most incriminating is that before she disposed of Sheena's body, she called Peter and had a long conversation, 'a long conversation of around 924 seconds, which is a call at odd hours and indicates his connivance and complete knowledge regarding the murder of Sheena Bora.' They also allege that since Peter gave 'false information' to his son that

Sheena was in the US and that he didn't go to the police, like Rahul did, he was privy to this information. The cover-up of Indrani using a fake email id in Sheena's name to resign and terminate the lease of her rented flat, it's all a teamwork, according to the CBI. Rahul couldn't even get the police to register a case, because the Mukerjeas insisted she had left him for someone else.

FROM WORLI TO ARTHUR ROAD JAIL

'I maintain that I had no knowledge of the alleged incident and was not a conspirator or an abettor. I was pacifying my son Rahul as he was naturally upset that his wife-to-be had left him. I was told she had left him for another person but I did not know who – I could really only console him and ask him not to worry – as she was fine.'

There's a rule of journalism which especially holds true of crime reporting – assumption is the mother of all cock-ups. As rookie reporters are taught across the world – nothing is as it seems and you never really know what actually happened, so go by what you know at the time. As Peter Mukerjea and I exchanged letters, the CBI gathered ammunition against him. He claimed it was perfectly natural for husband and wife to talk at all hours of the night, but the CBI found it strange. So who would decide? The CBI kept presenting angry emails and text messages between father and son showing Peter's evasion of the truth. But even after a year in jail, Peter maintains the same ground.

'I had no inkling that there was even the faintest possibility of me being arrested, as I wasn't here in the country when the alleged incident was supposed to have taken place, nor was I aware that Sheena was missing until 25 August 2015 when the police came home to arrest my wife, Indrani. All this while I believed Sheena was in the US and as there was no one else who seemed to be troubled by her being away. Her brother and family in Guwahati had never raised any alarm about Sheena's disappearance and Indrani would, from time to time, tell me that Sheena is fine and in the US and so on. Rahul, my son had initially been calling to enquire about Sheena, but after he was reassured by Sheena's brother Mikhail and the grandparents, there wasn't much he could do and left Mumbai himself in despair.'

In a strange kind of scenario, Rahul, who is the CBI's star witness backs up his father. In an interview to NewsX he said, 'I think it is ridiculous. He [Peter] shouldn't be in prison in the first place. He's been wrongly picked up by CBI, doesn't have any involvement at all. As far as I believe, my dad's not a murdering type of person. He could only have been believing what his wife was telling him. Why he wouldn't question her, I don't know. But he was just believing her. That's all there is to it, as simple as that. I don't think there's anything else to it. I don't think there's any conspiracy. I don't know why he's been arrested. That's just the investigative process that's going on.' When asked if he believes his father destroyed evidence, Rahul said, 'I don't know, I don't know, but I don't think so. He may have destroyed without knowing.'

Rahul's support for his father is perhaps the biggest source of relief for him. This support is what the Mukerjea family lawyers are putting forward in court, but in a family drama and crime like this one, how do you decide what's normal? For instance, Rahul's handed over his taped conversations with his father, in which Peter is dismissive about his concerns. But, why would Rahul record his calls to his father in the first place?

'I did continue to tell Rahul that Sheena would be back in due course so that is what I genuinely believed. Sheena's own family in Guwahati, brother and grandparents also told Rahul to leave her alone and that she has "moved to the US and is very happy with someone else". Recording conversations without telling someone that the conversation is being recorded is a personal choice and I can only assume that Rahul felt that Sheena would not do such a thing of her own accord and was not convinced about what he was being told.'

If his son is a star witness for the prosecution, all his family members are key witnesses in the trial. From the day of Peter's arrest, when Rahul and his brother Gautam and sister were with him, they continue to come and see him during each court hearing and also during *mulakats*. Peter Mukerjea knows that this makes him one of the fortunate ones in jail, that he has people who believe in his innocence. 'They know if I had known, I'd be the first person to report it to the police, as it was my son who was the most troubled at the time by Sheena's disappearance. And I would not let him suffer in that way. Also, I would have told my family instantly. If I'd known. The overall impact on my family was one of pain and anger at the injustice of it all but they were being very brave and doing everything they could to arrange legal support for me in this time of crisis.

'The hurdles, the hoops, the dramas, etc. that my family and I have had to go through these past few months – all of which are unbelievable and a horror story in itself... It was a regular day in the context of "regular" days, under the circumstances. My wife had been arrested 3 months prior, in August, while I had visited the police station (Khar) and the CBI offices in Mumbai, almost every other day, so it wasn't an entirely happy environment, obviously. We were all stressed as expected and I was called by the CBI to come in and do some voice sampling. They called me at 10, then changed it to 11 a.m. and so my brother, sister, son Rahul and I went along thinking this will take an hour or two. When we got there, they weren't ready and so we waited till the technicians from the forensic lab arrived. After doing all that was needed, the IO (Investigating officer) said I needed to wait as they were going to court to file the charge sheet against my wife, her ex-husband and the driver, all of whom had been arrested 3 months earlier. They let my family members go and have lunch but didn't let me go out, which felt strange and hadn't happened before.

'The arrest happened at about 7 p.m. after the CBI officers returned from court having filed the charge sheet. It was relatively dull as arrests go, as they informed me that they will be arresting me and that I was to stay in their custody overnight until I was taken to court the next day. I was shocked and horrified, specially as I wasn't expecting an arrest. I could have tried to get anticipatory bail, had I known this was coming.'

The surprise factor is always the same for those who have to go to jail. The media interviews, the CBI's clinical interactions, as Peter called them, threw him off into believing that they weren't suspecting him. Peter claims that he and his family were especially 'dumbstruck' because he'd been helping the investigators. A year down the line, Peter has been poring over law books, a source of 'solace' in a place 'out of my comfort zone'.

'I've been reading a variety of stuff although there's plenty to go round. Law books have been my favourite and Indian Penal Code, Criminal Procedure Code, The Indian Evidence Act, Constitution of India, Prevention of Corruption Act, The Hindu Marriage and Divorce laws are some that I've read over and over again. The jail manual too is a fascinating book written in the 1800s – although amended several times, it is still in need of some serious refreshment, as you can imagine. The others have been the Bhagwad Gita – which I'm still part way through, *Game of Thrones*, books on Buddhism and the Dalai Lama.' When I asked him if anything should be read into his reading the divorce laws, he said it was no different from reading the Telegraph Act and he was going to sit for the law exam soon. Months after, Indrani announced in court she was seeking divorce from Peter.

There are good days and bad days in captivity for all. On a good day, which could be the day your bail application seems to have had a positive hearing from the judge. That same feeling doesn't look so good when the hearing is adjourned and postponed weeks later, on a flimsy excuse. These ups and downs are captured in Peter Mukerjea's notes from jail.

On 28 September 2016, here's how he describes being in jail: 'It's like being in a spa – what can I say? No alcohol, no cigarettes, early to bed, early to rise, exercise for a couple of hours, lots of reading, plenty of time to think, no junk food – all very healthy. I've lost a few kilos – which is no bad thing and as I'm indoors most of the day, I don't get too much sunlight so my skin has improved.'

But the mood is totally different just a month later in his note on 24 October: 'Lock-up or jail is no "spa". That was a tongue-in-cheek comment and I hope you understood that. My day in the outside world was again a normal routine – which included gym, exercise, catching up with friends, occasional golf, TV and catching up on my housekeeping details. All of the above are what I'm unable to do now. So it's miserable, not fun and although it's an experience, it's not one that I would recommend to anyone. It's pathetic. Jails are overcrowded and far from being a reform centre, they're a grim reality check on life.'

The fluctuation of mood is not surprising. From being on the power list of business magazines, he was down to being on the criminal roll call at Arthur Road Jail. He was sleeping on the floor, next to strange people, with odd routine, barely a change of clothes. There were small mercies though like a permission from court to eat home food, which meant he still got fish to eat ('it's a diet designed to nourish than to be enjoyable!'). But as another Star News colleague Vidya wrote in a piece, in jail Peter was at the mercy of the whims of junior police officials. Despite the allowance from court for his meals, Vidya once caught the lockup police refusing to let him eat, insisting that he had to leave for Arthur Road Jail. That day, he went from pleading the police to the CBI officer to an absent judge, but he couldn't get his lunch. That was one of the times he realized what a great leveller jail can be.

At the courtroom, the first time he went he saw the judge, the bar, the line up of lawyers, the dock – all of which he'd never seen firsthand and felt out of his depth. 'I could not believe the outright lies the prosecution lawyer was alleging against me. I was in a state of complete disbelief and almost like I was in a bad dream.'

He was lucky though, because unlike the rough handling which Indrani had to go through at the hands of the Mumbai Police in the initial phase of the investigation, he was arrested by the relatively suave squad of CBI. Peter acknowledges this but says it's 'akin to having cancer of the lungs or cancer of the intestine. Both are nasty so it's not possible to compare.' You can't help but compare the impact though. While Peter continues to look almost the same, Indrani has changed completely. Her groomed look with blow-dried perfection is now replaced with all her grey roots exposed. In places like Delhi, married couples in jail are allowed to meet but in Mumbai, the women's jail is in Byculla and they only meet in court. It's unclear whether they have chosen not to see each other or whether they are not allowed to.

'I don't resent Indrani for anything other than for not telling me her complete life story when she had the opportunity to do so as then maybe I could have helped her overcome her concerns. Seeing her in court is disturbing.'

LIFE LESSONS LEARNT

So what does a millionaire CEO learn in jail? Maybe, it's about the lessons of simplicity, of enjoying the basics; in the midst of despair, finding someone to talk to and being appreciated. Sometimes Peter Mukerjea comes across as chatty and full of anecdotes, at others he says, 'What happens in Rio, stays in Rio'. Speaking of his 'fellow-travellers', Peter says: 'We share experiences, laugh and try and make the most of the learnings, each of us have had. I've made some useful contacts and they're mostly people I'd never have had the opportunity to meet, had I not been a guest of the "Govt of India" so I'm glad for that and it will make me a more circumspect person as a result. Some are incredibly rich and some incredibly poor and if I can, I will try and help those worse off than me. Everyone here has a common goal – to get out and not have to come back – so staying on the right side of the law is very important for most people I've met. The jail experience isn't pleasant, it's tough and not many want to ever repeat it. How long these new acquaintances last is something for the future, although it's true to say that being in jail gives you a good understanding and realization of who your real friends are and who were never really your friends. It's only a very few of them who you would call friends – once you're out of jail. That becomes quite clear.'

On another day, Peter writes in a more sombre tone: 'There's not a lot of laughing that goes on here – just in case the authorities think we're having a good time and make life harder still for us. We share experiences and it's amazing to learn how many people are in jails even though they are innocent and should not be in here. One day things will get set right.'

Stuck in a murder case himself, the only thing Peter could help the others with were the facilities of language. It seems the aspiration to learn English extends to prison too. So the Briton, when not reading and writing himself, spends time teaching. 'I set them reading goals, followed by writing passages from newspapers and getting them to improve their vocabulary by learning 10 new words every day – of which they only ever retain five but that's 30 words a week, which is really good and tough to maintain.'

If there's one thing any jail teaches a white collar man, it's how to make do on an impossible budget. It's one of the first things that Peter says he learnt. 'The economy within the jail is unique given there's no cash – but a really effective barter system seems to work. Home-cooked food is a rarity and is therefore a prized possession for those that have it. There are all kinds of services available from a savvy barber, a masseuse, a yoga class that's fully functional, a laundry service, a *darzee* (tailor) and lots more. Necessity being the mother of... is a well trodden path here and adaptability and innovation is phenomenal. I get a monthly spending allowance of a princely sum of 2500 rupees, which I get each month from home by money order and which is credited to my 'tuck-shop' account and I get to buy goodies with that – biscuits, nuts, mineral water and such like, but making that last the month is an incredible challenge. So when I get out, I'm going to look forward to existing on a pocket money of 2500 per month and make do just fine.'

As a year closes in on him, Peter seems less sure as he was before of getting out of jail soon. While his defence team keeps stating the same arguments about his innocence, it's only the prosecution side where the case is progressing, new dates, new witnesses, and so that's where the media turns to for new leads to the Sheena Bora murder story. The press is only interested in new developments and Peter's position seems yesterday's story.

'I'm getting to write, which I'd forgotten to do, almost, and as there's precious little TV, I'm glad I don't get to see the madness that exists on the news channels, every night, particularly the one-man band who plays the same time each night.'

In his last note, he says: 'Suffice to say – I wasn't there, I didn't know, I wasn't involved in any way, I didn't hate Sheena nor was I against their relationship and I did not lie to my son when I told him that Sheena had left him. But thanks to Arnab and his decibel levels, he's put me in here – which is the price I'm paying – but over time I'm sure it will get resolved and I'll then come on his show and take him on, happily. Maybe you'll see my point of view.'

It's perhaps apt to end Peter's tale of captivity and legal journey with this anecdote he dug up.

'When Pandit Jawaharlal Nehru came home to his father Motilal Nehru and his friends, most of whom were lawyers, and announced that he had successfully completed a particular case for his client in 6 months which he was very proud of, Motilal Nehru took him aside and told the young Jawaharlal, "I put you through all 5 years of law school while fighting a case for a client and so completing a case in 6 months is nothing to be proud of! You won't survive as a lawyer for very long if you complete your cases so quickly." There lies a tale.'

WAHID AND THE DIFFERENT SHADES OF TORTURE

It was a day before Independence Day in 2006 when 29-year-old English teacher Wahid Sheikh learnt the nuances of torture in custody. His students at the Maulana Anjuman-i-Islam Abdul Sattar Shoaib School, a government-aided school in Mumbai, had no idea that their teacher was about to go on a long, long break – several years long, in fact. They didn't know that when their teacher left the lesson mid-way that day on 14 August, he would be beaten by policemen and over the next two months, continue to come to class after spending torturous evenings with sundry crime branch and ATS (Anti-Terrorism Squad) officials.

But then, neither did Wahid. All he knew was that in 2001, he'd been arrested for being a suspected SIMI (Students Islamic Movement of India) activist and being summoned by the police had become a part of his life. 'Whenever there was anything happening anywhere in the country, they would call me. The local police, the CID, the crime branch would call me and question me and then release me.' He was acquitted in the SIMI case but he'd come to terms with the fact that if there were the Ghatkopar blasts, he'd be called, if there were blasts at the Gateway of India, he was questioned for that too. It was part of being a marked man, and the police would always question him and get his alibis for any blasts, so that they could rule him out. So, on 11 July 2006 when 187 people were killed as seven explosions shattered the first-class general compartment of seven Mumbai local trains, Wahid may have been listening to the breaking news with his neighbour Munna at his Mumbra flat, but he wasn't surprised at getting a call from the police later in the evening. As usual, they asked him where he was and with whom.

'They took my name, address and job and how many family members I had. They were speaking nicely to us. They said ok, please give us details of where you can be reached and your school number (since I didn't have a mobile). They typed, they wrote it down too. The senior inspector who was talking said stay wherever but we will call you again perhaps.'

He was let off after these formalities. Wahid thought that was the end of it, until the summons came yet again in the midst of his class VII session, where he was teaching a story from China. He remembers the moral of the story was that one should be honest.

Wahid, a teacher there since 1999 went to the headmaster's room and found three police officers waiting for him. They wanted him to come along with them to the Crime Branch office and knowing the drill, he told a colleague to let his family know since 'those people would not release me soon'. He had barely sat in the car when they started beating and abusing him. At the office of the DCP Railways near Byculla (W) railway station, there was some more beating and abuse, after which he was put in the lockup. He was photographed, his fingerprints taken and then the wait started for the boss,

Inspector Vijay Salaskar to arrive. The inspector, who was awarded the Ashoka Chakra after being killed in action during the Mumbai Terror attack of 2008, came at 9 p.m. and asked him about the train blasts. Wahid denied any involvement and after telling him not to leave the area, Salaskar finally let him go at 10 p.m.

After this 12-hour long interrogation and beatings, Wahid went to school the next day and they all took part in the flag-hoisting. Only his headmaster knew about his ordeal. There was a bit of a reprieve for the next two days, but then again on 17 August three ATS officers knocked at the door of his one-room flat at 2 a.m. His wife, his two-year-old son and a newborn daughter were also at home. Wahid told his wife what he was told, that he had to go with them but he'd be back soon.

This time, they didn't wait for him to get into their Tata Sumo. The beatings started as soon as he walked outside the building. The questions were now more intimidating than before – they asked who was with him during the train blasts, and when he said he didn't know anything about them, they responded with sticks and kicks. They picked up someone else from another building and then stopped the vehicles at Thane creek. As Wahid told the court under oath, Inspector Sachin Kadam placed a revolver on his head and told him that he'd kill him and throw his body in the creek and no one would ever know about it. Wahid started crying which led to further beatings. They reached the ATS Kalachowki office at four in the morning. He knew things weren't looking up when he was taken to a room where another person was being tortured. There, someone called Inspector Varpe stripped him and started hitting him with a belt.

This continued for the next 2 to 3 hours, while the inspector kept asking him about 7/11, and Wahid kept denying it. The same routine continued the next day too, with the only variation being the torturers and their rooms. In the evening, Wahid was handcuffed to a peg high up on the wall above his head. From somewhere in the vicinity, he could hear other sounds emanating, of someone undergoing what he had all day. Then, all the police officers – Khanvilkar, Tajane, Varpe, Sachin Kadam, Dinesh Kadam, Kolhatkar – all of them came in with their boss, ATS chief K.P. Raghuvanshi, and DIG Subodh Jaiswal. Wahid remembers Raghuvanshi slapping him and kicking him in his genitals while telling the other officers to tie him strongly. The session ended with Inspector Kadam renewing his threat of an encounter if he tried to run away or do anything else. Wahid had told the court all this several times over but 10 years later, what he still can't get over is that he was accused of being a terror plotter when he was actually going to the police station every single time he was summoned after 7/11.

Summing up the absurdity of the situation he says, 'Is it possible that a man after choreographing a bomb blast will keep appearing for questioning during its probe? That he will come for interrogation and then be released and then come back? They would keep torturing us – detain us illegally also. We never talked about torture vaguely. We talked and reported it from the first day. We gave specifics about who hit us, how many times we were interrogated, and we produced all details. Despite all this, the judge didn't listen to us… that's the tragedy.'

The same routine took place the next day too – on 19 August, this time in another police station and lockup. There at the Bhoiwada lockup, he saw a person with long hair, and scars on the limbs and swollen legs. Wahid didn't know it then but that man who looked scared was Faisal, accused number three (A3) who would go on to spend the next 10 years in jail with him. Things were turning strange because at one point, at the ATS office complex in Nagpada at Raghuvanshi's office, he saw accused number seven (A7), his brother-in-law Sajid. He later realized that they all were being 'investigated' for the terror blasts which were now more than a month old. Wahid didn't know then that the ATS had already assigned various roles to all of them. Faisal was supposed to be the local Lashkar chief who received arms training in Pakistan and sent the other accused to Pakistan via Iran for training. He was also accused of funding the train blasts through hawala money and planting the bomb at Jogeshwari station. Sajid was accused of getting the timer and other devices that were used in the attack, and Wahid was accused of sheltering and harbouring some Pakistanis in his house.

'They made us stay all day, and released us in the evening. The fact that they were calling us and releasing us daily was also registered in the daily diary. They would keep getting all of us, keep us in different places, even though they knew that we hadn't carried out the blast. They would pick us up for a week, release us, torture us for 10 days and then release us again. They were under pressure from media to have a breakthrough in the case.'

This routine of minor torture and release and then torture again, continued till 13 September 2006. By then Wahid had met a few others who were going to be part of his case. Like Tanveer Ansari who he saw limping out of what had now got imprinted in his mind as 'torture room'. Tanveer would later be charged with receiving arms training in Pakistan and then also surveying the sites of attack. But all this would become clear only on 13 September. Before this, it was all very unclear, a kind of groping-in-the-dark expedition for information that Wahid didn't have.

THE 180 DEGREES MOVE

On that day, as Wahid was yet again picked up from his school, his role was finally revealed to him. At the Kalachowki police station, the chief Raghuvanshi told him he'd just got some leads from Bengaluru about him and it was time to confess. Wahid was given two options: to become an approver or an accused. Some of the other accused were offered rupees 25 lakh like Tanveer, obviously the police followed the carrot and stick policy rather literally. Raghuvanshi said that on the day of the blasts, 4 to 5 Pakistanis came and stayed at his house and for three nights Wahid took care of them and then helped them escape. Wahid refused the offer and then he learnt that what he'd mistaken for torture wasn't the real thing.

'The earlier torture was to just strip you, starve you one day and force feed you another, give religious *gaalis*, deny you sleep for 9–10 days – it was first and second degree. In third degree, they strip you, stretch your legs at 180 degrees and tear it, so your private parts start bleeding. Sometimes, they take something called Surya Prakash oil and inject it into your anus – which creates burning. They use the *chakki patta* to beat your hands and feet and then waterboard you (put you on a sea-saw, head down and then put water, which gives you the feeling that you are drowning). The other forms are that they put you in a dark room for many days blindfolded so hard that your eyes feel like they are literally being corroded, and that even if you open your eyes in light, you aren't able to see anything.'

As he said this, something just clicked about the way our interview was being conducted. Wahid had put some eye drops, and was talking to me for 20 minutes with his face held high, and eyes closed. 'I am losing my vision and in a few years I will go blind. These eye drops just reduce the irritation in my eyes.'

And then I noticed other things. How he was not even 40, and he had an old man's gait. As he climbed the stairs, he walked a little slower and seemed to drag one leg. His hair and beard were liberally sprinkled with grey too. The one trait that was all about youth was his fierceness. That's why after being acquitted, after almost a decade of torture and incarceration, Wahid wasn't going to cower and recuperate somewhere. He was fighting for the brothers who were still inside, at least five of them on death row because they had given into the torture and confessed. Torture as described in court by Dr Tanveer: 'They hit us on our palms, soles and buttocks. The inspector said that ten blows should be counted. After beating one of us, they used to ask us to bang the palms and soles on the floor to prevent swelling and this was repeated after some time. A.N. Roy and the other officers were standing there and torturing us and inquiring during this period as to who had done the blasts. We all accused were saying that we do not know anything about it. We were then taken to other rooms and two accused were kept in one room each and again tortured. Jaijeet Singh came to the room where I was standing naked and as I was thin he abused me and said to me that if I am given a blow it would go through my body and I should tell the truth. He ordered to beat me only by hands and legs.'

These were still mild compared to what Faisal went through. Accused Dr Tanveer recalls how his torture also included being made to beat Faisal.

'I saw him (Faisal) bleeding from his nose, mouth and buttocks. He was not able to move or save himself as he was tied to the bamboo. A.N. Roy was asking all the others to beat him and all were beating him by belt. They gave me a belt and asked me to beat him saying that if I do not do so, they will beat me similarly. I was very frightened, therefore, I could not do anything. On seeing this, A.N. Roy started beating me and when I fell down he kicked me on my buttocks. The ATS constables started beating me... Raghuvanshi threatened to beat me as they had beaten the accused no. 3 Faisal, if I do not work for them. I saw that Faisal's condition was bad.'

There is another incident which is of unspeakable horror involving Faisal's father. Other accused and witnesses like Ehteshaam and Suhail Shaikh have told the court about that night in August at the Kurla police station.

'Some officers and constables, whose names I do not remember now, took me to a separate room, stripped me and beat me heavily. I was handcuffed to a window. I saw Tanveer, Faisal, Ehteshaam and Muzammil also handcuffed in the main hall and being beaten. This went on till late night. Faisal and Muzammil's father was brought there along with a veiled woman member of their family. We all were naked at that time and the officers and constables were using filthy and dirty language. They stripped Faisal's father's clothes, abused and misbehaved with him. Officer Dalvi scolded the woman and used bad language and took off her veil. Faisal and Muzammil were beaten heavily during this period. They were pleading and crying on seeing the misbehaviour with their father. When their father tried to hide his modesty, he was beaten on his hands and told to hold the hands high. The officers were threatening the brothers to tell what they did and even if they do not know they should take the responsibility of the blasts and that their father would take the responsibility. They also threatened me to take the responsibility of the blasts or else they would bring women from my family and would strip them in our presence and the drug addicts would be asked to molest them. This continued for the whole night. We were handcuffed to high windows so that we could not sit or sleep.'

Ehteshaam later also said: 'They threatened that if I did not sign a confession they would involve my father and brother in the bomb blasts case. They showed me photographs of my two younger sisters in their mobile and asked me whether I wanted to see how they behave with them or whether I am ready to sign. They told me that I had seen what happened with accused Faisal's father and they would do the same thing with my father and sisters. Because of this I told them that I would sign wherever they say.'

If they didn't use fathers or women of the family, then they just used brothers as they did in the case of Asif Bashir, the civil engineer who the ATS says was a plotter of 7/11. Bashir describes how they handcuffed his brother to a hook on the wall, stripped off all his clothes. While he was like this, Bashir was also stripped, and beaten with a flour mill belt for an hour. Then while repeatedly asking him to sign the papers, they stretched his legs, 180 degrees apart... till he lost consciousness. Bashir screamed for a doctor, but they refused and then turned to do the same to his brother. He lost consciousness too. They waterboarded both and hung Bashir upside down, asking if he was finally ready to sign the confession. He finally gave in when they put a cloth on his face and poured water. 'I was helpless and I told them to release my brother and that I would sign the papers. They removed his handcuffs and let him out. I signed on a paper at one place that they showed me, when I was satisfied that my brother was released.'

If you ask police officers about allegations of torture, they always point out that the system is now such that it is impossible to torture someone and get away with it. However, that's only half true. Yes, there are systems in place to check police excesses. Systems like mandatory medical tests for accused in police custody so that they can be physically examined for bruises, cuts, or fractures. But over and over again, in sworn testimony after sworn testimony, accused point out that the way the police officers get away with this is that they have an understanding with medical examiners. In this case, all the tortured point out that the doctors wouldn't even examine them because they didn't want to act against the police. As Muzammil described it, during his examination: 'The police used to give some ointment to apply on the marks and the marks used to go away after 2–3 days and then again I used to be beaten. It is true that I was taken to the hospital every alternate day during police custody. I was taken to the doctor on the days prior and after the day on which advocate Shahid Azmi came to meet me. But I was not examined and only my thumb impression was taken.'

These horror stories of tormentor policemen who were all decorated officers came out during the trial when the accused realized that the worst had already happened to them. They were already languishing in jail and they had no deals to make. But initially, they all kept quiet out of fear and threats and this was also used against them later when the judge asked why they'd kept quiet for so long. Wahid held his brother Javed back, he told his family to get the politician Arif Naseem Khan to stop calling as the ATS asked him to. He didn't let any of them complain that he was kept in custody from 13 to 26 September without being produced in front of a magistrate, which is illegal under any circumstances. Wahid's court testimony says that every time he'd plead with the officers to let him go, he'd tell them that his students were waiting for him. Finally, after two weeks of this illegal detention, Wahid was finally allowed to go home. And it was then that he realized that the police had also managed to threaten and beat a statement against him by his own relative. At the Bhoiwada police station where he'd been summoned just a couple of days later, he noticed the police with his wife's sister's husband, Mahmud Azim Quraishi. At that time Wahid didn't know that Mahmud would be both – a damning witness and a saviour for him. The police got him to say that after Wahid got married in 2003, he would have strange characters coming over to his Mumbra house and on 11 July, he saw these men (Pakistanis) in his house.

'The only thing they had against me was my relative's statement. They beat him up and threatened him and made him a witness against me. Now, if he, Mahmud Azim Quraishi had stuck to that in court, Madam, I wouldn't be sitting in front of you today. I would be languishing in jail.'

Why Quraishi didn't eventually testify against him in court, will come a little later. At that time, Wahid was about to be officially arrested. As they cuffed him and took him for his medical examination, they warned him not to say anything at all to the judge. His wife and his family had no idea that this was not going to be one of those short ordeals but this time he was going to be gone for years. They'd repeatedly wanted to complain against the police but Wahid hadn't let them. How could he? His body was being torn internally with the forcible splits that literally made him piss out blood, and if his own torture wasn't enough, he was haunted by the screams of others, all at the time telling him to keep his mouth shut. They'd parade the others like accused number 2 (A2) Tanveer Ibrahim without their shirts, so that the welts on their skin or the bloody, ruptured body would send clear message of threat to the others. When they weren't being lashed with these flour mill belts that broke their skin, others like Kamal were given electric shocks on their private parts.

The intimidation to not tell the judge continued for a few appearances, when they'd make Wahid also sign on some papers without letting him read it. Ostensibly there were permissions to conduct narco and polygraph tests on him – something that is not allowed by the Supreme Court and has been ethically questioned by many experts. These so-called scientific tests to extract the truth were also the setting for some imaginative torture sessions. They are meant to be done with proper consent and accused have the right to say no, but like Wahid, Sajid Ansari was also forced with threats to sign his consent for it. The two of them along with Naveed were taken for their narco together where Sajid says he was even threatened with an AIDS injection!

'Dr S. Malini misbehaved and slapped me twice before the test. They asked me to say some things in front of a video camera and beat me before asking me to say the sentences. She threatened that if I do not give correct answers she would give me AIDS injection. I became semiconscious after the injection of narco test was given. She asked me illogical questions while I was in this condition. The camera was switched on and first she asked how many bombs were prepared. I answered that I was not concerned and I was falsely involved. She slapped me hard and started pinching my left ear with pliers, because of which I suffered much. She then asked me what comes after six and I answered "seven". She asked me on what does the TV operates and I answered that it operates on electricity. She again slapped me and caught my ear with pliers and told me to say "by remote". When they played the CD of the narco test I was shocked to see that in place of my reply to the question as to how many bombs were prepared, the reply was "seven". Anyone could see that the CD was edited because the words were not in sync with the video. I said to Khanvilkar that the CD was edited, thereupon he started hitting me.'

Sajid Ansari applied under RTI to get a CD of his FSL test but didn't get it. He did complain about Dr Malini through

FIRs, and later on she did stand discredited in the CBI Sister Abaya case where they found her certificates also forged.

Accused Tanveer's father sent telegrams to the prime minister, to the home minister and to ATS chief Raghuvanshi that his son was being forced to undergo this test. Tanveer was taken physically ill with the procedure: 'I was falling unconscious and at that time I saw Dr Malini pinching my earlobes and nose by pliers and slapping me. I fell unconscious after some time and do not know anything thereafter. I regained consciousness in the evening. I was suffering from severe headache, severe pain in the stomach and feeling nauseous and weak. I realized that a large quantity of fluid was given to me, but even then my pulse was more than normal and blood pressure was very low and that I had become critical and they had resuscitated me.' There was no response whatsoever to these cries for help. Instead they would beat him even more on his hands and point out that he'd used these hands to write all the applications and complaints to the court. They'd handcuff him and make him stand all night and every time a police person would pass, he'd hit him so that he wouldn't sleep at all.

One of the factors why there was no response or no action despite the vivid descriptions of torture, was perhaps that one of the key players in ATS was a 26/11 hero, a martyr, Vijay Salaskar. Just two years after all of this happened he was not only credited with catching Ajmal Kasab but also lost his life in that battle. Who would want to pay attention to these allegations levelled against him by suspected terrorists? And yet, they are part of court records, throwing light on a different aspect of a national hero.

Here's just an extract from how Mohd. Majid Shafi describes Dr Malini's torture, apart from giving electric shock to his private parts. This is a confrontation the two had about his narco test: 'She told me to say that I had gone to Bongaon border and had brought some Pakistanis from there to Kolkata. I told her that I had not done this thing and would not say it. A cameraman was standing on my right side and recording everything in camera. He slapped me and my earlobes were pinched with pliers when I refused to say as she stated. I kept on refusing to say the things she told me. She then told me to say that I had not gone to the Bongaon border and that I had not brought Pakistanis from there. I repeated these things. I was then taken outside and made to lie down on a bench. At that time the saline was going on. I wanted to go to the bathroom after some time and they took me to a bathroom inside the room where my narco test had been done. I saw a bearded person lying there being tortured in the same manner as I was tortured. His condition was so bad that he had vomited on the floor. I realized during the judicial custody that the said person was Asif Khan Bashir Khan.

'I was brought back to the office of Vijay Salaskar and was shown a CD of my narco test and Salaskar said to me that I had told the truth. I told him that I had not said any such things. The CD showed that the negative statements that I had made were converted to positive statements. I was beaten and tortured when I started arguing about it and was asked to sign on some written and blank papers. When I refused to sign, Salaskar threatened that he would bring my wife and child there within two hours and molest her before me. I could not bear anything more because of the mental and physical torture and therefore I signed on all the papers.'

GOOD COP, BAD COP

It was around the time when the investigation was in full flow and the narco analysis of all thirteen accused was on, when cracks first appeared among the police officers. The continuous daily ordeal of getting confessions out of this group of men was taking its toll. The accused noticed that the police officers Sachin Kadam and Dinesh Ahir had an argument about their investigation on the way back from the narco lab in Bengaluru. 'Dinesh Ahir said that he knows what investigation they do, that they catch innocent people and do their encounters and that they have killed a poor person at Antop Hill,' said Sajid. Antop Hill was where a person was killed by the ATS just a month after 7/11, in August 2006. The ATS said they suspected some Pakistanis to be holed up there but responded with fire and a man called Mohammed Ali was killed.

It wasn't just these two officers who showed unease with their means, but also officer Khanvilkar. Wahid remembers how by the end of October 2006, he came and told him that he knew he was innocent, and that they had detained him illegally but he had to do what his bosses tell him. The same officers who had unleashed captive cruelty were now almost showing signs of remorse. 'He prayed with folded hands to forgive him and promised that he would do something to help me.'

Just a few days later, on 3 November, an anonymous letter written by an ATS officer emerged. The letter addressed to the president, to the home minister and others talked about the illegal detention of the accused, their innocence and the pressure that the officers faced in booking them for the entire case. The letter stated that ATS officers were ashamed that innocents were being framed, but the then home minister R.R. Patil reacted to this by saying no heed should be paid to all this.

That was perhaps because it was an anonymous letter, however, what needed to be probed was the allegation that the recent death of ATS officer ACP Vinod Bhatt was not a train accident that it was made out to be but a suicide. The letter alleged he didn't want to implicate innocent people as he was asked to do and that's why he preferred to end his life. When Bhatt's own colleagues said that he never travelled by train, how did he get run over by a CST local? The clue wasn't just in the anonymous letter but one of the accused – Ehteshaam Siddiqui recalled having a conversation with the dead officer which was published in the *Milli Gazette* in October 2010 titled 'My 75 days of Horror':

> In the police custody of 75 days, I never forget the words of Asstt. Commissioner of Police late Shri Vinod Bhatt, who committed suicide in the second week of August. Before his suicide, during interrogation he told me that he was under immense pressure from his senior officers to implicate us falsely in Mumbai train blast case and he also promised that he will try his best not to implicate all of you innocent people till he was alive. Unfortunately, Shri Vinod Bhatt committed suicide under tremendous pressure.

There were so many red flags going up, many inconsistencies in the plot that the ATS alleged, and while the odd piece made its way to the media, it wasn't loud enough to stir up any change. Accused were expected to claim their innocence and even if third degree torture was used, no one was particularly outraged as it involved 'terrorists'. As the accused were finally sent to jail and away from the clutches of the ATS by the end of October and early November, they presumed that the torture would end. There in the Anda Cell or isolation block of Arthur Road Jail, the high security accused finally met and exchanged stories, and realized that in their desperation they had also implicated each other in the blasts. When they'd ask why, the other would just say because they had no idea what they had said in their statement, they had just been forced to sign it. Since the ATS had invoked Maharashtra Control of Organised Crime Act, it allowed confessions made in front of a mid-level officer, like the Deputy Commissioner of Police level also to be admissible in court. And they could now finally complain to their Judge Mridula Ramesh Bhatkar, since they didn't have to fear the consequences once they left the courtroom. But they were wrong.

Wahid, in his detailed account of Jail Superintendent Swati Sathe, describes how the mistreatment continued in jail. 'When we first saw her we said, she's a woman, she'll be kind to us. The very next day, all such notions were busted. She called us to her chamber where ATS officers too were called and asked us to just listen to them. She would call us at various times in the middle of the night for these meetings. Those times, they would make us offers: we'll give you 25 lakh in cash, we'll give you a flat, we'll get your family settled, just become an approver, a prosecution witness. They would also call us individually and entice us. When we said no, the lady officer would threaten us. "I'll get you beaten. If you have to live here, you'll have to live according to my wishes."' Wahid found out later that Salaskar treated Sathe like a 'rakhi-sister', and even Raghuvanshi and other officers would drop by to harass the accused.

Swati Sathe wasn't just facilitating meetings with ATS officers, but, according to Wahid and others' complaints she would also try to block their pleas and complaints. In January 2008, when they complained about intimidation of ATS officers, Swati Sathe first refused to accept their applications, and then when it was sent to court, she confronted Wahid with violence. 'Superintendent Swati Sathe and her staff armed with sticks surrounded me when I was taken back to the prison and threatened as to why I complained against her. I told her that I am sick and she should not trouble me.

She again threatened me. I was intending to again complain against her as the regular date of the court was not near, but I knew that if I gave a written compliant she would not send it to the court.'

Now, till that period, it was all claims of the terror accused versus the police. But on 28 June 2008, an episode of torture took place in jail that was so severe that first a judicial inquiry confirmed excessive force against the train blast accused and then the Bombay High Court next year (2009) recommended action against the jail authorities. What happened was this: since the accused had informed the courts about their torture, the jail staff on that day used other prisoners to attack them. They also sounded the alarm for a jail riot, which empowers jail authorities to use excessive force in order to bring things under control. When the train bombing accused were seriously injured with broken bones and ribs, they weren't taken to the doctor for more than 20 days and that's what prompted the PIL. The jail authorities said that the accused were being transferred to another jail and because they resisted, they had to use force. A report of the principal judge Bombay City Civil and Sessions Court found that 'the circumstances and the statements of the doctors are sufficient to infer that even first-aid treatment was not given to most of the injured prisoners... This conduct of the doctors of Mumbai Central Prison speaks volume about the general approach of the jail authority and the doctors working in the jail. It can be said that the doctors helped the jail authority in falsifying everything and screening illegal actions of the officers.'

On the basis of this judicial report, no lesser authority than the Bombay High Court's Justice Bilal Nazki gave a judgement in July 2009 that asked for action against the jail officers. In a strong indictment, the High Court said: 'The conduct was shameful. All jail superintendents in a free democratic republic behaving inside the jail like a dictator is not acceptable. Such officials if left to manage the jail would negate all the principles on which our democratic set-up is built.'

What the High Court ignored was that such jail officials are perhaps in every single prison.

A FIGHT IN VAIN, FOR JUSTICE

So Swati Sathe was finally curbed with the help of judicial intervention but the Special Judge Mridula Bhatkar was proving to be as difficult if not more. In fact, the thirteen convicts of the Mumbai train blasts case were meeting one woman challenger after another. First Dr Malini, the narco specialist who kept pulling their ears with pliers if they didn't give answers she liked during their tests, then Swati Sathe with her *danda* in jail, and now Judge Bhatkar seemed to be standing by as a mute witness while violations happened.

For instance, Wahid talks about an incident in March 2008 when the hearing of the case was going on. There, just outside her courtroom, when Wahid saw an officer and some constables beating Ehteshaam in the corridor, he and Tanveer complained to the judge. Ehteshaam was so badly beaten, he lay down on the bench in front of her. They asked for medical assistance to be summoned, for the judge to take some action, and also filed official complaints, but nothing happened. Their applications were left pending.

Maybe, a beating was considered routine but when a prisoner's worst fear that was expressed in court comes true, can the judge ignore it? That's what happened when some of the accused told Judge Bhatkar that the ATS was threatening to book them in the Malegaon blast case. The case pertained to an attack that took place in September 2006 that killed 37 people near a mosque. But all of the thirteen accused were already in custody in September 2006. It was a threat that was used for many of the thirteen accused but unfortunately, it only came true for Sheikh Mohammed Ali and Asif Khan. Sheikh later described how his brother had submitted a written complaint about fears that Sheikh may be implicated. He gave the complaint on 7 November, and just six days later, almost on cue, Sheikh was allegedly identified by someone as involved in the Malegaon blasts. What was shocking was that both Sheikh and Asif were also granted custody of the ATS by the judge.

'The accused screamed and said, "Madam, we told you they would implicate us in Malegaon. Please we beg you not to send us to police custody." Even then she didn't say anything and sent them on police remand of fourteen days. We were very agitated,' shared Wahid.

In an unprecedented move, the accused said they'd had enough. They began protesting against the judge and they showed her black flags. 'It was the first time that court proceedings were stopped – the thirteen accused said that we don't expect to get justice from you, so we don't accept your court. You please leave your court and go.'

They sent complaint after complaint asking for a change of judge. And eventually she was removed but it wasn't because the accused were effective. In a strange irony, Judge Bhatkar's husband Ramesh, a well-known Marathi actor who stars in serials like *Hello Inspector*, was accused of rape. The authorities thought it was proper not to associate the high-profile 7/11 trial with any other controversy. Ramesh was discharged in 2010 and coming full circle, the appeal hearing is back in front of Mridula Bhatkar's bench as she is now a High Court judge. Asif and Sheikh, and the other Malegaon accused, were also liberated of their fake Malegaon case in 2016 after the ATS case was exposed with the NIA (National

Investigation Agency) saying it was Abhinav Bharat and not the group of men, allegedly from SIMI, behind the attack.

It took the Malegaon men 10 years to clear their name, and it took Wahid almost the same time. The twelve others have been sentenced to death. But for his freedom, Wahid had to credit his courage to not confess and his brother-in-law, Quraishi.

All the other accused retracted their confessions in court but the judge did not believe them. They accepted the police's clever manoeuvring in court. The police took the defence that the confessions they submitted, and if you look at the 2000-page judgement it is almost completely dependent on confessions, couldn't have been extracted via torture because then they would have submitted 13 confessions instead of just 11. They said Wahid never agreed, which they accepted and another accused changed his mind. And so all twelve of them were labelled guilty with Judge Y.D. Shinde saying: 'The prosecution has proved beyond reasonable doubt that all accused facing trial, except A8 (Wahid), were directly or indirectly connected and affiliated to a terrorist organization, i.e., Lashkar-e Taiba.'

If Wahid's relative Quraishi hadn't shown 'daring', as Wahid puts it, he too, may have been convicted. The police certainly tried to make sure he stuck to his initial statement which they took under pressure. But he came to court and called his own statement under section 164 'bogus'. 'This could only happen because my family was alert. Just days before his testimony, they moved him to some other location. They didn't give in to threats by the police and they carefully came to court, knowing that it was very dangerous.'

And so in 2015, the court finally told the English teacher from Mumbra: 'Prosecution has not been able to prove any independent circumstance to show that A8 (Wahid) harboured any of the wanted accused in his house, that he took part in the conspiratorial meetings and that he had any role to play in the subsequent activities leading to the bomb blasts. Hence, he will have to be given the benefit of doubt... Though it is proved that the A8 was also a member of SIMI, no overt act has been attributed to him and proved in connection with this crime.'

Wahid was finally free to go home to his wife and children, his daughter he'd barely known since she was just a newborn and his son only two years old when he was picked up. His wife, he says, never stepped out of home before but now was working as a school teacher because someone needed to pay for them. 'My daughter was never breastfed because of this.' Wahid's father died just a year after he went to jail, and so did his mother-in-law. His mother was in depression but now seems to be doing better. In January 2017, Wahid and his wife had another baby boy.

The other bright spark for Wahid is that his community has welcomed him back. Wahid went back to teaching in his school, although they are yet to give him his salary (the government says wait and watch in case an appeal is filed). His old students have been regular visitors, coming to check up on their teacher. 'The colleagues, students and neighbours, they all are fine with me, happy and welcoming. Only the Government of Maharashtra feels I am a terrorist, nobody else feels that.' In 2016, Wahid started a campaign called 'The Innocence Network'. It had only one objective – to get acquittals for the twelve who were still on death row and to campaign against the use of UAPA to harass citizens.

POST-SCRIPT: AJMAL KASAB'S ROOM

Wahid and company may have been in Arthur Road Jail exactly when 26/11 only-surviving terrorist Ajmal Kasab was there too, but they never even saw each other during those four years they were in the same jail campus. Initially, when Kasab was brought to Arthur Road Jail, they put a purdah outside his cell area, so that nobody would even be able to get a peek of his shadow.

Then, in 2010, a new cell (number 12) was built for Kasab. And his old cell was the one that Wahid was shifted to. When Wahid walked into that cell, he remembers that the walls were full of scribbled notes by Kasab – many of those were inspiring messages for Jihad. There was one line Wahid remembers very clearly.

Kisi diwar ne roka nahi, saile juno ab tak,
ye misra koi majnu likh gaya diware zinda par

(There's no wall or jail built, that can stop a man's ideology, this stanza has been written by a Majnu on this jail wall.)

When Kasab was hanged in November 2012, Wahid, like the rest of the country, was curious to know the details, especially because in jail there was a conspiracy theory going around. The rumour was that Kasab had been ill for a while and was suffering from malaria. He wasn't being able to eat properly either. So, the theory is that he wasn't really hanged but died of his illness. And so an operation was planned to make it look like there was a hanging.

'I asked Himayat Baig (of the German Bakery case) who was in Yerwada if he knew or saw anything. He said that he only saw someone being brought on a stretcher.' So was it his body or is this all bunkum and he was hanged as planned?

SOMNATH BHARTI &
THE ATTACK OF DON

'I didn't want to get arrested for domestic violence. If it was
for the Khirki episode, it would have been ok as it would
have been for the nation.'

– Somnath Bharti, August 2016

It was in June 2015 when the Aam Aadmi Party (AAP) minister
Jitender Singh Tomar had to step down because he was going
to Tihar Jail. It seems the minister of law had also broken the
law by claiming to be a degree holder, when he apparently was
not. Arvind Kejriwal, their boss and the Delhi chief minister,
decided to reinstate the law minister he had during his 59 days
of government, IIT Delhi graduate and lawyer Somnath Bharti.
'I was in Kerala when Arvind called,' Somnath recalled the
moment his luck looked like it might turn around.

Ever since he'd led a group of his constituents from
Delhi's urban village Khirki Extension on 16 January 2014,
against resident Africans egging the police to arrest them for
running prostitution and drug rackets, he'd had to keep a low

profile. Bharti, like Tomar, was booked for breaking the law as CCTV footage showed him leading a vigilante mob against some women from Uganda. He and his mob of supporters were charged with molesting and manhandling nine women and preventing the police from doing their work. And while there was public outrage about the apparent racism in Bharti's act, he had no trouble at all in winning back his constituents and the elections soon after. In fact, it may have been the key factor in boosting his victory margin from 8,000 votes in the 2013 elections to over 15,000 in the elections post-Khirki incident. AAP was a bit more circumspect and didn't make him a minister again, instead assigned him the southern states to work on as a long term investment plan. But as another law minister was heading to jail, AAP's moral high ground about not promoting anybody with criminal cases was becoming very tough to maintain.

'Arvind wanted to make me law minister again but I told him that it may not be a good idea as the Khirki case would come up again.' As it turned out, he underestimated his problems. Something even darker and murkier about him was just about to explode into the public space.

As the 40-year-old was relishing the thought of being back at the thick of things, TV news tickers were rolling out furiously with his mugshot – 'Somnath Bharti's wife goes to DCW (Delhi Commission of Women) against him' and 'Somnath Bharti booked for domestic violence'. In fact, it was exactly a day after Tomar's arrest and Somnath knew that his comeback was not possible now. He was a man wanted by law and claims it was all orchestrated by his wife. After their last altercation, she had apparently texted him: 'I will ruin your political career'.

As the police files document, Lipika Mitra or Bapi as Somnath called her, had met him through the matrimonial website shaadi.com in 2010. He claimed to be a lawyer with an international firm, and coupled with his IIT degree looked like quite an eligible match. They dated for nine months in which Somnath, being the true Aam Aadmi, refused to pay for anything. 'Yes, that's the only true thing she has written in her complaint. I didn't spend a penny on her because as I said, "If you love me, love me naked, strip me off everything."' Lipika wasn't impressed and in her complaint said she was cheated by his claims of financial wellness and security. The police claims she was under a lot of pressure to get married to Somnath and to pay for it all, because she was pregnant and their first child was born just five months after they had a court marriage. As with any domestic violence case, the police records go into really private and intimate details of a relationship, and with this one involving a politician, it played out in the public eye. From fights during their 10-day honeymoon to Sri Lanka and Maldives, to details of their emails and phone conversations, it was all dissected publicly by the police.

THE CHASE & ARREST

The charges against Somnath Bharti were very grave. He was accused of attempt to murder, of voluntarily causing hurt with a dangerous weapon (a knife) and of subjecting his wife to cruelty while misappropriating her property. If that wasn't bad enough, he was also charged with trying to harm their unborn child as Lipika accused him of causing her mental agony and hitting her while she was seven months pregnant. By September, it wasn't just the Women's Commission but the Dwarka police too wanted to question him. As the investigation picked up, Somnath went underground.

'When the FIR was lodged, I spoke to a senior police officer and asked him if they were about to arrest me. He said, "Not only will they arrest you but they will also be putting you through torture. So avoid it."' He went from court to court asking for interim bail and by the time the court's order came, he had spent all of September 2015 hiding. The police wasn't just looking for him. They were also looking for his golden Labrador, Don. It was a chase that Delhi police hadn't seen anything like since the summer of 2001 when they went looking for the mythical Monkeyman who was allegedly attacking people in east Delhi. During Somnath's bail hearings, the police produced an email by Lipika sent in March 2013 to her husband, which explained why they needed to 'interrogate' Don.

I could not manage to check the injuries inflicted on me yesterday by you & your dog because I was in too much of pain. However, today morning I have noticed that I have been bitten 6 times by your abnormal & violent Dog besides numerous other wounds/injuries on my neck, arms & right leg inflicted by you.

Your dog has bitten me at 3 places on my abdomen, at 1 place on my lower abdomen, there is a big wound at my Vagina (yes!!!), since now these days I cannot see my vagina because of my 7-month-old pregnancy, today I discovered the wound by seeing myself in the mirror & I was wondering since yesterday why so many of my pubic hair has been falling on its own. And off course there is wound on my thigh which is very painful. If you want proof of the same, I will photograph myself today & can forward you the relevant pictures. I don't think even a rogue will treat a 7 month pregnant woman the way you have treated me.

I don't see any reason for us to be together anymore! Therefore, I would request you to please move out from my home along with your dog at the earliest.

Of course, Somnath and Lipika had separated within three months of getting married but he would still visit her on weekends, and that's how she conceived a second time. The fight over Don in 2013 was just one of the many subsequent flashpoints that ended up with his being on the run two years later.

The police search went from one associate's home to another, from his constituency Malviya Nagar to Agra, prosecuting those who gave him shelter in a chase that lasted till 29 September. That's when the Supreme Court put its foot down and asked Somnath to join investigations immediately. He appeared at Dwarka police station on the same day at 10 p.m. and was arrested soon after. The police said they needed to arrest him as till he was not locked up, no witness would come forward to testify against him. They also needed to interrogate him in custody so that they could recover the assault weapon, a knife, and Lipika's jewellery, which Somnath and his mother had apparently snatched away from her.

So with cameras recording all the action outside Dwarka police station, and with top police officials like the DCP of the area present, Somnath would begin his time in custody. If he was arrested at 1 a.m., the mandatory medical examination in hospital took place at 3 a.m. Many prisoners who aren't as influential as Somnath are usually taken for their medical examination after they have been roughed up or beaten during their questioning. And they say even if they have very obvious signs of police excess, they have enough excuses to get by. Like 'He resisted arrest, so had to be subdued or grappled with in order to be taken into custody.' But those problems were far from Bharti's and all he had to worry about was how his incarceration was going to play out with his voters.

During the interrogation, the junior police officials, claims Bharti, were soon eating out of his hands. 'They wanted to know how I would get the dog to attack Bapi. They were asking me all kinds of questions but when the police heard the audio recordings, they immediately understood.' It's a strange thing to investigate what happened between a husband and wife, even if the husband is a public figure. How do you figure out if a relationship is abusive and violent or not? The Delhi Police used some routine and standard methods, like visiting their homes in Malviya Nagar and her rented and parental home in Dwarka and speaking to neighbours and their staff members. But there is a whole new generation of policing that's developed in the last 15 years, that goes by electronic evidences, no longer limited to Information Technology Act cases – Lipika and Somnath's social media profiles, their matrimonial ads, their emails to each other and of course, their call data records. Somnath had in fact even recorded all his phone calls. Why would anyone record conversations with their wife, though? 'It's an auto-feature on my phone. It has a call recorder so my clients' brief can be recorded and I would later give it to my secretary to transcribe.' While he claims his wife came across as scrappy, earning total disapproval from the police, in their charge sheet the police concluded his recordings were 'edited' and Somnath refused to give them the original versions.

IN CUSTODY

Confident that the police weren't going to get much out of him, Somnath says he stayed calm and smiling through the entire night in lockup. There was a certain degree of understanding which the junior police officials also exhibited about the nature of his case. But then, a certain ACP M walked in and barked at them that it was 4 a.m. and obviously they had been too easy on Somnath and hadn't been able to get him to admit to anything. '*Kya jaanch kar rahe hai aap? Yeh kya kar rahe hai ki woh hans rahe hai?* (What kind of investigation are you doing that he's still smiling?),' he apparently remarked. For the investigating officer's sake, Somnath claimed he looked less comfortable afterwards.

When the questioning finally ended at 5.30 a.m., Somnath was taken to the lockup to sleep. This is where he was going to spend the next five days before being sent to judicial custody. The 'bed' was the usual slab of concrete and behind it was a waist-high wall that was the enclosure with a hole on the ground which served as the loo. 'You won't believe, as soon as I lay down on it, it didn't take me a second to go to sleep.'

It's interesting how the politician-prisoners are the ones who always say that they had no problems in jail. They find supporters in fellow inmates, or among the police or security personnel themselves who make things easier for them. Even at the Dwarka Police Station where Somnath was, while ACP M had instructions to torture him (or so Somnath believed), the junior policemen offered him the station house officer's (SHO) personal toilet to use. Somnath said he turned it down preferring to imbibe the full experience by using the hole in his lockup. However, that experience didn't extend to having the lockup food. To control his diabetes, Somnath was used to having a diet of only fruits and raw vegetables with coconut water as breakfast. And that's where the VIP status really came in handy, to get permission to get this food from home. If the police really want to torture someone or pressurize them, they immediately cut off their daily needs like even vital medicines. And that's when the prisoner starts cracking. Somnath managed to get permission to get food from home but he remembers one day when he didn't get the food and how it suddenly made him feel stripped off all his rights.

For prisoners, the most taxing experience can be appearing for a court hearing. Prisoners are taken in the morning before

10 since there never is a fixed time about when their matter comes up. The prisoners are then kept in the court's lockup, which by all accounts is the dirtiest of all jails, since it's temporary and no one cares for it. There, prisoners spend all day sometimes, till their matter comes up before the judge. 'We left so early, I didn't have time to eat my breakfast and in lockup they gave *dal–roti* which I couldn't eat. That's when I started shouting, "I'm eligible for food, I'm not on trial, I'm not a convict. How can you treat me like this?"' This was just one day for Somnath, but it becomes a part of a prisoner's regular routine. Here's what one petition about jail conditions says regarding court appearances for female prisoners:

i. That the numbers of buses/vans allotted towards transportation for female prisons are extremely negligible in comparison to the number of female inmates already locked up in Jail No. 6. Due to the inadequate transportation for female prisoners they are made to wait and suffer in small and less ventilated Trial Court lockups in the court till 4.00 pm or beyond, which even lack the basic amenities. For example, if a female prisoner is produced before a court at 10 am and her case gets over around 11 am then she has to wait till 4.00 or 5.00 pm in the evening for all the female inmates to get over with their cases before they are sent back to Tihar Jail, unlike the male inmates who are sent back to Tihar Jail after their cases are over. The said wait in stuffy, unventilated lockup leads to inhuman condition causing serious health hazards to the life of female inmates.

ii. The buses/vans used for transportation for the female inmates lacks ventilation and the extreme hot weather of Delhi makes the van very suffocated which leads to dehydration. Thereby leading to vomiting and fainting in van. That basic amenities are not given any consideration and the undertrials are suffering to inhuman conditions and treatments.

(FROM THE HIGH COURT OF DELHI W.P. (Crl) No. 1352/2015)

A day after his arrest, NDTV carried a news report blaming police officials for making Somnath Bharti break down during his interrogation. While Somnath denies that anything so dramatic ever happened, he doesn't deny that the police made him undergo what's one of their favourite exercises during interrogation – to bring the prisoner face-to-face with the other party, which in this case was his estranged wife, Lipika Mitra. This was done so that the police could determine who was telling the truth about the night of 27 May when Somnath was supposed to have caused a knife injury to her, before heading off to Kerala.

That day was their three-year-old son's birthday and the immediate provocation for the on-off couple's fight was that Somnath didn't make an appearance. 'She called me saying, "How many kids do you have?" I told her my parents were in hospital, there was no one to cook at home, how would this go on? I told her you are there, I am here, this is not working!' Somnath claims that's when Lipika threatened to end her life and he called his mother-in-law, but also rushed to their flat in Dwarka. There he found her in the bathroom, sitting with a knife in her hand. He says he cajoled her and managed to take her to the bedroom, where he held her hand all night. But when he woke up in the morning, the tussle over the knife continued, with their two small children also present. Somnath says it ended with her mother being called to the flat and he leaving. The police case was that Lipika did threaten suicide and ask Somnath to collect the children but their version differed in that when Somnath came home, they said, he broke open the bathroom door and beat her and slit her arm with the knife. But Somnath says, 'There is no medical record of this, so how can they prove this?'

To make their case, the investigating officer needed to recover the knife. And so a posse of 20 policemen proceeded to Lipika's flat in Shri Ram Apartment of Sector 4 Dwarka with their MLA prisoner so that the couple could come face-to-face. The expectation, as one police officer explained, was that 'any false details given by either party becomes clearer for the investigators. They can't blatantly make up a false incident either.'

As NDTV reported, this confrontation between the husband and wife proved futile. They didn't talk during the entire period and at one point Somnath apparently asked his wife, 'Did you want all this?' The knife wasn't recovered there, or in Agra, where the police believed he was hiding, or at his brother and mother's flat in Vasant Kunj. Neither was any of Lipika's jewellery. The objective of custodial interrogation was proving to be futile. 'It was all *khanapoorty* (ticking the boxes)!'

There was only one thing left to be done during the police custody – another confrontation, but this time between the dog and his master. Don had been with the AAP MLA since 2004 and if Somnath is to be believed, was one of the sore points in his marriage. When they had a period of rapprochement in 2013 and he moved in with Lipika in Dwarka, she was the one who used to feed the dog. But she apparently would keep haranguing Somnath for letting go of Don. 'I said you made me leave my mother, my constituency, how can I also leave Don?' It was during this period in 2013 when Don allegedly attacked her on Somnath's command. He claims it was while he was away and that it was just a scratch. She has medical reports from Ayushman Hospital to show that it was actually a bite. Either way, it led to Somnath moving out again without realizing that it would be the main allegation against him two years later. Now the job for the police was to establish whether he could really order the Labrador to attack anyone, like Lipika claimed he had. She claimed that being seven months pregnant, Don's attack had threatened her as well as her unborn child's life. So now the police had to set up this situation with the help of a veterinarian from the government hospital at Palam Extension.

'They wanted me to order the dog around – get up, down, attack. Whatever I said, he didn't listen to me. That's because, as one press reporter also noted, Don only reacts to air-conditioning. He barks if it is switched off, and sleeps when it's on.' The Delhi Police looked into the eyes of the Labrador as they 'examined' him for one and a half hours and concluded: 'Keeping in view the opinion and as per advice of the said doctor the request has already been sent to BSF Veterinary Expert for imparting opinion regarding the assessment of the behaviour of the dog. The said opinion is still pending.'

In other words, it was inconclusive. With that done, Somnath Bharti was sent off to judicial custody.

FROM DWARKA LOCKUP TO TIHAR

If there's a jail cliché, it is this. Everyone who's been inside, whether it is the billionaire businessman Subrata Roy who had the ultimate luxury with a special office built inside the jail to conduct his business, to Somnath Bharti, they'll tell you that most of the people who are in jail have no business being there. 'Only 10 per cent of the people inside jails are criminals,' said Subrata Roy, 'rest are just poor, unfortunate souls.' Somnath Bharti, who the police declared as a 'habitual offender' because of his previous record, puts it rather philosophically – 'People are the same, inside and outside. It's not like you have all the freedom outside, do you? You are still limited by what you can do outside. It's similar in jail.'

Into this microcosmic world of 14,000 odd people, Somnath went to Jail Number 4 with all the trappings of a privileged guest. Those who faced charges like him of attempt to murder and cruelty to their spouse make up about 10 per cent of the jail population. However, while most of the others had no idea for how long they'd be locked up, Somnath knew he was going to get bail in a matter of days. 'I actually wanted to do Vipassana while I was there but that is for 10 days and they said you wouldn't probably be here that long.'

The time in jail actually provided him with an opportunity to meet and interact with other inmates, knowing that he didn't really share their ill-fate. Just as Subrata Roy had interviewed many other inmates for his book on the Tihar experience from his comfortable position and safe house-kind of jail, Somnath too profiled 53 inmates who desperately needed legal aid. They weren't living or sleeping in the same quarters though. His roommate was another well-heeled inmate. He was the protocol manager of the slain liquor baron Ponty Chaddha, arrested for his murder. The other inmate, since they never allow two people in a cell but either single or in threes, was another businessman involved in financial fraud. Somnath had wanted a solitary cell to himself, but he soon realized that he was far from slumming it.

'What can I tell you – the cell had everything. There were badminton racquets, books, a television, Complan and other drinks, there was even a cot which the other two would share, while I slept on the floor,' Somnath recalled. The toilet arrangement was similar to the one in the lockup – a wall to go behind with a hole on the floor. The flush would be a bucket of water. While his cellmates also bathed here, Somnath had the option of using the superintendent's toilet since that is where he spent the entire day.

'They were a bit scared about my security because there was a notorious gangster in the same jail. In fact, two men in Tihar had been murdered because of the gangs' infighting. So I had to sit in the office all day.'

The gang-fight Somnath was referring to was the bust up that happened just a few days before he arrived in Tihar. One of the inmates kept in the high-security ward, in isolation, was one of Delhi's biggest extortionist Neeraj Bawana. Bawana looked like any Delhi youth being just 24, but apparently coming to Tihar at 19 had made him one of the most dreaded criminals to look out for. His rivalry was with the Neetu Dabodia gang; and while Neetu was bumped off earlier, his gang members still had a running war with Bawana, whose latest stint in Tihar was since April 2015.

The story as media reported was that the two factions of the gangs were together on the way back from a court hearing. When a fight started, Bawana and his flunkies killed two members of the Dabodia gang, called Paras and Pradeep. 'I learnt that the weapon they used was the blade of an exhaust fan,' as per Somnath's insider information. Whether this was a myth or reality, it ensured that when Bawana and his followers emerged from the high-risk ward for the daily *chakkar* every morning, no one messed with them. 'Suddenly, everyone would go quiet and start whispering.'

Bawana may have been the big baddie but Somnath's own reputation also preceded him. September 2015 was just months after the AAP government had come back to power with an incredible 67 out of 70 assembly seats. And Somnath felt the fan base all around him in Tihar too.

'They kept asking about Arvind. What's he like? What's he

doing? They also wanted to know about the Khirki episode.' The largest proportion of foreign prisoners was Nigerians and maybe it's a good thing they didn't realize that one of the community's tormentors had now arrived in jail. 'There were black people in my jail too but I don't think they understood what I said.'

If there were dodgy characters like Bawana, there were also many infamous characters like S.S. Rathi, the police officer who was serving a life sentence for overseeing a botched up operation that led to the killing of two Delhi businessmen in Connaught Place. It was in 1997 when Rathi as a crime branch ACP had got a tip-off that UP's wanted man Mohammed Yasin was going to be in Delhi. Though all they knew was that he was travelling in a car with a UP registration number. A fatal mix-up and trailing led Rathi and his men to shoot two Delhi businessmen in the middle of a crowded marketplace. 'Do you know he is now doing his PhD after finishing his LLB and LLM?' Somnath expected him to be out in 2 to 3 years but that was all dependent on a larger PIL that the Supreme Court was now deciding on early releases.

The other character that Somnath befriended was the jail *nai* (barber), who had no such expectations of an early release. Serving a jail term for murder as well, his work inside jail was eerily reminiscent of what had landed him there in the first place.

'He apparently found his sister in a compromising position with his friend. His sister told him that she was in love with him but he still found it unacceptable. His friend used to drive a taxi so he went along with him one day, and while the friend was driving he took the blade and spliced his neck.'

In jail, the blade was still there and he'd charge inmates a few rupees for a shave every morning. And it made no one uncomfortable to know his past too. These kinds of strange coincidences are all over prison. One police officer had this story to share from one of his visits to Tihar. 'I went to meet my friend who is posted there and I saw one Nepalese boy bringing our tea and snacks. I was intrigued because he didn't look like the support staff. So I asked who he was. He said he was the domestic help accused of murdering his employers!' It was a particularly brutal case from Vasant Vihar where the help had not just killed the entire family, but had also not spared their adorable pet dog. But despite this horror associated with his work, he was still doing his mundane, lowly job. The police officer said, 'I felt really bad for those boys. They were servants outside, *aur andar bhi bicharo ko wahi karna par raha hai* (they were also forced to do the same job inside jail).'

So people like these poor sods worked, while Somnath caught up with his sleep for the few days he spent there. A politician's job is 24x7, posturing and working the crowds all the time, whether it was during his morning walks at Deer Park, or attending prayer meetings for the dead. But prisoners have no vote, and so Somnath had no one to win over while staying in Tihar, no promises to make to prisoners he met. All he thought about was ACP M and the humiliation he was put through. 'I got angry with the ACP when he asked me about my sexual relations with my wife. I said what the hell do you mean. He was briefed by the central government to embarrass me. Do you know that one day he asked me to take off my clothes? I don't know why but possibly to embarrass me. That was the only low point for me in police custody.' He only spent that one week in jail but is full of conspiracy theories – of the conspiracy to get him arrested for a domestic violence case; of the conspiracy to keep him there through a high level meeting in Sundar Nagar allegedly attended by top BJP leaders and the attorney general and solicitor general; and lastly, the conspiracy to sully his boss Arvind Kejriwal's opinion of him.

The last bit was because during this entire episode, Somnath's party had kept him at an arm's length. When he was on the run, Arvind Kejriwal just made this announcement on twitter: 'Somnath shud surrender. Why is he running away? Why is he so scared of gng to jail? Now he is becoming embarasment for party n his family(1/2).'

It was the only sign that things had changed for Somnath Bharti. The people who wanted their roads or their drains fixed, they didn't care whether he'd beaten his wife or not. In fact, many of them told me that these are matters that should be left between husband and wife. They only cared if he was available to listen to their demands and didn't appear to be corrupt. But Somnath Bharti's own mentor distancing himself, left him feeling abandoned. After being released on bail by the Supreme Court, Somnath headed straight to see his boss and all he'll tell you is that Arvind was very disappointed with him for running away from the law. 'I did what I did because I thought I had the right to seek relief from the top court of the land. So I just avoided the police,' he explains. Then pausing a little, he adds, 'I now think maybe I shouldn't have. Maybe, I should have surrendered right at the beginning.'

Somnath Bharti was released on bail in the first week of October and it was only four months later that the police filed their charge sheet. They were still unable to explain whether Don wilfully attacked Lipika at his command or not. But Somnath says it is something that is not possible. He's now working on his own book titled, *Chakkar, Devri aur Chakki* – about the three different places in jail. It will have the stories of those 53 people he met and spent time with in Tihar. 'After coming out, I met a BJP leader and we were arguing. I told him, "I have lost my wife and kids thanks to this. So now, I have nothing to lose. Nothing. So you guys just worry about yourselves."'

THE GANGRAPE OF A TRANS BAR DANCER IN CUSTODY

'What we learnt from the Bhanwari Devi case is that you never get justice.'

It isn't strange that Kavita Srivastava of the People's Union for Civil Liberties (PUCL) cites the landmark rape case that gave working women in India the Vishaka guidelines to tackle sexual harassment at the workplace, when she refers to Khushi's case. It may be exactly 20 years later, but the 1992 Rajasthan wasn't all that different from its 2012 version. In 1992, Bhanwari Devi was gangraped in Bhateri village outside Jaipur because she dared to stop a child marriage. In 2012, about 200 kilometres away from Bhateri in Ajmer, 24-year-old Khushi Sheikh was gangraped by three policemen inside a police station. The only difference is that Bhanwari's attackers were acquitted after a long drawn-out trial, however reluctantly conducted. Khushi's case never reached that stage, it never even got a judge, never got the dignity of a trial – because she is a transgender. She was raped in a police station and the police won't even file a charge sheet till the victim agrees to undergo a lie-detector test. Yes, you read that right. Her medical test may have confirmed signs of rape, but apparently that isn't good enough if you are a *hijra*. And there lies the story of Khushi and the Indian trans community. A jail story from hell.

IIII

The thing that you can't miss about Khushi is how beautiful she is. From her friends to the activists who are fighting for her, that's what they first tell you when they describe Khushi – she's stunning. In fact, she looks a lot like Aishwarya Rai, from the colour of her eyes to her slim figure. That's what made her a famous bar dancer who is proud to strut her stuff. And that's what her friends feared made her most vulnerable. 'She is very beautiful, glamorous, in fact. Basically, the cops wanted an excuse to get her into a *thana* and rape her,' Khushi's friend told me, adding, 'we never let her go alone for any hearing.'

The irony is that Khushi wasn't alone even in June 2012 when she was attacked. She and her group of *chelas* or entourage of *kinnars* or *hijras* had made elaborate plans to visit the famous dargah of Moinuddin Chisti at Ajmer. Khushi flew down from Mumbai with two associates while five of her *chelas* came by train as they had a lot of luggage. They were arriving just when the festival of Urs was beginning at the dargah, the week-long celebration of the anniversary of the Sufi saint.

As Khushi met her *chelas* after her taxi ride from the Jaipur airport, she had no idea that she would not get to see the inside of the dargah this time. All she wanted to do was offer a *chadar* at the dargah with some of her closest associates. In the *kinnar* society, she explained to me, there is a guru–*shishya* system. Everyone has a guru who is like a mother figure. And then they in turn adopt *chelas* who they mentor. For instance, Khushi's guru runs a 25-year-old social organization for *kinnars* which has several branches all over India. She helps the poor and orphans, assisting them in sorting out means for earning a living. The Karnataka PUCL report explains the system like this: 'Most hijras in India live in groups that are organized into seven houses ("gharanas") situated mainly in Hyderabad, Pune, and Bombay. Each house is headed by a "nayak" who appoints gurus, spiritual leaders who train their wards ("chelas") in "badhai" (dancing, singing, and blessing), and protect them within and outside the community. It is a system that replicates matriarchy, creating interdependence between the ageing guru and the "chela", who has been cast out of her family. Disputes among hijras are decided within the community by the "nayak" and senior gurus acting as law makers, and administering punishment such as imposing fines and expulsion from the community.' (Human Rights violations against the transgender community 2003)

Khushi wasn't an ageing guru, neither had she been cast out by her biological family. The transgender community is full of stories of abandonment by parents, of beatings or confinement, as parents or siblings realize that the trans person isn't conforming to their ideas of sexual norms. But Khushi who was born as an intersex – that is without typical male or female genitalia – defied these trends. She still lived with her mother and sister, and worked the night shift at a dance bar in Mumbra.

'My mother brought me up as a boy, but I was like a girl otherwise with all my mannerisms. I studied till class XII in a school in Ghatkopar. In school, everyone knew I was a little effeminate and I was ragged but I faced all that. I would listen to it but not be bothered about it.'

The struggle was compounded by their economic status. Her father was a driver and earned 5,000 rupees, which was never enough; being different in a lower-middle-class family makes life even more difficult. But from the beginning Khushi found an outlet in dancing. There were no lessons but just as some trans persons opt for sex-work as a viable option for sexual autonomy and financial independence, Khushi discovered that in dancing.

'I started going to shows and dancing for boys. My father was away in Riyadh and many people wouldn't talk to us. But slowly, as word spread, even those who never spoke to my mum said that I was very beautiful. Now in Mumbra, I am quite a celebrity because I am a famous dancer – that I am such a beautiful *kinnar*.'

In 2010, Khushi was doing well enough to pay for a vaginoplasty surgery that cost her five lakh rupees. There were complications and Khushi says it was totally botched up by the doctors and needed a second operation and she was confined to bed for months. 'My guru and the *kinnar samajik sanstha* helped me a lot. They filed a case against the doctors and fought because the hospital wasn't admitting me as the case was so very complicated. The doctors were basically doing whatever they wanted to – cutting up my stomach when they didn't have to.' This is also a classic example of abuse by medical practitioners who are negligent while dealing with transgenders who would like to get transition surgery. Vaginoplasty or sexual reassignment surgery isn't done in most government hospitals, and so those who can't afford to pay about 15 lakh rupees or more, end up going to quacks.

But despite all these struggles, by the time her father died in 2012, Khushi had achieved what is impossible for many trans women. She was a successful professional and breadwinner for her family. She also managed to retain her biological family and become a mentor to others in the *kinnar* community.

However, it was in June 2012 when Khushi's *chelas* would witness the most gruesome episode of her life. It all started harmlessly enough on the morning of 4 June. The group was near Delhi Gate in Ajmer when the police stopped their auto, telling them that vehicles weren't allowed further. The constable, who the FIR names as Bhawani Singh, said they could take the auto if they paid him 50 rupees. It is hard to say if they had paid this cash as bribe Bhawani Singh would have gone his way, continuing in his path of petty corruption. As it happened, they argued and slowly Bhawani's insults became worse.

'*Tu kahan se aayi hai, kinnar hai ki ladki hai?* (Where have you come from? Are you a girl or a trans?),' he wanted to know.

The auto-rickshaw driver, the *chelas*, the police, all got involved and suddenly Bhawani Singh started trash-talking. Khushi mentions that it is believed that *kinnars* or *hijras* are only good for entertaining. But it was when Bhawani's language progressed to wandering hands, her *chelas* got enraged.

'*Tu ladki asli hai ya nakli,*' Bhawani Singh said, and reached out and touched Khushi's breast. A physical fight started with Khushi's *chelas* and the police personnel. The PUCL report of the incident quoted onlookers, who said, 'Khushi's group got aggressive and beat up the police constable badly and hurled abuses at them and they were rescued by the nearby shopkeepers and all eight were taken away to the Dargah police station.'

Out of all her *chelas*, Zoya was the loudest and was fighting the most. Khushi said she had to intervene to make them stop arguing and agree to move it to the police station, but that turned out to be a wrong decision. 'As soon as we went in, they started beating us.' And here's where the law or lack of its coverage for transgenders plays a part. According to the Code of Criminal Procedure (CrPc), you have to have women personnel present in order to handle a woman inmate. Khushi and her *chelas* identified with women, but their *hijra* status meant that they didn't have that protection under law.

'The male policemen started hitting us all. Zoya wanted to save me, so they hit her a lot.' The physical abuse was just one part of it. The case hadn't even been registered and processed yet, and all of them were paraded in front of the media. 'The police said that these people hit them. So everybody accepted it and no one was willing to listen to any of us.'

It was a day of abuse and humiliation. The arrest meant they had to surrender all that they had – 87,000 rupees in cash and jewellery. They were also treating them like slaves. The FIR notes Khushi as saying, 'Some touched my cheeks, some touched my hair and some waist. If I spoke, I was beaten.' At one point, one constable apparently told them, 'Walk the ramp and show us.' It was as if the bored men in khaki had got some comic relief with their arrest.

When they were bored of these games, they moved to more dangerous ones. At 11.30 p.m., they were summoned one by one. 'They hit you, so you hit them with *chakki ke atta ka patta*,' she heard one telling the others. It was an individual beating session. When Khushi went in, she saw Bhawani Singh and Vijay Singh Chaudhary and she started talking in English to explain what had happened. She thought if only she could convey to them that she was educated, she would be able to defuse the situation. But that didn't work. They beat her even more so. At midnight, Sub-inspector Lakshmi Narayan Singh left her, warning that he would be back later in the night.

At 3 in the morning, Khushi was woken up by Bhawani Singh, who was now in his civvies, and Lakshmi Narayan Singh. After only serving them beatings and abuse all day, they promised her *paratha* and *jalebi*. They dragged her by the arm to another room, isolating her from her *chelas*. Apparently, then Bhawani Singh said to her, 'I asked you *ki asli ya nakli hai, abhi khol ke bata* (I asked you whether they were real or fake. Now take off your clothes and show me).'

'First Lakshmi Narayan forcibly removed my clothes and then all three of them removed their clothes too, and then they raped me one after the other,' records the PUCL report. The three policemen put their legs on Khushi's legs so that she wouldn't move. All she could do was cry and scream.

In her 164 statement recorded in front of a magistrate, Khushi said, 'One more constable was present there who had a white mobile in his hand. I don't know the name of this constable but I will identify him when he'll come in front of me.' This constable shot Khushi's ordeal on his mobile phone and when Khushi screamed for help, a woman constable came running. She was shooed away with, '*Aapka yahan koi kaam nahi aur aap yahan se baahar jaiye* (You have no business being here so get out).' Constable Sarita did leave but she also raised an alarm with the others. Soon, Zoya rushed into the room to rescue her guru.

'A lady constable came there and she saw me in that condition, there were no clothes on my body and she also saw these police constables were in their undergarments. The constable who had a white colour Samsung [phone] shot my video in that condition. This lady constable narrated the whole incident to my friend Zoya. When Zoya came she saw me in the same position. All of them started beating Zoya mercilessly.' (Statement under 164 CrPc)

If the rape and the beating wasn't enough, both Khushi and

Zoya were threatened with fake cases of narcotics possession. By early morning, they were made to sit in the *murga* position (with their heads between their legs) and asked to say that they were the ones who made a mistake, it was all their fault. Khushi said what she had to, but when the SHO came in that morning, she immediately reported the rape. However, if she was expecting some kind of reaction, there was none. The SHO said he knew everything and in fact, Khushi discovered that out of the 87,000 cash that was deposited, the records showed only 47,000 rupees. The rest had just gone off the books. The magistrate didn't say anything and sent her, the rape victim, to jail.

Now if you go by the PUCL report titled 'Human Rights Violations against Sexual Minorities in India in 2000 and 2003' and another one done by Ondede on the 'Human Rights Violations of Transgenders in 2014', you will know that Khushi's case just follows a pattern. A chance encounter with law enforcers and the lack of any clear law protecting transgenders leads to rampant sexual attacks on them. In the 2014 report, one trans woman called Richa almost has an identical experience as Khushi. When some neighbourhood boys got aggressive and started attacking them for paid sex, it resulted in a huge neighbourhood fight. The police was called, and here's how Richa describes her night at the police station: 'It was a nightmare. Firstly, we had no blankets and it was really cold. Secondly, when we would sleep, the police pricked me with sticks on my breasts and vagina. They asked us if what we had was real and asked if they could touch our breasts. We didn't know what else to do as we just wanted to go out.'

'Are your breasts real or fake?' That was exactly the question which Khushi was asked as well, and if you go through testimonies of trans women in various reports done by human rights organizations, it is a recurring theme. Of course, asking prying questions is the least of indignities they have to face, as sexual attacks like Khushi had encountered are not uncommon at all. It is as if the curiosity about the trans person's body manifests itself into violence and sexual attacks, especially by law enforcers like the police. What made this attack different was that here Khushi refused to accept it.

Soon after she got bail in four days, she went back to senior police officers to report and follow up on her complaint. When she arrived at the Dargah police station, one of the perpetrators threatened her. Khushi's statement to the magistrate read: 'Lakshmi Narayan held my shoulders tightly and said, "Don't you dare tell anyone about the rape, otherwise you remember (sic)." At that very moment my friend who had come from Mumbai scolded Lakhsmi Narayan and asked how dare he held my hand?' They went inside and told senior police officers about the rape and loss of their money. Instead of registering a case and suspending the accused policemen, the police tried to dissuade them. What was the point of saying this? She couldn't keep travelling to Ajmer to follow up on the complaint? When the DSP didn't heed their word, Khushi wrote about the entire incident and took it to his boss, the ASP and finally on 10 June, her FIR was registered, along with a separate FIR about bribery or theft of her money. This second case for the minor offence of theft was the only one which led to some action, and the eventual punishment when station in charge Vijay Singh Chaudhary was transferred.

The only reason that happened was because of the presence of a witness. 'The lady constable had witnessed it all. She vouched for the rupees 87,000 rupees being deposited and so Vijay Singh Chaudhary was suspended.' However, neither the witness's testimony nor the video recording of the rape could get them past the FIR stage of investigation. The forensic report of that mobile is still not out after years, which even by our regular delay yardsticks is something to gasp about. Although, not as shocking as the comments that activists heard when they met various police officers to pursue the case. Here's what they said in defence of not taking the rape allegations seriously: *'Bedaag hain, tabhi to job main hain* (They are unblemished, that's why they still have their job),' – this was the response received when asked why the rapist policemen hadn't been suspended. The other responses were: *'Hamara thana toh itna chota hai ki agar mein apne room mein chhikoon to uski awaaz poore thane mein sunai padti hain* (Our station is so small, even if I sneeze, everyone can hear it). *Aur yahan par market mein itna crowd hota hain ki raatko bhi subaha jaisa mahaul rehta hai* (The market outside is so crowded that even at night, it's like the middle of the day).'

When the activists asked if Khushi was lying, one officer said, 'Eunuchs cannot be raped as they themselves tear their clothes and are always ready to make their bodies available.'

Not everyone was as insensitive though. When days later, Khushi's medical exam was done to look for signs of rape, the doctors were almost reverential towards her.

'When they saw me, they first thought I was a girl. The doctor was a little afraid to touch me because I am a *kinnar*. She said, "Please forgive me as I will have to touch you. My God will be very angry." I had tears in my eyes. I said you'll have to, otherwise how will I be able to report my rape. She said it was the first case of *kinnar* rape that she was examining.'

The doctor's behaviour stemmed from the belief among many Indian communities that *hijras* because of their atypical reproductive organs were linked to divinity, that they had special powers. Khushi was fortunate to experience this not just from the government doctors but also in jail. She says of the guards there: 'When they were checking me, the lady constable kept apologizing. *Kinnars* are called "buaji" by some and she kept saying buaji, please don't give me *baddua* (curse). I don't want to touch you but it is my job.' The jail guards ensured Khushi and her *chelas* were kept in a separate barrack and there wasn't any kind of harassment they experienced in the police custody. But this isn't the typical experience for other transgenders.

The PUCL's 2003 report gives several testimonies of brutal rapes inside the prison system. Here's what 27-year-old Nasir said of his experience in a Karnataka jail in 2002:

That night at around 11 p.m., about twelve men came to me, and one by one they forced me to have anal and oral sex with them until the next morning. Because of this I got a severe back ache and my anus started paining; when I went to the toilet to answer nature's call, I could only see semen coming out of my anus like water from a tap, along with blood. Already I was extremely tired and weak because of the pain and the sleepless night, now I also started feeling scared after this. When I told some of the prisoners about all that had happened to me I was told to keep quiet, they said if I tell this to the police then I as well as the persons involved would be punished severely by the authorities.

The report adds,

Jails are custodial institutions where feminine behaviour by men is always at a greater risk of mistreatment by both authorities and inmates. Jails are closed institutions with a strict segregation based on sex. This ensures that male wards in general are highly masculine spaces with no heterosexual contact. The cult of masculinity promoted by the jail environment necessarily entails a targeting of those considered not "masculine" enough.

Khushi's attack didn't continue in jail but she couldn't get over that night in Ajmer police station. 'Even after two years, I have to go so far for all the proceedings. It is very, very depressing.' They asked for the case to be transferred to Mumbai, but that was rejected. In fact, the police almost reject the entire case. Her medical report notes that she had 'bruises over body, blue bruises on the thigh and vaginal injuries.' While the report also notes her breast implant surgery and vaginoplasty and talks about 'abnormal development', the police said that it proved she was a female and not a transgender. Senior officers told PUCL that 'there was no prima facie evidence found against the rape accused, the clothes which were provided for examination were not found to be torn or in bad condition.'

And so that was it. Two year later, the police charge sheeted SHO Vijay Chaudhary for extortion, but the rape case drags on. 'Due to mounting public opinion against the police, it became clear that the Ajmer police had decided to work on the lesser crime and not take any action against rape in custody, as if it accepts that then the Ajmer police will get a bad name and also action will be taken against all policemen present and also authorities will be made culpable.' (PUCL)

The police want to put Khushi through a lie-detector test, which neither she nor the activists have agreed to. The police are also pursuing a case of assault of policemen and trying to use that as leverage in the rape case. There is a lot of pressure to compromise and reach a settlement.

'My mother had rushed to Ajmer when this happened. I am the only one who takes care of her. She is a kidney transplant patient and it was very difficult to save her life. It was a major struggle for us too. A person can't stay on dialysis for very long. She needed a transplant. We have managed it somehow.'

Indeed, all this did take a toll. Khushi is now undergoing treatment for depression, questioning why she had to go through such extreme brutality. Why, even now, the forensic reports aren't out? 'I kept calling the chief minister to meet me, but she didn't respond or wasn't interested at all. As a woman, she was least interested.'

If there is one thing that keeps her going, it is her dance and her job at a Thane dance bar where she has been working for the last six years.

'In dance bars, we never get harassed. It is a very positive place. People just come for entertainment. There is lots of security around, so no one can harass or do anything to us.' And that's why Khushi's guru has been pushing her to settle the rape case, to get on with her life and as time passes, Khushi feels that she should give in, take back her allegations against all. Travelling back and forth to Ajmer, fearing for her security, have just become too much. The pressure from activists meant it is being probed by the CID but there hasn't been any progress. Kavita of PUCL, who has been fighting for Khushi from the beginning, perhaps understands this. She knows Khushi has already made a statement with the fight she has fought till now. She isn't calling it quits, and. also continues to visit the dargah every time she is in Ajmer.

'I am very proud of the fact I am a *kinnar*. The kind of respect I get as a *kinnar*, I feel very happy. Even women don't get that much respect.'

FROM PURNEA JAIL TO TIHAR

'Is it true, Pappuji, that you started the VIP ward in Tihar? And, that you actually made it very comfortable and also started a gym there?' I asked the five-time member of Parliament (MP) from Bihar a little hesitantly. Most politicians don't really like talking about their time in jail unless it was during the Emergency, which is the only event in which the jail tag is worn with pride. Most MPs would not even like to admit that they created any 'VIP' category or asked for special treatment. But Pappu Yadav isn't like most MPs and the reason he doesn't deny his 15 odd years or more spent going in and out of jail is because that is where he discovered his caste identity, saw his wife for the first time, became gangster Arjun Yadav's protégé and also fought and won elections from Purnea, Bihar. If there's one person who knows how to survive the worst jails of India from Bhagalpur to Beur, it's 50-year-old Rajesh Ranjan, aka Pappu Yadav from the Kosi region of Bihar. Pappu's rather large frame, which at one point weighed 175 kilograms and is now a trimmer 125 only, has even undergone several surgeries in prison. It was only in 2013 that the jail tag finally left Pappu Yadav when he was acquitted by the Patna High Court for the murder of Communist Party of India's (Marxist) Ajit Sarkar. However, he was soon on the brink of going back in 2015 while flouting a bandh in Bihar.

'Yes, it is true,' he replies to my query as if it was the most normal thing in the world, as if I'd asked him if he'd helped poor people or not, whether he'd spent some money from his MP funds, as if it was the daftest thing to ask. He didn't elaborate but the answer writ large on his face was: 'Don't you think I will try to make the place where I was sentenced to spend my entire life comfortable?'

We meet at the lawns of his MP bungalow early mornings for our interviews. Ever since he was acquitted by the Patna High Court, Pappu Yadav had carefully cultivated a different kind of image. 'If you Google me, you will no longer read that I am a *bahubali*, or a don.' This was true. Among the things that he'd hit the headlines for were more cerebral issues, many outside Bihar. Like the Kashmir issue, or dalit atrocities and there were several mentions of his perfect attendance and enthusiasm for participating in parliamentary debates. In fact, his interests were bordering on cerebral even though he was a man who had completed his entire education in jails. He took his class XII or inter exams while he in was in Bhagalpur Jail, did his master's from Beur Jail, and then later during his days in Tihar Jail, he got himself an additional degree in Disaster Management and Human Rights from the National Open University (IGNOU). In his writings, Pappu remembers a jailor in Hazaribagh Jail who had maintained an excellent library where he had read about the Irish Revolution that inspired Bhagat Singh. Also, it was here that he became acquainted with the works of Mahashweta Devi, especially *Jungle ke Davedar*, a novel on the atrocities committed on Santhal tribes by the landowners/ zamindars in late eighteenth century.

Every morning, I'd find the former history sheeter for crimes as wide ranging as murder, illegal possession of arms, and kidnapping, sitting with his reading glasses (which had a furry holder), carefully going through all newspapers, and getting feedback on the phone from his aides on the ground. He'd be in track pants and a T-shirt and wearing either Crocs or some trendy trainers.

Sometimes I'd find him surveying barracks behind his bungalow at the Balwant Rai Mehta Lane in Lutyens' Delhi. He lives in number 7 allotted to his wife and Congress MP Ranjeet Ranjan. And their offices are at number 11, where the barracks house all those who come to Delhi for medical treatment from their constituencies of Madhepura and Supaul in Bihar. '*Kya babua, hum dikha dein kaise saaf karte hain?* (Shall I show you how to clean?)', he tells off the cleaner by trying to wrest the broom from his hand. People are housed in small makeshift rooms and a courtyard outside. Some families that accompany the sick are given these rooms while others are in more communal wards and Pappu looks out for any sign that takes away the sheen from his bungalow. There are some rows of toilets that are part of the barracks and also a large area that serves as a community kitchen, although those with individual rooms do their own cooking. '*Kya bana rahe ho?* (What are you cooking?)', he'll ask the cook, who promises to send him some *bhaaji* (vegetable dish) for his approval later. Pappu Yadav tells me that they cook for 200 odd people every day in that kitchen, and as he passes each of his temporary guests pop out with their hands folded to show their gratitude. Yadav has created what may be illegal construction to give shelter to those who would have been sleeping on the pavement outside AIIMS, waiting for days, sometimes weeks, for crucial doctors' appointments. When the caretaker tells him that ten people arrived the night before, he asks, 'Where did you adjust them?' The caretaker said he arranged some space to sleep for four of them but the others had to sit around.

'*Kya karein*, madam,' he said to me, 'can I turn them away?' It's perhaps actions like these that have earned him the tag of Robin Hood and ensures that he keeps winning poll after poll. When he called the Indian Medical Association (IMA) Indian Murderers Association, doctors from Bihar threatened to go on strike, but his constituents loved him because he was demanding an end to the exorbitant fees that doctors charge. And the doctors in his own area of Madhepura live in fear of what he'll do to them if someone complained they'd charged them unreasonably!

Even when he was in Delhi, where his son was at Hindu College playing Ranji Trophy for the state and his daughter studying at Delhi Public School, help-seekers would all turn up, asking for Pappu's help for admissions or job interviews, and he'd always oblige with *pairavi*. *Pairavi* or lobbying for your work to be done isn't just a word in Bihar, it's actually a guiding principle or a way of life. As his aides would bring in requests on slips of paper, he'd sometimes make these calls in front of me. '*Ji, main Pappu Yadav bol raha hoon*,' he'd start. 'There is a boy who's been selected in the exam and he's appearing for the interview. Yes, yes, he's of your caste. I'm just whatsapping you the details.' Not sure whether the strategy actually worked or not, but the supplicant definitely felt better when Pappu made the calls. Apparently, these calls never stopped even when he was in jail. According to a report filed by the Press Trust of India, in December 2004, Pappu used his sister's mobile in Patna Jail to make almost 22 calls every day, which amounts to more than 600 calls in a month. The news agency said that the call detail records showed that Pappu had had long conversations in jail with various ministers, including the one responsible for jails, the irrigation minister and the one responsible for power. And of course, there were calls to his wife Ranjeet Ranjan too. Obviously jail officials were helpless in stopping him from making these calls because instead of cracking down, they told the Supreme Court that they were going to install signal jammers in Beur and other jails.

Of all the jail stories from when Pappu Yadav first went inside Purnea Jail as a 17-year-old to when he was finally released at the age of 46 from Tihar, the most interesting one is how he met his wife Ranjeet. A former national-level tennis player, the two are quite a romantic pair. In the midst of our interview, he'd sometimes suggest, 'Madam, *aaj coffee peene ka man kar raha hai*. Will you come along?' If I'd agree, he'd ask me to follow him to Khan Market to their regular hangout of Gloria Jean coffee shop where Ranjeet would meet us after her morning walk in Lodhi Gardens. They'd have omelettes, grilled vegetables and muesli for breakfast and then leave on their individual Harley Davidson bikes – carefully guarded by the Khan Market parking boys, who would also dish the latest gossip like which woman the eligible political heir was now bringing with him for coffee. 'They're all from Bihar so they tell us everything,' chuckles Ranjeet. Followed by their personal security officers, as Pappu had Y-category security, the two looked an unlikely pair – he overweight by many, many kilos and she, tall and physically fit – both riding together into Lutyens' Delhi.

ROMANCE FROM BEHIND BARS

As Pappu recounts in his memoir *Drohkaal ka Paathik*, which literally can be translated to 'one who walked the path of rebellion', it was in Bankipur Jail in 1992 when he first saw a photograph of Ranjeet. The story reveals as much about their relationship as it does about the flexibility of rules in jails. At the time, Pappu was particularly upset because the National Security Act was enforced on him yet again, which meant that he could no longer be in the comfort of Patna Medical College Hospital, which Rabri Devi would give him the benefit of, but had to stay in jail.

In this despondent state, he would apparently keep staring out of the jail superintendent's office every day and what brought him relative comfort was to look at the kids playing outside the jailor's window. It went without saying that he had access to the superintendent's office as he was a VIP prisoner. To add to that, Pappu also recounts how he befriended the children outside by ordering *jalebis* and *samosas* for all. 'So you're very honest in your writing about the facilities you had,' I asked him, 'that you were able to order snacks even in jail?'

'Oh, that! We would do that whenever we wanted.'

As the story goes, one of the young boys playing outside, Vicky, became particularly friendly with Pappu and once brought some family photos to show him. That's where he spotted a girl in a 'green polka-dotted dress'. She was Vicky's sister, Ranjeet. And that was the moment his life changed for good. As Pappu remembers: 'In jail, I was privileged but with conditions.' This meant that he could use the superintendent's phone which was unthinkable for anybody else. The only condition being that he couldn't call anybody between 11 a.m. to 2 p.m. as this was the time when the superintendent himself would be in his office. So, over the course of the next three and a half months, Pappu apparently used the phone to first make blank calls and then finally started talking about the weather and other inane things with Ranjeet. When he got bail, the then MLA followed her around till the object of his affection finally reciprocated in a mutual manner, although she's quite aware that they make an odd pair. 'When I first saw him, his picture had come in the newspapers – some story about his arrest,' giggles Ranjeet now. 'I remembered saying, *Kitna mota hai* (How fat is he!). How was I to know that I'd end up marrying him!'

The story may be amusing to others but Pappu isn't amused at all. He gets upset when I ask Ranjeet how she, as an upcoming tennis player, could be attracted to someone who had already gained notoriety. He also wasn't happy when I asked why his daughter never visited him in jail along with Ranjeet even though he was sentenced to life imprisonment. Jail was where he grew up and flourished but it was still not the place to take children to visit their imprisoned father, however long he was away from them, and so many years after emerging from imprisonment, Pappu still gets agitated talking about it.

'*Mulakat* or meeting time is the most hellish thing.' In Tihar Jail, Pappu says, it all depends on how much money you have. If you pay 500 rupees, then you may get some uninterrupted time. Else it was everyone all together shouting over each other to be heard across the iron mesh that would serve as a partition between the prisoner and their visitors. Children, unable to meet their fathers in custody, would often start crying, making the atmosphere even more desperate. 'They start hustling you even before you have started speaking to your families.' In Purnea, when he was far less influential than he was in Tihar, Pappu recalls how there were just two windows for all the visitors who had come to meet the inmates. Two windows for hundred or more people! 'In that small place, people would try to exchange food, they'd try to talk, they'd try to exchange crucial information – can you imagine what that's like? The same hand would search everyone, the same hand would receive the food, and the same hand would give the food.'

There were other tortures too during *mulakat*. Most prisons in India don't allow families who have come to meet to hand over cash. However, they are allowed to give money only in the form of coupons which can then be used to buy food at the canteen or toiletries like soap and other essentials. But how do you bribe officials if you don't have cash? So many would try to sneak it in and the convicts acting as guards or regular guards were aware of it. So, they'd search inmates soon after the *mulakat* to retrieve this cash and take a cut from it.

'*Pag pag paisa aur sharir, jail mein bikta hain* (At every step you have to offer, it is either money or your body up for grabs).' Everything in jail is for sale, even your body. Even if you want to use a working toilet, you have to pay. That's the only way to survive.'

There was no dearth of money for Pappu but he still insists that the prison system in India is like death, only designed to subject pain and not to reform inmates. An idea, he insists, that has only maintained the worst of the British criminal justice system. 'When I write my book "Jail Yatra" it will rock the world,' he says, declaring, 'the law is the illegitimate mistress (*rakhail*) of the powerful.' Pappu uses very dramatic phrases but in a way, he's not too far from the truth. The Death Penalty India Report of the National Law School, (that came out in May 2016,) cites how families that come from other towns spend nights outside prisons and have to offer bribes up to 1,000 rupees just to have a meaningful conversation during *mulakat*. As most of the inmates are from poorer backgrounds, many families don't bother to visit, leaving the prisoner even more desolate. The report cites a case of a young man who was serving life sentence for raping a minor.

He remembered his mother visiting him in the initial years but hadn't had any visitor for the last eight years. The authors of the report tried to track his family down but found no one living anymore at the address he gave. He was truly forgotten by the outside world.

Pappu Yadav's experience, though was not that tragic, but his story of going to jail for the first time as a 17-year old is poignant nonetheless. It was 1984 and till then he and his friends' escapades were limited to targeting the local cinema, Chitramani hall, which would play adult or 'blue films'. 'My friends Anand, Munna and Prakash and I would carry out demonstrations on various issues. For example, we'd say – "English *mitao*, Maithili *lao*" or "English *mitao*, Bhasha *lao*" (Get rid of English, Bring in Maithili; Get rid of English, Bring in the Vernacular). When they saw that the morning show at the local cinema was getting quite a draw, they decided that it needed prompt action, so they went there with banners and posters against such 'immoral' movies, also lighting explosives, leaving the cinema to burn down.

'We went in there and lit a long string leading to some local explosives we had assembled,' he said. They quickly left the hall to make sure they were not caught but when they came back the next morning, it turned out that the bomb had proved to be a total flop! 'We came back and asked, did anything happen here? Any explosion? But there was no explosion or any destruction.'

Though it wasn't this *krantikari* Pappu with revolutionary ideas who landed in jail. What actually happened was that they went to the Ginny Cloth Shop in Purnea because one of them wanted to buy material for a pair of trousers. Pappu claims that they were only going through the various options but the salesman accused them of ruffling his wares. The owner of the shop was upset and apparently he insulted them by saying they had no money and should leave immediately. Pappu says that was provocation enough for them to start beating him and that's when the police was called. Pappu and his friends were taken to the Khajanchihat Police Station and locked up and beaten. They only stopped when he told them he was a school student.

In 1984, states were governed by state juvenile laws and the Bihar Children Act of 1982 preceded the Parliament's Juvenile Justice Act of 1986 that would apply across the country. According to the Children's Act that was enforced at that time, a 'child' meant a boy below 16 and a girl below 18. That's why Pappu Yadav was taken to the local district jail. He remembers how in the van that took him to jail, he hid his face between his knees and contemplated suicide just thinking about the shame that it would bring to his family. His family belonged to the Anand Margi sect, and Pappu says that before this incident, his family had planned to send him away to the US for further studies.

As Pappu entered jail for the first time, he was apparently still in his school uniform, and seeing a young boy the other inmates descended on him asking all kinds of questions. One particular question would define him, not just during his first jail stay but throughout his life. When he told them his name was 'Rajesh Ranjan', they immediately wanted to know what caste that was. His jail papers said 'alias Pappu Yadav' and the word of a new Yadav boy's arrival reached the local *dada* or goon, Arjun Yadav.

'When you arrive in jail from a good family, you are asked your caste. In Delhi jail, there is a Jatav gang or a Jat or Gujjar gang,' explains Pappu. And in Purnea Jail, the crying young man was ushered towards his caste identity. The alternative to being a gangster like Arjun Yadav's boy was to be left at the mercy of everybody.

'I became a "paniya", which literally means the water boy.' Fetching water for the other inmates is the least of the dirty work inmates are made to do. Some are given the task to clean the toilet commode by wading into the shit with a piece of brick, and that's not all. 'Young, beautiful boys become wives in jail. And if a big *dada* takes a fancy to you that means you won't be touched by anyone else.'

The rest, as Pappu witnessed, had to go through initiation rituals that involved sadistic sexual exploitation. Most of the time this wasn't at the hands of prison guards but resident convicts, who in many jails become jail employees, were the worst perpetrators as they had nothing to lose. One of the factors behind their behaviour, he noted, was that they were just acting out the cycle of violence which they'd experienced as inmates themselves. As new prisoners came in, they would be termed 'chikna' or 'gora' or 'londa' or other terms of endearment, and some others would instantly be received with cusses: 'You fair bastard with long sideburns, motherfucker, I'm talking to you,' or, 'This is a jail, you son of a bitch, not your father's *sasural*!' These would then be punctuated for some with kicks and slaps, just to show them their place in the prison hierarchy. They would make all the new ones strip, then they were searched over and over again, touching their genitals till they got off. And this wasn't just once, but repeated at various checkpoints in jail. The only way to escape these perversions, in case the local *dada* didn't fancy you, was to pay your way through. Apparently, there was a flexibility to the amount of bribing – if you were rich, the pay-offs could be a lakh and if you were poor, then even some stolen contraband like tobacco would act as a valuable bribe. And whatever bribe was given would go down the line, from the guard stationed at that particular ward to the jailor in-charge. Those who had no money at all to bribe were the worst of the lot in jail. They were the ones who were left to clean toilets because, according to Pappu, the real cleaners were too busy working for senior jail officials to actually do their work. The undertrials, considered innocent until proven otherwise, were therefore left to do all the hard work.

So you were lucky that Arjun Yadav was there, I asked him. 'Not lucky, Maha-lucky,' Pappu was unequivocal about it. While others were made to sit on their haunches and then picked out for various tasks, Pappu was taken straight to Arjun Yadav's ward where he didn't even have to eat the jail food of uncooked *rotis* and *subzi*. The mafia don would get special food from outside and his entourage, into which Pappu was embraced, got to partake of home-cooked food. And yet, at 17, the idea of being in the midst of all this and the possibility of being attacked were real, and he recalls how he would keep looking for a place to cry, constantly. Even to sleep at night, they had to look for space as the ward would be full, some new entrants would have to spend the night sitting up, because there was literally no space to lie down. Pappu found some space next to the toilet and even now, he recalls how the stench from it pervaded his sleep. The heavy-weight man who is said to be a terror everywhere the Kosi flowed, has no qualms in admitting that he let his tears flow uninterrupted in that stench-filled loo. Everything worried him, potential tormentors in jail, his felony record, and the shame on his parents.

RISE OF THE HISTORY-SHEETER

Pappu was bailed out soon enough but it was certainly the beginning of a new journey for him, and not one where he would be going off to America to study. His release was smooth but he was aware that even when someone's release order was signed, it didn't mean freedom. Even here, there were enough red tape available to hold someone back. If an official didn't like you or you hadn't paid them off, they'd make sure that your release papers disappeared or weren't signed. All of these observations, these experiences, led to instilling rebellion in Pappu, a rebellion which was soon followed by getting expelled from the district school. 'If you've been in jail for even six months, you cannot be reformed,' he explains, although denying that he was 'spoilt' by his jail term. 'I was expelled because I fought with upper-caste boys, that's all.' I asked what his fights were about. 'What *are* school fights about? They said you can't sit here, and I wanted to sit there even though we were Yadavs. They said you can't talk to that girl. We said no, we will talk to that girl. All these fights happened and our principal, who was from upper caste, took it out on us.' The caste awareness may have created a deeper imprint during his first incarceration, because in his assessment 90 per cent of those in jail are backward castes, only 10 are upper castes. The actual data from 2014 prison statistics showed that in case of detention, 38.1 per cent and 43.2 per cent belonged to the OBC and SC/ST categories respectively. While only 18.8 per cent detainees were from general category.

The statistics were less stark for convicts and inmates across the country. In case of undertrials, statistics revealed that 37.4 per cent were from the general category while 31.3 per cent were OBCs and 31.4 per cent SC/STs.

When you read Pappu Yadav's memoirs, what's refreshing is that there is no airbrushing. Writing from a vantage point as an MP, he candidly reveals the dark twists in his journey. Things like how he stole his mother's jewellery to buy weapons and how he actually ran over the superintendent of police's leg because he was in a hurry to get somewhere! By that time he was known as Arjun Yadav's right-hand man, who perhaps taught him at 18 how to run an election campaign, with the mafia don himself in jail and Pappu coordinating things outside. Arjun Yadav's enemies, apparently all caste-based, became Pappu Yadav's enemies too, and there lies a long trail of bloody battles, of assassination attempts and evading the police. Of course, according to Pappu, all the cases against him were part of his agitation against caste-based atrocities but they may not have appeared so to the outside world.

For instance, he decides that Rajputs were the enemies of the Yadavs and part of that fight was to assassinate a local goon called Dalip Singh. So he casually mentions a motorbike chase and how he hurled bombs at Dalip Singh in order to kill him, although he didn't end up dying. Or he talks about another incident where he is forewarned by his informers that his rivals had planned to attack him on a train. Mentally prepared for such an ambush to take place, they decide to go on the offensive, and he with his followers started a fight with who they thought were his supposed attackers. He talks about another instance while fighting for MLA elections. He admits that the charge of mass booth capturing was wrong but admits that he and his men were able to capture 'only 20–30 booths'. 'You can capture booths only in areas where 80 per cent of the people are with you. Then you can tell the rest, look everyone is voting for us so you should also vote for us. But you can't do that in an area where 80 per cent are against you, can you?' he says, putting these figures into perspective. While in some instances Pappu acknowledges his own involvement, in some cases he claims he was totally framed, like his role in the plot to assassinate the Speaker of the Bihar Assembly Shiv Chander Jha. The case led to a hide-and-seek game with the police; Pappu even escaped to Nepal, but eventually he had to surrender at some point.

Antics like this ensured that Pappu Yadav became a regular at most jails, and his reputation started travelling ahead of him. He was moved from one jail to another – Bankipur, Buxar, Bhagalpur, Beur, Hazaribagh – with the assumption that constantly moving him would ensure that he didn't stay long enough to set up a system of comfort. Nevertheless the assumption proved to be wrong, as Pappu recounts how in most of the jails he was given special treatment, so he got by with ease.

A HOSPITAL FOR PAPPU

'*Itne bade VIP hain hum. Khana kisi din canteen ya kahin se banwa lete the* (I am such an important person, I would arrange my meals from either the canteen or somewhere else).'

Sometimes the VIP treatment came from unlikely quarters. The other and more famous Yadav of Bihar, Lalu, is Pappu Yadav's sworn enemy these days. They are an example of the classic frenemies pair that are abundant in Indian politics. Pappu says that whenever Lalu was a little insecure about Pappu's influence, he'd transfer him to another jail. However much of a VIP you are, this is hugely inconvenient for anybody. Moving to some other place meant that he had to start all over again in fixing contacts, officials, guards, in order to ensure a life of reasonable ease even within jail.

While Lalu would transfer on a whim, his wife Rabri Devi, says Pappu, had a soft spot for him. And when she was in the hot seat in Patna, she gave Pappu the biggest gift of all – allowing him to get himself admitted in the Patna Medical College Hospital (PMCH) for treatment. Pappu was thrilled with this development, it felt like an early Diwali.

He explains: 'If you are admitted to a hospital then you have two major flexibility. One, you can meet whoever you want to. And second, you can also eat whatever you want.'

Looking at Pappu Yadav's frame you know that food is a big part of his life. Whether it's breakfast at Gloria Jean's or *bhaji* and *chura* which he has at home, or the food those staying in the barracks in his bungalow send for him, he relishes it all. The deepest cut of the jail experience for him was how prisons are designed to starve. '*Jail ka khana janwar bhi nahi kha pata* (Even animals cannot eat jail food).' He describes in detail how the arbitrary authorities would give two *rotis* to some, four to others and then they wouldn't even be cooked properly. Their raw, dark patches are etched on his mind, haunting him forever. That's why he constantly obsesses about what he feeds to those who are staying with him. 'Ay, you must make sure on festival days you serve *puri* and *kheer*.' In jail, he remembers how everyone had to bribe even if they wanted an extra *roti*. Again, those who couldn't take the hunger anymore, those who didn't have that extra cash to buy coupons that would get them canteen food, would sell their body just for food. 'If you can't fill your belly, if your food has no oil, no taste, then you will get desperate,' says Pappu.

Of course, as cruel as the conditions in jail were, with no non-vegetarian food allowed, the inmates were equally innovative. Some would instruct their families to mix finely pounded mince into a *saag* dish. This would hopefully be delivered to them during their weekly *mulakats* with the families. Others desperate for a high and even a tinge of alcohol would ask them to mix it in curd. Of course, somebody did get caught and that meant *saag* or spinach and curd or yoghurt was banned for all. At least for sometime till a new official came and had other ideas.

So, to escape from arbitrary and wide-ranging rules, the hospital was the best option. Either God was kind and you actually fell ill enough to be recommended to the OPD, or you paid off the doctor who sent you to hospital. Pappu was a special category whose hospital term came from the top office in the state. 'But I did have two genuine surgeries,' he said. 'The only advantage I took was that I stayed much longer than was required.' That was an understatement for sure. When he was serving his jail term for the murder of CPM MLA Ajit Sarkar, the Supreme Court found he had spent 450 days in hospital in four years – that's a year and a quarter in hospital!

'The best is when the doctor writes you have tuberculosis. Then your diet will have to be non-vegetarian too, and you get extra milk.' Hospital stays ensure that you have a grave sounding medical history which you can use to avail other benefits in jail. 'Why do you think when politicians are sent to jail, they land up in hospital first thing?'

Prison doctors can take on a diabolical role inside jails, so much so that people like Pappu Yadav refer to them as 'Ravans'. First of all, they are often the only ones who have regular contact with the outside world as they, unlike the other officials, don't live in the jail complex. So, for a fee they can be couriers. Being doctors, they're also free from stringent frisking.

The other thing that doctors can easily do, according to Pappu, is exploit their legitimate and easy access to drugs. For prisoners desperate for a high or any form of intoxication, the doctors can be facilitators, of course for a suitable fee. In fact, many report that the jail dispensary never seems to be stocked well because the medicines have all been illegally sold to the inmates for a price. Doctors can also help you avoid court hearings by writing you have some condition that doesn't allow travel.

Pappu doesn't admit he spent that much time at AIIMS as he did in PMCH, but he was there when Parliament was attacked in 2001. Being an MP who is lodged in jail is quite an exercise for jail officials. Every morning, while the other inmates were getting ready to slave at their menial duties, Pappu would get ready to leave the jail complex. Accompanied by guards, he'd arrive in Parliament and on that day in December, he headed to Central Hall as proceedings were adjourned.

'As people were screaming and ducking, part of me thought that maybe we'll be better off if these terrorists kill us all.'

That wasn't the only historic moment he experienced first-hand from custody. When the vote of confidence for Manmohan Singh's government over the Nuclear Deal happened in 2008, Pappu and Ranjeet Yadav's votes became crucial.

'I remember at that time BJP leader V.K. Malhotra came to meet his colleague H.S. Balli who was also in Tihar because of his demonstrations against the shifting of illegal units in the Capital. He met me too, and asked us to cooperate with the Opposition.' But the lobbying was on from both sides and Samajwadi Party's Amar Singh met Pappu Yadav to ask him to vote with the UPA. 'He came to meet me in AIIMS. But that wasn't required as my wife was very influenced by Sonia Gandhi and so we decided we would vote for the UPA. All American dalals were moving around Delhi at that time and the going rate of each MP was 40 crore rupees.'

When you ask Pappu Yadav what kept him positive, what kept him going for 15 years in jail, he immediately answers that it was reading and playing sports. 'We would win everything – we played volleyball a lot, and also kabaddi.' An inmate of Jail Number 2, whose team was defeated by Pappu Yadav's team, promises that even in prison games Pappu Yadav used *pairavi*. 'He bought our team members tracksuits. Yes, I think he did some match-fixing which is also why his team won.' I couldn't find the courage to ask Pappu Yadav to confirm or deny that charge.

WAITING FOR JUSTICE AT 70

When the Jawaharlal Nehru University (JNU) Campus became the setting for a nationalism debate in the spring of 2016 after a group of students wanted to mark the anniversary of Afzal Guru's hanging, there was one person watching things very, very carefully, from not too far away in west Delhi. Sixty-nine-year-old Kobad Ghandy, who with his few thousand rupees allowance that every undertrial was allowed, managed to still subscribe to three newspapers in jail – the *Times of India*, the *Indian Express* and the *Hindu*. He scanned the papers every morning during that period for the fallout of what happened that February night in JNU. And what he read – about three students being sent to jail for organizing this event to commemorate Afzal Guru, about the central university being called anti-national, about pro-Pakistan slogans being made – disturbed him. And while so many across the country jumped in on the debate, no one cared for Kobad's thoughts. What they didn't know was that Kobad Ghandy, the man accused of being a member of the banned organization, CPI (Maoist) and arrested in 2009, was perhaps the only one who knew Afzal Guru in his last three years and is also the only one who can describe from inside jail how his hanging took place. (See Kobad Ghandy's letter to the author on page 259.)

'They all kept misrepresenting Afzal Guru,' he told me inside the Cherlapally Jail in Hyderabad, in August 2016. 'There was so much talk about Afzal being anti-national. He was not.' Afzal Guru and he became thick friends from the moment he walked into prison till 9 February 2013 when he was hanged. It's not based on any solid, scientific evidence. It's the impression of one prisoner of his co-prisoner in a high-risk ward. One was branded a Maoist ideologue, the other a convicted terrorist who plotted the 2001 Parliament attack. But why was Afzal Guru not an anti-national according to Kobad? One of the main reasons Kobad cites is Afzal's knowledge and love for the thirteenth-century poet and Sufi mystic Rumi. 'Afzal had all six volumes of Rumi's works.' And over the course of their three-year association, Afzal Guru seems to have transferred this love to Kobad Ghandy. When they'd have their morning tea and slices of bread together, Afzal would familiarize him with verses from Rumi. No wonder Kobad quotes Rumi in a letter to his Doon School batchmate of 1963, Gautam Vohra, written just a month after the hanging:

> Those loves that are only the pallor of the face, Are not
> love at all,
> But only in the end disgrace,
> For like the peacock's plumage,
> And like the finery of many a king,
> The outer allay of beauty
> Became the inner enemy of ugliness.

It's extraordinary that the man who was hanged to 'satisfy the collective conscience of the nation' influenced his neighbour in jail to such an extent – he left a legacy not of violence, or of hate speech, but of poetry that is serene and beautiful. Even though they were surrounded by criminals, even though Afzal Guru was destined to die, and Kobad faced more than 14 cases of the deadly Unlawful Activities Prevention Act (UAPA) across the country, which meant at 69 there was no guarantee that he would ever live to be a free man, the two would sit in Tihar Jail and talk about mystical verses. Often Afzal would read and speak about Rumi and Iqbal, and Kobad would take notes.

Of course, Kobad makes a distinction between Afzal and the other Islamists in jail, who he couldn't have a proper conversation with. He clearly remembers how 9 February in the year 2013 unfolded. From the moment they took him out at 6 a.m., the other Kashmiris started shouting slogans against the hanging. They were all locked in their cells but the protests became so loud that the law officer had to come to calm them. 'He explained that they were only following orders.' The older man remembers how Afzal had no idea when he left his cell that he would never come back again – thinking it was a regular search; he apparently said: 'Will come back after namaz.' It was only when he realized that he was the only one being taken out of the cell, the real reason dawned upon him.

'The jail staff was very impressed with Afzal, he was not at all nervous.' This was also corroborated by the then Director General of Tihar, B.K. Gupta. He doesn't like to publicize it much but says he was saddened at Afzal's hanging. His force, however, wasn't able to work out all the arrangements. For instance, they couldn't manage to find a hangman and so it was one of the jail staff members who had to work the gallows. Law officer Sunil Gupta who was in charge of the execution recalled Afzal telling him: 'I'm getting compassion from your eyes.' When Gupta apologized for what he was about to do, Afzal apparently told him, 'People call me a terrorist but I am an activist, fighting for the marginalized. My fight is against the system. I have no regrets'. There was one last request Afzal had for Gupta – that death should come swiftly. 'I assured him there wouldn't be any pain,' Gupta said to me, later. As they pulled the lever that took away the ground he stood on and jerked him to death, Sunil Gupta remained in front of Afzal as he had requested him to. Afterwards, the prison authorities did everything they could to erase all traces of him. As Kobad said: 'My milk jug which he had borrowed was in his cell, but they refused to give it back to me. There were some whose books were with him, they refused to return those too. We all wanted to get his diary which we knew he maintained, but nothing was allowed and they destroyed it all.' Nothing remained except memories and a love for Rumi.

THE ARREST & ACQUITTAL

Just as poetry and reading made Afzal Guru stand out for Kobad Ghandy, the same literary qualities made Kobad stand out amongst other prisoners. Born in a well-off Parsi family in Mumbai with a sprawling, sea-facing flat in Worli, this Doon School and St Xavier's graduate and chartered accountant from London, now spends his time in Cherlapally Jail and before that Tihar Jail, reading books and studying psychology. Take a look at this note he sent to his friend Gautam Vohra, to whom he would write at least once a week:

> Gorky wrote of Chekov in the foreword: No one even understood life's trifles so clearly and intuitively as Chekov did, never before has a writer been able to hold up to human beings such a ruthlessly truthful picture of all that

was shameful and pitiable in the dingy chaos of middle-class life.

Of course, he wrote at the end of the nineteenth century and early twentieth century when there was much turmoil in Russia. The last two decades of ultra consumerism seems to have killed the sensitivities of the earlier period, but now I think a new sensitivity will grow as a backlash to the tremendous alienation that this culture creates... Jail life is tough, but it has also given me an opportunity to reflect (and read) in spheres I never got an opportunity to do outside. (2010)

Yes, there is no doubt that Kobad came from privilege and fine education. But steeped in the Left ideology and way of life, he didn't have the wealth that would have bought him comforts in Tihar Jail and so his story of incarceration becomes one of an ageing man struggling with his disintegrating body to cope with challenges of confinement. There are files, and more files, and reams of papers, filled with his small, neat handwriting, sometimes written in A4, sometimes in a schoolboy's notebook, begging for his medicines or describing his condition. He has to write application after application asking for his medicines for kidney ailments, for skin infections, for his irritable bowel syndrome. He documents his experiences in letters he writes to friends like Gautam Vohra and also his lawyer Ravindranath Balla in Hyderabad. They are perhaps the most exhaustive and poignant documentation of a life in jail.

But first, how did the genteel son of a finance director at Glaxo end up in custody? In his own words, Kobad's ideology first developed when he was studying in London. Writing in February 2011, Kobad explains: 'It was in UK that I began to think socially, seeing the racism there towards Indians. The period I was there – 1968 to 1972 – was one of great worldwide ferment and it was some Marxist groups that were fighting racism. By then Naxalbari had taken place and I thought serving the country meant participating in this.'

He came back to India and met his wife Anuradha Shanbag, who was doing her bachelor's at Elphinstone College at the time. It was their work in the slums of Mumbai that brought them together. Together they saw the tumultuous years of the Emergency and when it lifted, they got married. It was during her stint in Jharkhand, educating the tribals against oppression of women in their society, when she contracted cerebral malaria. Anuradha died of the disease just before Kobad was arrested in 2009.

'This was the time we also joined the then People's War Group (PWG) and shifted to Nagpur. Anuradha took up professorship in Nagpur University and I worked as a journalist with *Hitavada*. We continued our work amongst the poor and lived in a Dalit basti. But in 1987, we split from the PWG due to differences in our ideology. Since then, I have been working in Nagpur and Mumbai amongst workers and slum dwellers. But I remained a sympathizer of the movement, helping them out by writing economic and social articles/books for their publication. And through these years I also kept in touch with Maoist and other Marxist parties abroad. But the Andhra Pradesh Police, to gain credit, has blown things up in media.'

'Blown up' may be an understatement. Despite dealing with a senior citizen, on 16 September 2009, the Andhra Pradesh Police picked him up from Bhikaji Cama Place in Delhi, dragged him into a Sumo; blindfolded and drove him around the city for eight hours before keeping him on the outskirts of the city for three days for interrogation. After that they handed him over to the Delhi Police. Later, they filed 12 other cases against him, in areas where Kobad claims he's never been to. It wasn't just the Andhra Pradesh Police, but after his arrest, police from states like Punjab and West Bengal also registered cases against him for being a Maoist. It was as if state police forces were just waiting for a high-profile 'Maoist' to be caught who they could attach cases too. For instance, a year after this arrest, in 2010, police in Surat charged him with conspiracy for organizing the unorganized sector to 'create disaffection and violence'. At the time he was supposed to be in the Delhi Jail, the state police said he participated in a meeting in December 2009 to 'promote violent agitation for demands of adivasis for autonomous council and separate council state.' The charges are outrageous and yet after so many years, while all the co-accused have got bail, Kobad is still treated as a wanted man in this case where the court is waiting for him to appear in person. This time too, the police have charged him with the deadly UAPA but as Kobad points out, it is a little incredulous as in 2010 at the time of its occurrence, he was already in Tihar. Surat isn't the only far-fetched case. There was also one in Patiala in which he was later acquitted.

'In the Punjab case the High Court rejected my bail. This is such an absurd case, I do not know what the lawyers were up to. All the case says is that two people while on a morning stroll at Patiala University saw a person giving a speech on the lawns. They say they recognized the person as me after my arrest. That's all. On the basis of this supposed speech (I have never been to the Patiala University) they have slapped charges against me under the UAPA. That too there was no FIR registered on that date. The precise date is not mentioned – nothing. There is really no case. Still no bail! I have never even seen Patiala University – I told them I had toured the Bhatinda cotton belt for 10 days in 2006 to do a rural study on agrarian relations, debt and studies.' Similarly, he had never heard of a place called Tenugarh and had to ask people where it was once there was a warrant from there against him.

This would have seemed like the obvious denials of an accused but since Kobad Ghandy has been acquitted in the main Delhi case by the trial court in 2016, and also been acquitted by the Patiala court, the police operation stands totally exposed. The police allegation was that he was a politburo member of the banned CPI (Maoist) and looking after their international department. They said, 'There is all likelihood that this underground (wanted) cadre who has wide contacts and extensive network may be conducting recce of targets in Delhi to commit offences.' He was also accused of attending a meeting of Maoists held in Bhimabandu Forest of Bihar in 2007 which resolved to 'create large scale violence throughout India' and 'to conduct multi-raids on police establishments'. His trips to Belgium and Germany in 1996 were used in the charge sheet as evidence for Maoist activities. The police's last charge was that Kobad Ghandy was using a fake name and posing as 'Narsi Patel' to receive treatment from Sitaram Bhartia hospital in Delhi.

As it turns out, this fake name to receive treatment for his prostrate was the only charge which the police was able to prove against him. As Kobad wrote in June 2011 of the time he was produced at the Karimnagar court by the Andhra Police: 'During the day, while I watched TV they wrote a "confession statement" in Telegu, saying I was involved in many actions. Though I denied this the very next day in the court, and also said that I do not know its content not knowing Telugu – they used this "statement" to implicate me in a number of on-going cases.'

The police showed no sympathy for his health, and submitted in court: 'Kobad Ghandy did not cooperate with the IO [investigating officer] and kept on complaining about his ill-health and didn't disclose any material facts about his associates and about the illegal activities of his banned outfit.' The police also didn't like the fact that Kobad didn't agree to undergo narco-analysis – a flawed system that involves pumping chemicals into the brain and which many human rights organizations have found to be a tool abused by the investigating agencies. When his lawyers cited ill-health, they got doctors to say that he was fit for narco so he had to move the High Court, to secure a stay order.

On 10 June 2016, just nine days short of his 69th birthday and after almost eight years in custody, Kobad Ghandy was acquitted of all charges under the UAPA. The court of additional sessions judge Reetesh Singh upheld the defence arguments that CPI (Maoist) was banned only in June 2009 and none of the evidence submitted predated the ban. The judgement also demolishes prosecution witnesses and the evidence saying that they were unable to hold up the police story. 'The above circumstances cast a serious doubts (sic) as to whether any articles at all were recovered... There is difference regarding date and time of recovery between what is stated by way of documentary evidence and testimonies.'

While acknowledging that Kobad Ghandy was using fake IDs, the court said:

> The gap between using fake identities and membership of the said banned organizations cannot be filled on the basis of suspicion... The material relied upon by the prosecution was not at all reliable and admissible to be considered to establish the charges under sections of UAPA. Hence, in absence of any evidence in support of the charges, Kobad Ghandy is acquitted for the charge framed for the offences under UAPA.

While pronouncing the sentence for forgery, the judge said:

> Kobad Ghandy is 68 years of age and has faced trial in this
> case for almost seven years... The offences for which they
> have been convicted have not caused any loss or damage
> to any person or authority... I therefore impose upon him a
> term of imprisonment already undergone by him.

You would think that this perhaps would lead to a final
vindication, and an end to his time in jail, but only half of
that came true. As he celebrated his 69th birthday and the
last few days in Tihar, Kobad Ghandy got ready for the
next round of cases in Vishakhapatnam in Andhra Pradesh,
Mahbubnagar, Belampalli and Adilabad in Telengana, Surat
in Gujarat, Bokaro in Jharkhand and Salboni in West Bengal.
It took seven years for one case to be concluded, so it can be
anybody's guess how long it would take for the others to get
over. Before the year was out, Kobad was also acquitted by
the Patiala Court of being a CPI (Maoist) member but the
other cases were still a long way to go. The Patiala case may
have been the flimsiest, but the judge also finished the entire
trial process in a record 20 days, during which Kobad stayed
in Patiala jail. Writing about these erratic trial durations
ranging from 7 years to 3 weeks, Kobad says:

> If this case in a district could be finished in 20 days in
> an ordinary court, why did the Delhi case have to drag
> on for six years and 9 months!! ... At least I should have
> been given bail. Even that was not the case. Let alone
> that in June 2010 the Lt Governor clamped 268 of CrPC
> on me, which meant that I could not travel out for any
> other cases until the Delhi case got over. This was revoked
> in March 2015, but except for Patiala not a single

production warrant was out. Now that Delhi case is over, all my other cases begin from *scratch*, thereby denying my constitutional right for a speedy trial. This seemed a conscious conspiracy... At the age of 70 with all my health problems, this amounts to nothing but judicial murder. (3 November 2016)

The irony is that Gopal Ansal, who was the same age as Kobad, had been held guilty for causing the death of 59 people, many of them children, in the Uphaar tragedy, but was declared 'too old' to go to jail after having spent less than six months in custody. In February 2017, another bench reversed this but his brother Sushil Ansal was still spared because he was in his late seventies. Another influential accused, DGP SPS Rathore, was convicted of sexual harassment of a teenager who later committed suicide but he too, at 70, was held as too old to go to jail. Kobad wouldn't have been too surprised at these arbitrary decisions. Much before his acquittal, in 2011 he wrote about the unfairness of not getting bail: 'It is true, technically, judges are supposed to be independent. But here in jail, it is common talk (amongst criminals) as to the going rate for bail, parole, etc. Such judges easily buckle under pressures from the government and police. At the trial court it is difficult to find such upright judges.'

'This one' did acquit but it took seven years and Kobad had spent all that time in jail, even trying to mobilize Doon School associates like Kamal Nath and Mani Shankar Aiyar, to get himself a place in the senior citizen's ward.

THE PERILS OF AGEING IN JAIL

When you interview young men who've spent time in jail, they react with revulsion at the conditions in jail. One can only imagine the state of someone who is elderly and has serious health conditions which need constant medication and supervision. Kobad suffered many ailments.

He had a bad knee, slipped disc, arthritis and cervical spondylitis. Lifting heavy objects gave him tremendous pain. And yet, a regular part of jail life is the surprise gift of searches. When certain high-profile prisoners were found using cell phones, suddenly these surprise checks increased. Sometimes conducted daily, it involved the Tamil Nadu Special Police (TSP) coming into your cell while you took all that was dear to you outside and waited for them to ruffle everything together. 'They are geared to harass as they throw everything around.' For Kobad, to take all his things and move them in and out regularly was torturous and he describes it in an application to the High Court later. Kobad asked for help or a 'sewadar' for a payment, which is routine and many other inmates use. But as he asked officially, he was denied. The doctor had recommended Kobad to use hot water 'fomentation' to ease aches. The only thing was that Kobad had no access to hot water in the high-risk ward. The other wards had access but there was no one willing to get it for him and the authorities weren't bothered to help him despite many letters of appeal.

What kept Kobad Ghandy going in jail was reading and writing but that was threatened too. Slowly, his left eye's vision was fading and in his letters to Gautam Vohra over a period, you can sense his frustration.

> Unfortunately, I have to cut down on my main pastime – reading/writing as my left eye is damaged. For three months I have been trying to see the doctor, but for us in high-risk, this also is a difficult process. Finally, got to see him a couple of days back. The doctor said there is damage, but they have no real instruments here, and to be sent to a hospital outside is a long procedure (if at all). So, for now I

have to take 'tear' drops and B12. But I do continue to do minimum reading, though I know it will damage it further. Anyhow… (7 July 2011)

In two other letters sent almost within a month, he shares:

They finally sent me to DDU for my eyes. But it was more a formality (they have an arrangement with the jail). The doctor merely repeated what the jail doctor said without doing any test. I am applying to a proper eye hospital as a cataract operation may be needed. But not sure there will be any response. (5 August 2011)

My eye problem continues. In the last 6 months, the number of my left eye has increased by 2 points. The reason given by doctor in jail is cataract. Sister consulted and said not cataract. Can't read or write. Trying eye exercises shown by someone (not docs) to prevent deterioration. (23 August 2011)

Finally, I got to go to AIIMS for my eye. But that was only after lawyers argued with the jail visiting judge (who refused) and a letter to the DG Prison (who instructed to go). The exact cause of the deterioration I could not understand. I have to go back in six months to check for further deterioration and development of the cataract. But the specs nos. given to me by the jail doctor was wrong so I have once again to change the lens; that they say, may be the cause of the pain. Also, I have taken permission for a switch in the cell so that I can turn off the bright light when I sleep. Here everything takes time and enormous effort. (September 2011)

Now I also have a cataract developing in the left eye and have been told to have an operation by the judge. Trying to make some arrangement, but the problem is all senior staff have recently changed – DG prisons, DIG prisons, jail supers and two medical officers. So, with such changes, there is no continuity of people knowing my health conditions and needs... prefer to do at a private hospital as it involves a sensitive organ (for me the most important). (September 2012)

Rebecca (lawyer) asked for interim bail for a few days and that the cataract operation be done privately. But the judge was not amenable... when all the discussion on the operation was taking place in court, the judge casually asked me which was the doctor I had seen at AIIMS. When I recollected, he smiled and said, "Oh, you are in illustrious company, he did the operation of Manmohan Singh – one Dr Tityal." I am worried about the type of place they put. And the present SMO (medical officer) is a real nasty chap. (16 November 2012)

The problem only gets resolved much later when the Doon School alumni association, rallied together by Gautam Vohra, contributed to pay for Kobad's cataract operation.

Kobad already had a condition of hypertension but what Tihar gifted him was an erratic heartbeat. He documents that he complained of chest pain on two occasions when he wanted to be taken to the jail's emergency room. Apparently, it took five hours to do so.

At the time of his arrest Kobad was getting treated at Sitaram Bhartia Hospital for suspected prostate cancer. And even years later, there had been no relief or diagnosis. Even when I went to meet him in Hyderabad jail, he complained of being restless since the prostate problem kept him awake at night.

Irritable bowel syndrome was another condition that affected Kobad, making him predisposed to bouts of diarrhoea and dysentery. As his lawyers and activists told me, buying mineral water which was a necessity to tackle this condition, ate considerably into the allowance that he was given inside jail. The rules seemed arbitrary. Because the jail officials felt kindly towards him in the first couple of years, they would give him two bottles of mineral water a day. But officials got transferred, and the new people had new rules, and then even when he requested a bottle of boiled water or a good water purifier, it was denied. As always, their excuse was security.

The conditions of Tihar also presented Kobad with a contagious fungal infection of the toes. It got so severe, he had to go to AIIMS for a minor surgery but the problem persisted. As he wrote at one place about the hygiene:

> I have been down with flu, have had to cut down on my yoga and reading. It is all over our ward and spreading from one to the other. While, with the younger people they are able to throw it off in a couple of days, with me it always tends to cling for a long time. Hope to get over with it soon, so that I can return to my reading and writing. The mosquitoes have now increased as the hygiene level in our ward has gone down. But it has gone up where the elites are. But all said and done, things are ok. (18 November 2011)

Kobad reports rotting teeth due to unavailability of proper toothpaste. He had to also extract one tooth which had become totally rotten.

All these conditions, related with health, were heightened by irritants like his vitamins being suddenly stopped. He would get them from his lawyers during their meetings but at some point, the vitamins, too, were considered a security risk. Then there are incidents like what happened on 5 March 2013. Kobad's sister came to visit and, considering the poor diet he was getting in jail, brought with her dry fruits and health foods and vitamins. The TSP confiscated all of this even though the deputy superintendent of the jail had cleared them. Kobad was in fact allowed to have them for the previous three years, but the TSP apparently said that the new DG of Prisons had 'banned' dry fruits. Of course, Kobad couldn't get a response to his question that dry fruits comprised only three of the nineteen items his sister got for him, so what happened to the rest?!

These complaints, pleadings, requests and applications form a thick file full of his woes in prison. Younger, abler men and women somehow find ways to get these amenities via bribes. Though Kobad cited court judgements, jail manuals to fight for it, they didn't work. So he wrote letters to the National Human Rights Commission (NHRC) and applications to the Delhi High Court because his letters to jail authorities went unheard. An excerpt:

1 November 2011

To
The Director General NHRC
Mr Sunil Krishna,
Faridkot House,
Copernicus Marg

Dear Sir,

This is in continuation of a discussion you had held with Dr Gautam Vohra On October 17, 2011 at a national consultation on human rights. The discussion, according to Dr Vohra, had veered around the question whether I should be treated as a political prisoner or like any other petty criminal.

After ruling of Honourable Supreme Court Judgement 4/2/2011, bench of M Katju and GS Mishra which has raised some constitutional points and so it is not a crime to be a member of a banned organisation. If the individual is not linked with any form of violence.

I have merely been charged under sections 10, 13, 18, 20 of UAPA together with section of IPC regarding impersonation. In the entire charge sheet, there is no charge of violence. There is no charge of any criminal activity or criminal intent, which is normally accompanied with charges under UAPA. I have merely been put behind bars for my views and my work amongst the poor, who comprise 80 per cent of our people. Even from within Tihar, I had put forward a model of economic development at a seminar held in Delhi, which was covered by media.

SIR, even under British colonialism, a political prisoner status was granted and that is why Nehru and others could devote their prison time fruitfully and produce such seminal works as *Discovery of India*. I continue my writing on such issues in jail; but such study and writing is exceedingly difficult given the humiliating and difficult conditions in jail. This has been compounded by my old age – 64 and poor health. For example, recently, I had to give up reading/writing due to some degeneration in my left eye. It took me after enormous efforts, 5-6 months to get proper treatment and the right number for my glasses (the prison eye doctor number given was faulty and so did not help).

I am terribly handicapped in this because of the jail conditions in which I am kept, for no fault of the authorities, but a system wherein even individuals like me are treated as petty criminals and not political prisoners.

It is in this background that I write this letter to you, with the hope that the NHRC can intervene on my behalf. Earlier, I had sent you a letter on police methods deployed against me, but that was defacto ignored.

Anyhow, I do hope in this case, you are able to give it some thought, and if possible, initiate some action.

Yours faithfully
Kobad Ghandy s/o Adi Ghandy
Tihar Jail-3, Ward 8, Hari Nagar,
New Delhi-110064

Kobad followed this up with many letters to the Human Rights body. If this one focused on a political prisoners' ward which he would get later in Hyderabad, the others talked about his need to be in a senior citizens' ward and the dangers of being constantly transferred to other jails within Tihar, as that meant setting up the painful process of re-acquaintance yet again. In a handwritten appeal to the High Court sometime after 2014 (the appeal was never filed as his lawyers anticipated that he would be acquitted before it could be filed), Kobad cited various Supreme Court judgements and precedents before summing up saying,

As an aged inmate with numerous health problems I had been provided western toilet (arthritis), single cell, wooden bed, medical diet, etc. But at the time of a transfer, the superintendents refused to sign a request that these facilities be provided in the jail transferred to. These need not be provided and will thereby further affect my health. Also, the medical facilities provided in the earlier jail often takes months before the medical officer in the new jail gets to understand the case and take necessary steps... During transfer the jail authorities do not even provide any assistance and the inmate has to himself carry the bags, etc. Thus, on humanitarian grounds requested that the petitioner be transferred to the senior citizens' ward in Jail 3 or kept in Jail 1 without transfer. Also that in either place, he continues to enjoy the facilities now given – single cell, western toilet, wooden bed, table and chair and medical diet.

When the jail authorities or any other body didn't respond to this, Kobad resorted to hunger strike inside jail in June 2015. His lawyers issued a press release and due to the subsequent media pressure, the director general intervened on the sixth day of his fast. 'Alok Verma is a good man and he assured me that I could go back to Jail number 3 which had the medical facilities.' So after one and a half years of torture, Kobad could finally get some relief.

The NHRC didn't intervene. Eventually, much after he had moved to the more humane Hyderabad jail, he received this response from the Human Rights panel on 31 August 2016:

Superintendent, Prisons, Delhi sent a report stating that Kobad cannot be kept in senior citizen ward of Central Jail No 3 due to security reasons. It is submitted that hot water is provided to prisoners if medical officer recommends for the same and personal sewadar is not provided to prisoners. It is also submitted that Shri Kobad has also sent a letter to DG (Prisons) thanking for transferring him back to Central Jail No 3 which has a hospital having proper medical facilities. Since the grievances of the complainant have been resolved, no further action is called for. Reports are taken on record.

Fortunately, this letter arrived when Kobad had already shifted to Cherlapally Jail, because the fact that he was being even denied hot water may have been too distressing for him and caused more erratic heartbeats.

BLADEBAAZ & THE OTHER JAIL CHARACTERS

If there's one tribe in jail that everyone's scared of, it is a pack of boys called 'Bladebaaz' – a group of slashers that are found in every jail and can strike at any point of time. From Pappu Yadav to an elderly person like Kobad Ghandy, everyone in jail lives in the fear of being attacked by this breed, usually young, petty criminals like pickpockets who slash faces because someone's ordered a hit, and sometimes for no other reason but because they are pissed off. Bladebaaz are often used if two people are warring inside jail.

The charge for setting a bladebaaz on you could cost anything between 5,000 to 10,000 rupees. The cutting usually happens on a court date as that allows the slasher to get access to a blade. And it usually happens on the bus, because that has loopholes of security. 'If we get attacked on the bus, police can't come inside as that is a security threat, and in the melee someone could run off. The protocol is that the bus won't be stopped even if people are fighting inside, till it reaches its destination,' shares a jail insider.

A bladebaaz spree on the bus sometimes results in 25 people being cut at one go. 'A cut on both sides of the face is like trade marking that you've been inside. They come and ask, show me your face. If you give up meekly, then the cut is

smaller. Else they will hold you down and give a bigger cut.'
All this while the police just sits and watches the jungle rules
of jail being played out.

While most VIPs don't encounter them because they are
in VIP wards, segregated from others, people like Suresh
Kalmadi were threatened with a knife during a court
appearance. Apparently, someone had hidden the blade in
their anus before bringing it out to threaten him. Just the
threat was flashed by news channels, while for other inmates,
even stabbings doesn't raise too much of an alarm.

There's also a standard operating procedure about the boy
who does the cutting. If they are disciplined in any way and
put into a punishment ward, the one who ordered the hit or
slashing, to be more precise, takes care of him for at least a
couple of months. The slasher may get paid in cash outside
prison, with the money sent to any person of his choice, but
they also have to be paid in kind. The one doing the bidding
also sends breakfast, lunch and dinner from the canteen for
the slasher boy for 30 days or however long they are in the
punishment ward. Also, what is inevitable is that if you order a
bladebaaz, the person who's been cut will also send a counter
bladebaaz after you. So, there is no escaping this vicious cycle
of violence inside, yet another big worry that plagued Kobad.

In November 2011, he writes:

Life becomes an even bigger hell when "bladebaaz" are
dumped in our ward. Lately, the most notorious one has
come here – we have 4 to 5 of them out of the 30 odd
in the ward. These people who make life hell for others,
slash peoples' face for any petty reason (not giving respect,
money, food – even just like that for publicity). Those are
also the jail mafia who control/run the illegal activities.
These are supposed to be put in a special "Kasuri" ward,

but are regularly put here. Just one month back one of our inmates was stabbed (he had to leave his intestines stitched up) and another had surface stitches. About 6 to 8 months back, two of the most notorious were put here and I just about escaped an attack. Now they are back and vitiate the entire atmosphere. It is difficult to concentrate on anything. Ordinary criminals are bad enough but these are impossible.

Then again, just a couple of months later (January 2012), Kobad writes to Gautam Vohra:

At least if there is a decent atmosphere one could concentrate on yoga, reading and writing. But with this criminal atmosphere one has to be tense about everything as even the hot water, food and any item gets taken away if one is not alert. Just the other day, I was physically attacked by a drug pusher when I confronted him about 250 rupees coupons taken from my cell and wrongly perceived taking of my eggs, it was taken by another. In such an atmosphere it becomes difficult to concentrate – not to mention the numerous other forms of harassment.

If it wasn't bladebaaz, then there were other characters including psychopaths.

In my ward I have that Delhi serial killer (psychopath) – Jha. People say he revels in showing off photos of chopped up torsos. Well, still, it is not too bad, but all this may have been easier to take at a younger age. (December 2010)

The other 'disgusting fellows' he met were the rapists involved in the 16 December 2012 gang rape case in Delhi. They were lodged in the same block as Kobad for a year and he recalls how when they'd see Nirbhaya's mother speak on TV, they'd say things like: 'She needs to be raped as well.' These boasts by convicted or undertrial rapists aren't uncommon, neither is the 'tit-for-tat' that such rapists face in jail. Just before Vinay Sharma, one of Nirbhaya's rapists attempted suicide in Tihar on 25 August 2016, Kobad told me how Sharma had told other inmates he'd been raped in Tihar. 'It's something Vinay Sharma told many people. But considering some of the things that happen in jail, rape isn't the worst that can happen.' Vinay Sharma's lawyers shared with media his client was tortured but the sexual assault is something only jail insiders speak of.

So, how do you survive and hang on to your sanity in such an atmosphere of fear, pain, and revulsion. Many turn to drugs to just suppress their anxiety. They would have charas for their morning smoke, paying in cash or kind to obtain the contraband. Others like Kobad found comfort in any living thing that he saw around him, since there was limited human contact, at least the desirable ones. He befriended a little cat who he fed in jail, and after winning the permission to walk around the grounds, he began a bit of gardening. In his letters from Tihar to Gautam Vohra, he described how these two hobbies were progressing:

Here in prison one can only express it to the walls around us on the squirrels that chirp around in the grounds outside. I have never appreciated this quaint little creature and their playful ways, as when I now watch them within these barbed-wire four walls. They are indeed, my main source of pleasure in here. The superintendent has kindly allowed me into these grounds due to health reasons. (21 June 2011)

Here in the compounds inside jail (fortunately I and another only are allowed), I planted tulsi plants and guava last monsoon. Of all those I planted, one tulsi and one guava survived. But since the last three months, the tulsi leaves have been badly attacked by insects. With the rains physically breaking off the infested leaves, I think I have been able to save it. But our chap from Rajouri village says they use ash to kill the insects. He says that is very effective. I will try. Let's see. It was a real battle to save this one tulsi plant as the other two (which are very prolific) died last summer. The compound has some lovely big trees – peepul, neem, jamun, it's the only soothing place in this environment. (August 2011)

Earlier those with costs (lots of it) could get into this (VIP ward). Now the bulk of the elites are in this ward and they have probably done it up further. Now it is strictly out of bounds for all. While life is a bed of roses for these people, it is hell for others (unless one is a gangster). And even the roses that I planted were some discarded plants thrown here, which I retrieved. Now even to water them and khurpi them is in spite of the difficulties of the authorities. No instruments so we hunt for sticks from the compound, then the machine like guards burn them – "no sticks allowed".

Talking of cats, a baby one came here some fortnights back. It was malnourished. We started nourishing it – more out of self-interest, as the mice had become a menace of late. It really loves its rats and only drinks the milk and biscuits when it cannot get any. Oh it is 1 p.m. – there she is waiting for her milk (everyday at this time she drinks a little). And guess what – I planted about 15 rose plants. So now looking after the rose and tulsi plants is quite a job as no one is particularly interested except myself and a farmer from Punjab. (October 2011)

Now the cat no longer seems to have much mice. Earlier, she would hardly touch the milk that we gave, but now she has most of it – it seems all the mice have run away (good for us). Actually, we also discovered that another cat (coloured) slyly comes and drinks up all the milk – while our meek little one now probably has less (or not) mice and less milk. (November 2011)

Now it is freezing here. The cells are quite damp and cold and the sun in one ward disappears after noon. The cat is still around and I have made a little house for her outside my cell with two jail blankets. At least, for the present we are mice free, though the human vermin around are much worse. (December 2011)

Cat not drinking milk only egg that I give her. It seems it will die soon. Today I tried mixing some antibiotic powder in the milk. (23 March 2012)

This year with late heavy rains, I closely observed my pot in the compound and found that virtually everything was sprouting. How easy it must be to create a forest. Seeds from the neem trees and tulsi plants came up in hundreds, even seeds from them sprouted many plants. The inmates who threw mango and date seeds after eating them sprouted and by no means is this compound soil fertile and there are a lot of white ants in the soil. So I was thinking how easy it would be for the government to develop afforestation involving local people. (October 2012)

When I brought this up with Kobad later, he noted how this part of the ground came in the Phansi Kothi compound. So some time after Afzal's hanging, they sealed it with huge walls around it. All the plants were destroyed.

His letters and applications are often repetitive in their themes, especially when it came to describing the discomfort he faced.

But that may be expected, with very little family left, and only visits from activists and his lawyers, writing was his only outlet. Kobad's sister, who lives in Mumbai, is the only family member still alive. She oversees his cases and visits him but age prevents her from following up too actively – whether it was the insensitivity of the authorities regarding the heat conditions inside the jail or their refusal to listen to his complaints. Some of these critical writings also appeared in the press which embarrassed the government, and the Ministry of Home Affairs once asked for an inquiry on how the jail authorities allowed such writing to get out. 'I told them I gave it to someone in the courtroom. They made me give that in writing and that's how it ended.' They didn't bother to fix the problems that he actually wrote about in his pieces. For instance, while officials had air-conditioners in their rooms, prisoners had exhausts which didn't have that much power to cool during the summer months. Jail inmates would throw water in their surroundings to bring down the temperature to some extent. 'Unless you are 2G and in the VIP wards, no one would wish to stay even a day in Tihar. I was in Hyderabad jail… in comparison, it was far better.'

A MULAKAT IN CHERLAPALLY

Two months after Kobad Ghandy was acquitted by a Delhi court of all charges of being a Maoist, I went to Cherlapally Jail in Hyderabad to meet him. I wanted to meet him in Delhi, but his lawyers, the activists who were fighting for him, advised against it. Going to meet someone in Delhi Jail means a day-long excursion and you have to be on the list of a handful of people that is cleared by security and background checks. After you've been cleared to visit someone in the high-risk ward, you would have to call a landline to seek an appointment. Getting through this landline is an achievement by itself. Once you get your time slot, which is usually late afternoon, you arrive at around 1.30 p.m. After a wait of a couple of hours, you then get 30 minutes across the glass screen and communicate through mikes and headphones. 'You couldn't have just dropped in to meet me,' smiles Kobad Ghandy.

Actually, in Hyderabad, I did just drop in to meet him. His lawyers, who represent the association of political prisoners, Ravindra and Savithri, told me they'd take me along when they'd go for a visit. I asked them which days they were allowed to visit. They said that in Telengana he was allowed to have visitors at any point of time, all days other than public holidays, but they'd only be free on a Saturday. There were no phone appointments required, no long queues. While Ravi and another lawyer Dasrath didn't need to sign in as lawyers, I was simply asked my relationship with Kobad, to which I said, I was his friend. They took a photo grab of me and issued a visitor's pass. Apart from me, there were about 15 others, women and children included, who had come to see their relatives. The waiting rooms were clean, there were places to sit around, and an organized atmosphere with token numbers being issued for the *mulakat*.

Like Tihar, there's also a waiting period to see the prisoner. Our meeting was going to be face to face because unlike the Delhi jail, Telengana had given Kobad Ghandy the respect and status of a political prisoner. 'When he arrived in Hyderabad, the jail superintendent came to his cell to welcome him to the jail. That immediately shows the difference in their attitudes,' said Savithri.

There were many other significant differences. Whenever Kobad was produced in a Delhi court, it would be in the police van with an iron cage inside it. The door to the cage had three gates – imagine a medium-sized truck with three gate-barriers inside, and how suffocating the small cage can be. 'It would be hot and suffocating and the only blessing was that I wasn't handcuffed.' And at every gate there would be a different layer of police security, which meant that every time this senior citizen stepped out of jail, he needed 25-strong security cover led by an assistant commissioner of police. Once the animal-like transfer to the court was done, he'd be put in the stuffy lockup and then finally the court appearance, where even carrying a pen would be seen as too much of a security threat. This was only limited to Delhi and only for prisoners considered 'dangerous'. Neither in Punjab nor Telengana would such security measures be taken.

In contrast, in Hyderabad, Kobad would be taken in a jeep with five security personnel. While we waited outside the jail, I saw posters stating: 'Telengana State: First to declare all its jails corruption-free'. It's quite an announcement to make. Ravi and Dasrath were carrying a bag of items that Kobad had asked for – Bata slippers, some food items and lots of stationery. After one and a half hours, the jail authorities were ready to let us in and Kobad was waiting for us in the jailor's office. This was also a courtesy he got being a political prisoner. In Delhi, this privilege is only given to politicians and the rich who've paid people off. The privileges that political prisoners got in Telengana and Andhra Pradesh were the result of an agitation by Naxalites and political prisoners in 1994 and 1996 that got a lot of support from civil society.

I'd read so many of his letters in despair, I expected a tired, ageing man. Kobad, in a check shirt and track pants, was smiling. He was happy to see Ravi and Dasrath, who are obviously much more than lawyers to him, and he was also in a positive frame of mind to talk to me. The change of scenery had done him a world of good – and he told me how he had grounds in front of his cell where he'd walk and do yoga too. The Naxalite barrack where he was staying had a lot of fruit trees, a ground that had generally improved his quality of life. His irritable bowel syndrome and other stomach ailments were also much better thanks to the better food that the Telengana jail was serving him. I asked him how he was feeling – 'I am 70, so I do have certain health problems,' – he smiled to indicate that unlike Tihar, this jail wasn't making him ill.

As we chatted, as Ravi and Dasrath discussed his cases with him and joked and laughed, it struck me how brave Kobad was. How could you possibly remain positive at 70 when you know that you still have to wait for justice? His lawyers tell me that they are planning to file a special petition in the Supreme Court which would plead for a provision to club all his cases together so that they could get fast tracked or that he could at least finally get bail till his cases were resolved. But whether that materializes or not, Kobad seemed optimistic. He was happy to use his time in custody studying his favourite, Erich Fromm. He just has this advice: 'Everything I found inhuman, everything impersonal was in Tihar. If you have to go to jail, go to Kerala or Tamil Nadu, Telengana or Andhra Pradesh. The judges are also much nicer – mine tells me to just take care of my health.'

As we leave, Kobad comes close to the gate to receive the items that Ravi had brought for him. At one point, he comes close to the exit gate, when the guards stop him and they all have a bit of a laugh. I look back wondering if he's really smiling at the thought of the outside world, and how distant it must be to him. I couldn't see because they had already shut the wicket gate.

APPENDIX
Kobad's Afzal Guru and the Last Walk to Phansi Kothi

Cherlapalli Central Jail
Cherlapalli
Raiga Reddy district
Hyderabad 501301

17 September 2016

It was 21 September 2009, when I first entered Tihar, at about 7 pm. It was my first entry into an Indian jail. After going through two sets of humiliating searches, I entered the high-risk ward of Jail Number 3. The inmates had already been locked up in their cells. And as I entered the ward of Block A (there are 2 blocks in this ward), I found Afzal Guru at the gate of his Cell 1, with a huge smile on his face saying, 'Welcome to Tihar, I was expecting you here.'

He said he had been reading about me all over the newspapers and said we will meet in the morning. I was led to Cell 4 and kept with three others, including Delhi's most famous Don, Kisan Pehlwan.

The next morning, I was moved to Cell 8 with two Khalistanis. The death sentenced Khalistani, Bhullar, was in Cell 2. That morning I had tea with Afzal which was a practice I continued till the day he was hanged on

9 February 2013. It was Afzal's standard practice to fill the thermos flask of Tihar's watery tea and add to it milk powder and a few tea bags purchased from the canteen to give an excellent brew. For the next three years, each day we would have this, together with the two slices of bread supplied by the jail authorities. This was followed by a walk in the ground adjoining the ward. A regular practice through the years. This was the same ground that adjoined the Phansi Kothi where he was later hanged and buried.

And through the years I found in Afzal a very humane person, warm hearted and simple. A person who had a deep affection for his mother, his school teacher wife and only son. They would regularly visit him every Raksha Bandhan day when the lady family members were allowed into the jail to be with their relatives. His needs were very limited, living off the ₹1000 a month his wife sent from her meagre earnings.

Afzal Guru was exactly the opposite of what the media has portrayed him as – a fundamentalist fanatic. No doubt he was a staunch believer in Islam, and did his namaz five times a day, observed *roza* and other Islamic customs. He also had great faith in the other world – Jannat – which gave him his enormous courage to go to the gallows with his head held high and apparently without an iota of fear.

Philosophically, Afzal believed in the Sufi tradition of Islam with its emphasis on humanity, love and equality. He was a great admirer of Rumi and Iqbal. He had all the six volumes of Rumi in Urdu which was his regular companion; many of the excellent verses he translated for me over our morning tea. Through Afzal I learnt much of the human essence of Islam, so vulgarized by the dogmatists and fundamentalists.

Afzal was not only vehemently opposed to the methods of the fundamentalist of bombing/killing, the innocent public, he also had a deep dislike for the Pakistani/ISI. He would often say they were worse than the R&AW and were responsible for the killings/assassinations of large number of intellectuals who were for Azaadi and not for merger with Pakistan. Particularly during the JKLF upsurge in the 1990s, which was then not pro-Pak. Afzal said large numbers were killed by ISI besides the Indian government. He also gave me a concrete picture where virtually every aspect of Kashmiri life was controlled by the army making the entire valley like an open prison. He would regularly compare the life of Kashmiris to that of the Palestinians. He was of the opinion that the Pakistanis were doing more harm to the Kashmiri's struggle than assisting it – Kashmiri people were being used as a mere tool in Pakistan's conflict with India, the sacrificial lamb of the India-Pak conflict.

Afzal had also great respect for communism (unlike the fundamentalists) and even repeated Iqbal who had said: Communism + God = Islam. Afzal was very well read having a nearly equally good grasp over both Urdu and English. He had read people like Naom Chomsky and other progressives from the West. He loved ghazals. In jail, the prison authorities had no complaint against him, notwithstanding the humiliations he apparently faced during the earlier period of his confinement.

Two days before Afzal's hanging we were told to immediately move to the block at the back (and those in the B Block were temporarily moved out) as white washing had to be done. But when we went to the B Block the gate leading to the ground which over-looked the big compound that housed the Phansi Kothi was promptly closed so that we could not see what was going on outside. But we soon gathered hectic work was going on in the Phansi Kothi. All sorts of rumours were spread by the staff that a foreign delegation was visiting; maybe Bhullar (who was by now shifted to the mental hospital) was to be hanged, etcetera etcetera.

Afzal would say if anyone was to be hanged, it was not Bhullar but himself. That evening though the fear was there in everyone's mind, Afzal seemed as cheerful as ever.

The next morning the staff turned up half an hour late, at 6 am. When they opened Afzal's cell, Cell 1, he was heard saying that if there was to be any searching, do it later as they will first say their namaz. But after letting Afzal out, they locked his cell and did not open any other. It was then that he and we too realized what was to happen.

He was led away to his original cell in A Block where the law officer met him. He was told that the hanging was to take place at 8:00 am. He requested to speak to his family and son on the phone, which was refused. That all other legal norms had already been flouted by the Congress government are already known. He did his namaz, was given tea and biscuits; he had a bath and said his final namaz.

At 5 minutes to 8, he was led across the same ground we walked everyday, wishing all the staff present, and asking the authorities to treat them well. We were told later much that the staff had tears in their eyes as he wished them all well and fearlessly walked to the gallows. The prison authorities, at the behest of the government, refused to hand over his belongings, diary or even body to his family. He was buried two feet away from where the other Kashmiri leader, Maqbool Bhat, was buried. Ironically, Maqbool Bhat, too, seems to have been anti-Pakistan as well, as recently the books by him were banned by the Pakistani government.

And with this ended my association with the most humane, honest, straightforward and simple person I met during my seven years of incarceration in Tihar. Most Kashmiris were not like Afzal, except one Rafique who had much of the same characteristics as Afzal. But none were as well-read as him. It is surprising why the Congress government sought to snuff out the life of the more rational voices in Kashmir, pushing the movement into the arms of the fundamentalists and pro-Pak elements.

The Khalistanis with whom I was put was also a great education. I learnt that the movement no longer stood for its original ideal based around centre-state relations and the Anandpur Saheb resolution. They had turned the movement into a fundamentalist movement where the main target was now the Deras (mostly supported by the SCs and lower castes as they were denied a place in the gurdwara) who they claimed were vulgarizing the Sikh religion. They have turned puritanical, oppose meat-eating and are fanatic. Ironically, as I gathered, all their leaders were in Pakistan. Many, like one of my cellmates, were involved in smuggling drugs and arms from Pakistan. They idolise Bhindranwale and ignore Bhagat Singh. But the two recounted many stories of Sikh bravery in their history much of which was not known to me. I felt sad that such a heroic history of a community had degenerated into such sectarian fanaticism. It was these two who in fact brought out the secular character of the gurdwara and the excellent tradition of all in the gurdwara, big or small, during manual labour (Kar Sewa). Guru Nanak's great social reform, anti-caste traditions seem to be in strong reversal from what I learnt from the Khalistanis.

Kobad Ghandy

ACKNOWLEDGEMENTS

The stories I write about in this book are personal – very intimate accounts of the lowest points of people's lives. Some of them were raped, sexually abused, beaten, humiliated in custody. Most of them don't want to talk about it and yet they shared their stories with me. And so, I am deeply grateful for the trust they put in me, in narrating their experiences. Each one of them knew that this book was likely to impact their public image and even their legal case, and yet, they agreed to open up, which was incredibly brave. Some, like Wahid and Khushi are tired of the system which has been incredibly unfair to them and yet, they again talked me through their trauma. I sincerely hope that this book is able to have some impact on their fight for justice.

Getting in touch with my subjects, with all these incredible stories, took all the professional contacts I had built over the last 18 years of my career. This next list of those who helped is definitely not exhaustive – my colleague and friend Tanima Biswas who put me in touch with one of the key subjects in this book and then helped me meet endless police officers and lawyers and get copies of judgements; Rona Wilson for all his time and advice; IPS officer Madhur Verma for great insight and suggestions; Manisha Sethi for help in identifying subjects and then helping me with resource material; Anup Surendranath of the National Law University whose 'Death Penalty Report' provided valuable insight; all my lawyer friends – Karuna Nundy, Ashish Dixit, Sushil Kumar, Manan Verma, Rebecca John, Bhavuk Chauhan, Vijay Aggarwal, Ashok Verma, Savithri and Ravindranath Balla (who is now in jail himself accused of being a Maoist sympathizer) and Indira Jaising, thank you all for the help, big and small, that you provided. Thanks also to Shahbaz Sherwani, Lesley Esteves and Kavita Shrivastav of PUCL who dug up precious papers and transported them to me, and Gautam Mukerjea and Gautam Vohra for all your invaluable help.

I want to thank my employers, NDTV for sending me on so many challenging assignments, each of which provided insights and inspired me to follow stories. Barkha Dutt, who remains a huge source of encouragement was the first one to jump at this book idea while my friends Nirmala Ganapathy, Suneel Sinha, Mustafa Quraishi, Mansi Midha, Prachi Bhuchar, Samit Basu, Hridayesh Joshi and Rasheed Kidwai helped with regular doses of pep talk and title suggestions. From the word go, the publisher had to be my old friend and colleague Priya Kapoor because she got exactly what I wanted to do and I trusted her implicitly (Okay, friends can work together, Priya, you are right!).

Everyone talks about how tough it is to juggle work and home, especially if you are a mother. Well, not if you have a son like mine. Neel, or Tiny as we call him, was super excited about my book. I don't know any six-year-old who would keep pushing his mother at her desktop with interjections like: 'So, mama, how many chapters have you done now?' And quietly play Lego while I worked. Thank you Tiny, you made it super easy. Of course, it's also because the rest of the family chipped in to take care of him, both sets of grandparents – Ma, Papa, Ma and Baba, Bachchu, Charlie, Bhai, Vasudha, and little Viren. I love you all. I owe this book also to Gauri who is a second mother to Neel, allowing me to chase projects like this. And Sudeep, you will always make up my biggest cheering squad and yet again, you let me be ambitious for both of us.